1 Small Boat, 2 Average Lovers,
and a Woman's Search for the Meaning of Wife

The Motion
of the Ocean

Janna Cawrse Esarey

A Touchstone Book
Published by Simon & Schuster
New York   London   Toronto   Sydney

For Talia and Savai,

in hopes that you dream big, too.

Touchstone
A Division of Simon & Schuster, Inc.
1230 Avenue of the Americas
New York, NY 10020

First Touchstone trade paperback edition June 2009

TOUCHSTONE and colophon are registered trademarks of Simon & Schuster, Inc.

For information about special discounts for bulk purchases, please contact Simon & Schuster Special Sales at 1-866-506-1949 or business@simonandschuster.com.

The Simon & Schuster Speakers Bureau can bring authors to your live event. For more information or to book an event contact the Simon & Schuster Speakers Bureau at 1-866-248-3049 or visit our website at www.simonspeakers.com.

Designed by Ruth Lee-Mui

Manufactured in the United States of America

2   4   6   8   10   9   7   5   3   1

Library of Congress Cataloging-in-Publication Data
Esarey, Janna Cawrse
The motion of the ocean : 1 small boat, 2 average lovers, and a woman's search
for the meaning of wife / Janna Cawrse Esarey.
p. cm.
"A Touchstone book."
1. Esarey, Janna Cawrse, 1971—Travel. 2. Esarey, Janna Cawrse, 1971—Marriage.
3. Ocean travel. 4. Sailing—Pacific Ocean. 5. Pacific Ocean—Description and travel.
6. Man-woman relationships. 7. Marriage. 8. Adventure and adventurers—Biography. 9. Seattle (Wash.)—
Biography. I. Title.
G530.C38 2009
910.9164—dc22   2008045977

Author will donate a portion of proceeds from this book to Wild Fish Conservancy and Teach For America.

Southern Cross
Words and Music by Stephen Stills, Richard Curtis, and Michael Curtis
Copyright © 1974, 1982 Gold Hill Music Inc. and Three Wise Boys Music LLC. Copyright Renewed.
International Copyright Secured. All Rights Reserved.

A portion of chapter 10, "The Net," was written and produced as part of the Jack Straw Writers Program.
Page xiii, 1, 43, 87, 171, 217, 253, 301 photographs by Graeme Esarey
Page 131 photograph by Doug Eck

ISBN 978-1-4165-8908-2
ISBN 978-1-4165-9681-3 (ebook)

I used to think that going to the jungle made my life an adventure. However, after years of unusual work in exotic places, I realize that it is not how far off I go or how deep into the forest I walk that gives my life meaning. I see that living life fully is what makes life—anyone's life, no matter where they do or do not go—an adventure.

—MARIA FADIMAN
National Geographic Emerging Explorer

Author's Note

t here are three things you should know before reading this book:

1. This is not an old mariner's sea story that ends with us in a life raft, bending earrings for fishhooks and contemplating eating each other's limbs. Rather, this is an adventure love story that happens to take place on a very small sailboat. If that's not your cup of tea, please, for your sake, go fish.

2. My husband will tell you I have a very shrewd memory . . . particularly when it comes to his past missteps. But, in reality, my memory is just as good or bad as anyone else's. And so, while all of the following events really did happen, I have taken liberty with some details, always with the goal of revealing what sailing into the sunset is really like. Where the narrative required, I have consolidated conversations, events, and time. Most boat names, people names, and incriminating details are real except for a few cases, where they've been changed to respect people's privacy.

3. Despite appearances, my name is actually very easy to pronounce:

Janna Cawrse Esarey
"banana" "of course" "yesiree"
Graeme's name is easy, too—like "graham cracker."

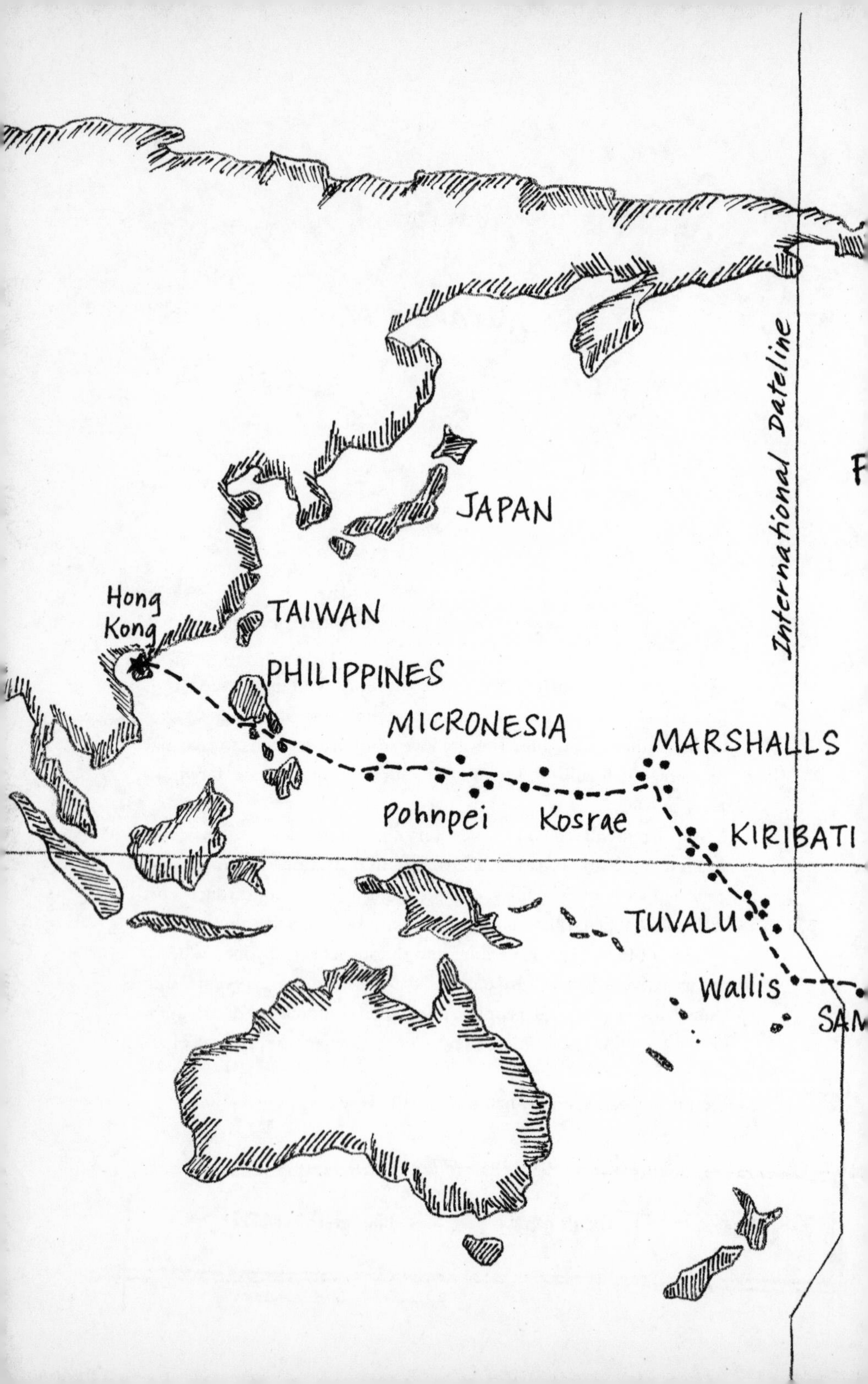
JAPAN
Hong Kong
TAIWAN
PHILIPPINES
MICRONESIA
MARSHALLS
Pohnpei
Kosrae
KIRIBATI
TUVALU
Wallis
International Dateline

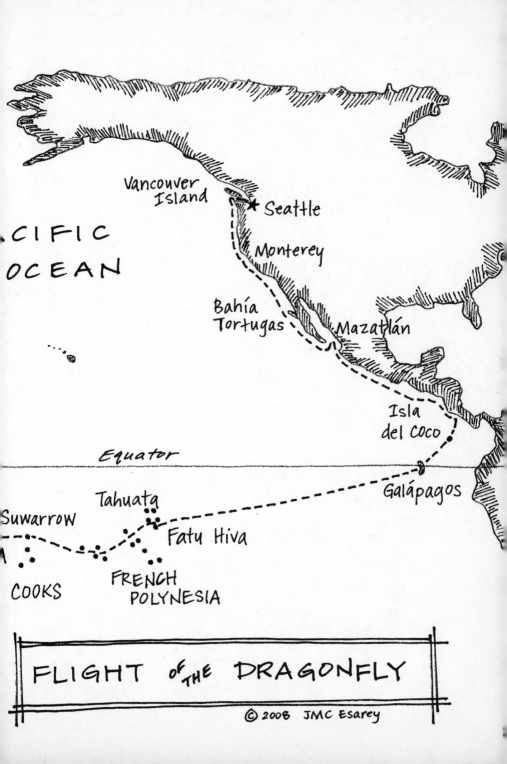

PACIFIC OCEAN

Vancouver Island

★ Seattle

Monterey

Bahía Tortugas

Mazatlán

Isla del Coco

Equator

Tahuata

Suwarrow

Fatu Hiva

Galápagos

COOKS

FRENCH POLYNESIA

FLIGHT of the DRAGONFLY

© 2008 JMC Esarey

Contents

Prologue

From First Date to First Mate

S o m e w h e r e   f i f t y miles off the coast of Oregon I realize the skipper of this very small ship is an asshole.

He also happens to be my husband.

He's down below, cooking Top Ramen, which will be the fifth time we've had Top Ramen in almost as many days. Not that I'm mad about *that*. Actually, he's chopping carrots and cabbage and onions—and I can smell the garlic from here—so it's bound to be good. Which makes him sound like a kind, nurturing, non-assholey sort of guy, cooking a meal for his bride on a boat that's rocking like the fun house in *Grease*.

But that's not how I see it—au contraire. I sit in the cockpit, braced behind the wheel, glaring at the stainless steel waves lifting and lowering our boat, *Dragonfly*. The sky is pixeled blue-gray, and the clangs of my husband's cooking punctuate the whitewash of wind. Running through my brain is Olivia Newton-John's signature phrase "You better shape up"— minus the chipper "doo-doo-doos." I *assure* you this guy is an asshole. And he's only in the galley to get as far away from me, his perfectly reasonable and charming wife, as possible.

Now it's hard to imagine why a guy on his honeymoon would be yearning for personal space of all things. (Another quickie? Right on! But *space*?) The fact that we're cooped up on a boat the size of most people's kitchen is a clue. The big fat fight we just had about sailing is another.

Every time the topic of sailing comes up we argue. It exasperates this skipper no end that his first (and only) mate—that would be me—displays neither aptitude nor interest in the technical aspects of sailing. Now this is a problem, as we've only gone, oh, 319 miles so far. And all told this trip— from Seattle to Costa Rica, from the Galápagos to the South Pacific, from Micronesia to Hong Kong—will span over 17,000 miles. So if we can just avoid talking about sailing for the next two years or so, we'll be fine.

OK, so maybe I should try to learn a bit more about sailing. The thing is, every time I ask a question, Graeme launches into a lecture that is so Physics 101 that it sails, as it were, right over my head. Take his response a few minutes ago to my inquiry about boat speed.

> GRAEME: It's logical, really. Just think about how an airplane wing works.
> ME: [blank stare]
> GRAEME: You, of course, already know how lift is created by *blah blah blah* vectors and velocities *blahbedy blah* maximize driving force *blahbedy blah blah* square root of waterline multiplied by the age you lost your virginity [OK, so I amended that last part] which determines your maximum hull speed. So it's really quite basic, right?

Right.

I feel stupid and confused. Graeme feels frustrated and criticized. And I . . . well, things generally deteriorate from there. This recent fight ended with this parting shot as he retreated below to cook noodles: "If you'd just stop and *think* about it," he muttered.

And that's what I do. I stop. And I think. About the fact that I'm a lousy first mate. And my husband is an asshole.

As dismal as I am at seamanship, Graeme is equally and inversely terrific at it. He sails like he makes love, all feel and instinct and attention. He knows this old boat like he knows my body—her angles and lines, her moans and her hums. And if there's something he *doesn't* know, he asks someone even more expert. In the case of sailing, a salty old soul he meets on the dock. In the case of sex, me.

And while I find it quite handy to have two experts on my body on board, it'd be nice to have two top-notch sailors aboard, too. But I'm a slow learner. It takes me a long time to realize when I should ease the main (the center sail), sheet the genoa (the forward sail), or put up the mizzen (the rear sail). And when it comes to a more technical fix (tighten the vang, adjust the block, pat your head while rubbing your tummy), I'm clueless. So, as long as *Dragonfly*'s moving in the right direction at an acceptable rate, I prefer to pretend this is—call me crazy—a romantic honeymoon cruise. I settle with close enough.

But close enough's not good enough for my husband. He flogs this 20,000-pound tub like she's an America's Cup yacht. Our approaches to sailing are like motor oil and water: When he's on watch he actually spends every single moment *watching*. The sail. Its position. Its shape. Its overall mood and body language. The boat speed. The wind speed. The wind direction. The ripples on the water. The current. The clouds above. The clouds forming on the horizon. The list is endless. He makes minuscule adjustments—an inch here, a centimeter there—and, most important, *he loves every minute of it*.

So imagine his reaction to my personal watch strategy: I check the general direction of the wind, point us in the general direction of our destination, and set the sails in the general configuration I think will get us there. Then I flip on Willie, our trusty autopilot, and cozy up on a cockpit cushion to read a good book or inhale the sounds of the sea. And of course I check the horizon for ships and squalls every ten minutes. I love every minute of *this*.

It's only now, as we set out across the largest ocean on the planet, that it's finally dawning on Graeme just how little his blushing bride knows or cares about the technical, mechanical, and strategic aspects of sailing. In the year leading up to our trip, instead of following a watch schedule, we would euphemistically sail "together"—which inevitably meant him at the helm (tweaking, analyzing, calculating) and me stowing fenders or preparing snacks or huddling from the rain or sunning on deck. He was so busy paying attention to the sails that he didn't realize I wasn't.

Now you may wonder how two individuals, with their attention so diverted from each other, could end up in a boat together. Crossing the Pacific. As their honeymoon. But there was a time when this man could pay attention to little else but me. And his gaze was like the sun.

Of course, he was barely a man back then, more a walking, talking sack of testosterone. It was college, I was playing pool, and he was propping up the beer-stained wall of a party-packed basement. He says it was love at first sight. I—an insecure freshman with a recessive gumline, low-grade acne, bowed legs, and a penchant for serious intellectual inquiry—say it was love at first beer goggle. Either way, beer goggle translated to lust, lust turned into love, and I had that boy's full attention.

Until a year later, when I didn't. At which point he broke my heart. Frayed it. Splayed it. Twisted and burned it. Like a seaman splicing line. Our relationship went something like this: I became a nag—a dishy, loveable nag, mind you—but a nag nonetheless. And Graeme, by then a senior, was feeling The Pressure: What was he going to do with a degree in philosophy bought on credit for $13,000 a year? He just wanted to play rugby and tend bar and party until graduation. He didn't need some girlfriend whining about needing more attention, not being at the top of his priority list, being overlooked and underlaid.

Finally, after feeling neglected for too long, I gave Graeme an ultimatum. Standing on the green lawn outside my sophomore dorm, I said, tears streaking my face, "Look me in the eye and tell me you don't love me anymore, and I'll walk out of your life forever."

Graeme countered with the most searing look of loathing I'd ever seen. He said, "I don't love you anymore." Then he turned on the worn heel of his flip-flop, and walked out of my life forever.

When you marry someone you've dated seriously once or twice before—and then climb aboard a very small sailboat for a very long honeymoon—it's important to leave behind as much baggage as possible. But huddled in this dinky cockpit, wind whipping the split ends of my hair despite my red sou'wester hat pulled low, I feel crowded by these memories. The wind's blowing harder now, the rig is ringing like a wineglass, and I'm even more upset than I was before. I should have known he—

Bam!—*Dragonfly*'s broaching. Tilting over on her side. Green water flooding the cockpit. If I don't do something quick we could be knocked all the way down till our sails slap the sea. I've got my life jacket on, but I'm not tied to the boat—and while a knocked-down sailboat will always rise back up from the water, an untethered crew member may not.

I scrabble and claw upward, toward the high side of the boat, and reach instinctively for the mainsheet.

"*Release! Release! Release!*" Graeme's voice rises above the din of rushing water.

But my fingers are already there, around the thick white line, yanking it from the cleat's jaws. The line sings out of my hands as the sail staggers violently over the sea on our starboard side. Tension eased, *Dragonfly* lumbers to her feet, still lurching in the waves, jolted, soggy, and off course. When the next gust hits seconds later, her sail is slack; she barely flinches. My eyes search below to find Graeme's. He's staring at me, one hand on the lid of a pot that is still, miraculously, on the stove. Miraculous because the edge of *Dragonfly*'s deck wasn't just kissing the sea, it was molesting it. Our cockpit swirls with water and begins to drain. I wipe the salty spray from my mouth and begin to cry.

Graeme's got his arms around me now. "It's OK, it's OK, it's OK," he intones. "You knew exactly what to do. You did just the right thing. You did *great*."

I'm hiccoughing and crying and wiping snotty tears on the sleeve of my yellow foul weather gear. Graeme holds me and rocks me. He doesn't mind that the sail is slapping and the boat is yawing and we're no longer following the red rhumb line of our course. "You were perfect," he says. "You *are* perfect. I love you."

I cry a bit more and let him smooth my back because it feels so good. I wait for my heartbeat to slow. Finally, after a few last sleeve-wipes I manage: "I love you, too."

Feels like I've never meant it more.

So now I'm gazing fondly at the husband-formerly-known-as-asshole. He looks damn cute slurping that Top Ramen, and I'm reminded of my girlfriend's old adage: *Marry a guy you're attracted to, because even when you think he's an asshole, at least you'll think he's a cute asshole.* Right now I'm back to just thinking Graeme's cute—period. Especially since the steaming bowl of noodles he made feels like some exotic spa treatment, its sesame scent mixing with the salt air. I hold the bowl slightly away from me, arms fluid but legs braced, to keep *Dragonfly*'s rhythmic gate from spilling it in my lap. Her sails are reefed and set back in their (generally) correct places. She's moving with the sea instead of fighting it now. Graeme's and my battle has blown over, too.

Of course, there's still that pesky question of why I would sign on for a trans-Pacific honeymoon if I'm not, as seems clear, fanatical about sailing. Well, the truth is I *do* love sailing. If by sailing we mean traveling to the most beautiful and remote islands on earth with our home upon our back. Or getting to know ordinary people with extraordinary lives. Or riding the broad back of the ocean, under the raw power of wind, with the man I love. That, I do love. The maximizing of boat speed, the perfecting of sail shape, the tweaking of every line and vang and block to make the sailing vessel a version of Descartes's divinely tuned watch? Nope. Don't love that. Just doesn't float my boat.

And I hope Graeme can accept this. Because ultimately this honeymoon of ours is neither a race (as Graeme likes to think) nor a happy-go-lucky cruise (as I pretend). It's a test. Of our boat, our seamanship, and most important, our relationship.

We were repeatedly told before we set sail: *If your marriage can survive this, it can survive anything.*

This always sounded overblown to me.

Now I'm not so sure.

Part 1

Home

Looking for That Woman-Girl

Day after day, day after day,
We stuck, nor breath nor motion;
As idle as a painted ship
Upon a painted ocean.

—*Samuel Taylor Coleridge*
The Rime of the Ancient Mariner

A Year and a Half Before the Voyage Begins

Shit. Shit. Shit. I've done it again. My watch is set five minutes fast, and still there's no way I'll make it on time. I have to finish this e-mail, print tomorrow's assignment, and make copies of—where did I put that book of engravings? Did I tell my sophomores Coleridge was an opium addict? Is there a faculty meeting this week? I could have sworn I put that book—

Focus, Janna, *focus*.

I type:

Mitch's writing shows great improvement, and our support will only further his progress. If you have any other concerns, feel free to contact me.

OK, that's fine. That's tactful. It's fine. Now end with *Best* or *Sincerely*? *Best*. OK. Reread. Reread. Reread. OK. Ready to send. No, *Sincerely*.

SEND.

The student desks sit idle. My classroom is dark and cool. But someone has twisted the knob on the bathtub toy in my chest. *flapflapflapflapflap*. I start shoving stuff in bags—laptop, student papers, an illustrated copy of *The Rime of the Ancient Mariner*, and the red brick that is my bible: *Norton's Anthology of British Lit*. Now, faculty meeting this week? Check desk calendar. Yup, Wednesday. And 6:30 A.M. student government tomorrow. And community service permission slips due Friday. Last Friday. *Damn*.

By the time I lock my door, walk halfway down the hall, return to get a book for my philosophy elective, lock my door again, go to the office and make copies, go to the faculty room to print out the assignment I forgot to print in my classroom, go back to the office to make more copies, and rush to the front of the school, I'm twenty-five minutes late. My boyfriend, Graeme, who's always on time except when he's early, has got to be pissed.

I open the passenger-side door of his blue 4Runner, and the stale smell of Taco Bell wafts out. "Sorry. Sorry. Sorry," I say, bunching my shoulders. He's listening to the Mariners' game and doesn't respond. I look to the back of the SUV, which doubles as Graeme's closet: climbing gear, wrinkled work clothes, a spare tire, an outboard motor for his twenty-four-foot sailboat. Not a lot of room. So I haul my laptop case, my purse, and my book bag into the passenger's seat with me and weave the seat belt beneath the whole mess. Then I turn to him.

"Really, I am so so sorry for being late," I say.

Nod.

"Graeme?"

He leans into the sound of the radio. Dave Niehaus's voice booms, "And the Mariners retire the side. No runs, no hits, no errors. Mariners five. Indians two."

Silent as a paperweight, Graeme puts the car in gear. The engine growls as we pull away from the curb. The mountain of bags on my lap is heavy, so I toe aside travel mugs and Taco Bell wrappings and Diet Coke bottles in the foot well, and stuff my bags down, bowing my legs around them. I lean toward Graeme and give my creeping underwear a tug. Then I fold my hands in my lap to wait.

I'll just be silent, I think.

Let Graeme cool off.

Wait till he's ready to engage.

Then I blurt, "Look, I really am sorry. So will you please just say something?"

His voice comes out slowly, stiff as cracked mud: "You want me to say it's OK. Like I always do. But the thing is, Janna, sometimes it's not." He clears his throat and looks away; confrontation for him is like the turn-and-cough test at the doctor's office. But he's had plenty of time waiting in the car to get his gumption up. "Being late is a sign of disrespect," he says. "It makes me feel like you value your time over mine."

Graeme continues for another two blocks, laying out "I feel" statements as gently as he would eggs, just like the couples counselor taught us. Everything he says is dead-on. Everything he says hurts.

"You're right," I say, when he's finished. "I'm so sorry I was late." The air between us hangs for a moment. Against my better judgment I add, "But I had parents to mollify. And copies to make. And. And"—my voice is wavery and thin—"there's just so much—"

"I know there's a lot to do, Janna. I work for a living, too, remember?" He takes a deep breath and softens his tone. "You've got to prioritize. You've got to put yourself first sometimes. You've *got* to find balance." I glance at him, and when he moves his hand from the steering wheel I think he's going to put it on my knee.

He shifts into fourth. "You spend your school nights planning lessons. And your weekends grading papers. And your evenings going to proms and basketball games and who knows what else. Our relationship gets the scraps of your spare time, and meanwhile you're more stressed than ever." He sounds genuinely concerned, which, aside from being nice and all, feels like a medicine ball on my chest; it'd be easier if he just picked a fight. Then he says, "At some point you've got to add me to your priority list."

My mind flares. *At least I'm prioritizing teaching, not rugby drink-ups*, I think, recalling our college days when I elbowed for his precious time. "You know, Graeme," I say, picking a fight of my own, "teaching isn't just a job. It's kids' lives."

"Yeah, well. It's my life, too," he says, hitting the gas through a yellow light. "And I need you in it." He pauses under the weight of what he's just said. Yet it's what he reveals about me next that touches the back of my neck: "The real you. The flesh and blood you. Not this stressed-out ball of teacherly perfection that's unraveling before my eyes."

My defenses jerk: *Teaching takes time! It takes energy! It takes commitment!* But as quickly as the thought comes, I see that a relationship needs time and energy and commitment, too. And my brain feels thick now, muddied with revelation. *I was always the caretaker in the relationship; he was the taker. When did all that change?* I cross my arms, close my eyes, and lean my temple against the cool of the window. The tears are coming now. *What's happened to me?* I think as I feel the car stop at a light. *When did I become such a stressed-out whacko?* My insides mix the cement of my thoughts. *And when did I get too damn busy for love?*

This time when Graeme moves his hand, he puts it on my knee. "I love you, Janna," he says. Then after a while, "Life's not supposed to be all work and no play."

I swipe my eyes dry, and the trees begin to tick by: Evergreen. Evergreen. Deciduous. Evergreen. To my silence he tries one last tack: "Look. What happened to the girl I knew in college? Who was fun-loving and up for adventure? The girl who wanted to sail around the world someday?"

The houses threaten to swim again, and I bite my lips in that monkey face that comes before crying. More sad than bitter, I say, "Don't you remember, Graeme? You broke up with her."

I was fifteen years old when I decided I wanted to sail around the world. . . .

I sit cross-legged on the living room floor, my parents' record collection surrounding me like flower petals plucked and tossed in He-Loves-Me-Not fashion. I record every album to cassette, analyze the lyrics for double meanings, and transcribe quotes from Cat Stevens, the Grateful Dead, and Simon & Garfunkel onto my denim-blue school binder. I think: I've been born in the wrong era.

But then, on Crosby, Stills, & Nash's *Daylight Again* album, I hear a song called "Southern Cross." And though I've missed the boat on Woodstock and war protests, I'm carried away by something else entirely: the Dream of Sailing the World.

"Southern Cross" is about a guy who mends his broken heart on a sailboat voyage to the South Pacific. It's painfully beautiful. Catchy, too. And that day, as I teeter between girlhood and womanhood, the idea of making the passage from love for someone else, to love of oneself, speaks to me.

I take out a blue batik-print pad of paper and, with my ear to the speaker, write down the lyrics in block letters. I listen over and over to get the words right. These get pinned, among photos and dried carnations and green honorable mention ribbons, to the bulletin board beside my bed. Then, in my family's gray atlas, I look up the places in the song: Avalon, the Marquesas, Papeete—words that roll like primary colors off my tongue. And my dad explains the nautical terms "reach" and "off the wind," "waterline" and "following sea."

After dinner, I steal the globe from my brother's room and run my finger from California's Santa Catalina Island across four knuckles of open ocean to Tahiti. One knuckle = 1,000 miles. On my Walkman I press PLAY and REWIND, PLAY and REWIND.

> *I want to sail a-rou-ou-ound the world.*
> *I want to be that woman-girl.*
> *Who knows love can endure.*

And so I fall in love with the sea. Not the literal, wet, let's-go-surfing sea. Nor the Cousteauian get-a-degree-in-marine-biology sea. But the lyrical sea. The transformative sea. The sea that inspires me, years before @ is anything more than shorthand, to end my senior quote in the 1990 Mercer Island High School yearbook with: FindMe@SthrnCrs.

To the extent that women-girls have pickup lines, "I'm going to sail around the world someday" became mine. Boys eat that shit up. None more than my college boyfriend Graeme.

Before meeting me, Graeme's great loves had names like *Ingrid, Emma C*, and *Henrietta W*—the names of commercial fishing boats his family owned and operated up and down the Pacific Northwest coast. Graeme first went to sea at age five; his job was to keep the boat on course while his parents hauled in salmon and halibut and tuna. By age six, he was gutting fish himself. And at age seven, he was so used to boat rules (can't go on deck without your tether) that one day on shore, he asked his mom for his life jacket so he could go outside to play.

By the time Graeme reached college he'd been fishing for thirteen years. And while he didn't harbor any mad dreams of living at sea (been there, done that), he thought it a good sign that his girlfriend did; it showed she was fun-loving, carefree, adventurous. The kind of girl he might like to marry someday.

But ten years later, during that fight in Graeme's 4Runner, I realized how far I'd traveled from the woman-girl I'd been in college. I no longer felt carefree or fun-loving. Or loving. Period. I felt stuck. Like Coleridge's Ancient Mariner, painted into a picture I couldn't get out of. A picture that, until that day, I wasn't aware I wanted to get out of.

Because as fervent and romantic and unrealistic as my long-lost sailing dream had been, so had been my teaching dream: I thought I could change the world one student at a time. And while the efficacy and advisability of this scheme is highly debatable, I passionately loved my job. I just didn't love the person I'd become through my job: a harried, perfectionist, martyring workaholic.

1 anxiety attack
3 major fights with Graeme
5 months' soul-searching
and innumerable therapy sessions later,
I came to understand that I was ready for a change.

Which is how I end up on the back of a Honda 650 motorcycle speeding toward what Graeme and I have dubbed the B-HAG Brainstorming Summit. The past five months of fights and freak-outs have convinced us we need a B-HAG (that's Big Hairy Audacious Goal, in Graeme's business speak) to give us a new direction together. Whether a few months' adventure or a long-term lifestyle change, we're not sure, but it needs to be mutual, something beyond his obsession with mountain climbing and my obsession with teaching. And we need to do it now—while we're still young, still childless, and still crazy enough to go for it.

I've dressed up for the occasion in a buttery beaded sweater set, cute black pants, and my number one accessory: a smooth-and-lift bra. But then Graeme tosses me a crusty, old rawhide jacket that looks like it's been in a wreck or two, which is precisely why he insists I wear it. And even though it's a hot August day, he vetoes my open-toed sandals in favor of hiking boots, and gives me gloves the size of moon boots to wear. "Safety first!" he says. When I pull on Snoopy-style goggles over my (neon yellow) helmet, the damage is complete. Sexy biker-babe Barbie? I'm Skipper, her dorky little sister.

Luckily, when you're riding on the back of a motorcycle going 50 mph with your arms wrapped round the man you love, sexy comes rushing back. We pull up at Anthony's, a splurge of a seafood restaurant at Seattle's waterfront, and in one swift arc I swing my leg off the back of the bike. I pull off my helmet and shake out my (limp, mousy brown) hair like in the movies. It's Saturday night. I'm ready to brainstorm.

Graeme locks the helmets to the bike while I rummage through my bag for my strappy sandals. There's my wallet, there's a condom, there's a tin of curiously strong mints. There are no cute, black, strappy sandals.

Shitfuck.

"Shitfuck" is the expletive my dad invented years ago to show my brother and me how silly we sounded saying *shit* and *fuck* every other word. It was so dorky it actually stopped us swearing for a while. But now, in my thirties, it's my invective of choice.

Shitfuck. No sandals.

I take Graeme's arm, push my shoulders back, and clomp gracefully toward the tall doors of the restaurant. I soon realize that if I had my (neon yellow) motorcycle helmet cradled under my arm, the hostess would at least have some context for my ensemble. But as it is, the expression on her eye-shadowed, diamond-nose-studded face reads: "Seattle fashion sucks."

When we reach our raised half-circle booth with its fantastic view of the water, I remove the jacket, scootch into my seat, and fold my feet clunkily behind the table's metal pedestal.

And that's our big, hairy, audacious start to the evening.

Anthony's is crowded and loud, and it takes a while for the server to get to our table. Graeme orders a 2000 Côte du Rhone—big body, soft finish, hints of black currant—and the B-HAG brainstorming begins: Move to Mexico. Bike across France. Become truck drivers. Of course, I don't bother mentioning that some couples our age go after that big, hairy, audacious goal called Marriage. Because every time the topic comes up, we argue. And, anyway, a wedding isn't going to get me out of this rut, or lower my stress, or help me find balance.

So we're sipping our wine and coming up with crazy schemes and looking out over the water. I'm off on a tangent about driving Graeme's orange and white 1973 Winnebago cross-country. "I bet we'd go to some pretty remote places," I say fingering the stem of my wineglass, "and maybe that would lead to some exotic outdoor, mm, extracurricular activities." My eyebrows do calisthenics on my forehead.

At this, Graeme turns back from the window and slaps both hands on the table. I think, *He's taking this outdoor sex idea more seriously than I expected.*

But then he looks me in the eye and, in a why-didn't-I-think-of-this-before voice, says, "What about your old high school dream?"

I'm puzzled. "You mean marry Tim Fries, have two-point-five children, and impale myself on a white picket fence?"

"Noo," he says. "I *mean*"—he points to the sailboat masts swaying in front of the windows—"do you think you might like to buy a sturdier boat"—he's smiling really big now—"outfit it for the ocean"—his fingers wriggle like centipedes—"and sail it to the South Pacific?"

I look at him and I don't think, *I like my outdoor sex idea better.*

In fact, I don't even think: *Do we have the sailing skills? Can we afford it? How do I leave my dog? my friends? my family? What if I get seasick? What if pirates attack us? What if a tanker or whale or hurricane hits us? What if he falls overboard? What if I fall overboard? What if we capsize? What if we die?*

I just look at the man sitting across from me. The man I've loved off and on since I was nineteen years old. The man who's asking if I think I'd like to sail to the Southern Cross with him.

And I say, "I do."

Over Penn Cove Mussels in saffron and white wine broth, we plan: We'll buy the cheapest boat we can find. We'll take sabbaticals from our jobs. We'll sell our cars. We'll rent our house. And we'll go on a strict B-HAG budget: No more movies. No more restaurants. No more fancy wine.

By the end of the evening, we're both fully on board the Sailing Dream. All that's left is the biggest, hairiest, most audacious part of the plan: telling our parents.

The Best Sea Stories Are Love Stories

O ne thing you should know about my mom is that I can tell her anything:

Age sixteen: "Mom, I'm thinking about having sex." *Check.*
Age seventeen: "Mom, I had sex." *Check.*
Age twenty-two: "Mom, I'm using my $60,000 education to work on a dude ranch in Wyoming, be a ski bum in Park City, and milk cows in Bavaria." *Check.*
But age thirty: "Mom, I'm quitting my job, buying a boat, and sailing across the Pacific with my on-and-off boyfriend of ten years who still hasn't found the *cojones* to propose"?
No can do.

Nonetheless, that's precisely what I intend to do. Even though I have personal reasons, beyond the obvious, for not wanting to tell my parents that I intend to sail the world in a small boat. Namely:

1. Mom and Dad haven't always been crazy about my boyfriends in general, or this boyfriend in particular.
2. I have no open-ocean sailing experience.
3. Mom and Dad sailed, not the whole Pacific, but a tiny hangnail of it in a small boat years ago.
4. That's how Mom and Dad nearly died.

So, it's an Indian summer day in Seattle, and Graeme and I have come to share our Big News. My folks live on the shores of Lake Washington in a house that displays all the *objets*-they-consider-*art:* an old ship's compass, a framed sailboat burgee, numerous nautical prints, a foghorn. Every room has floor-to-ceiling views of the water. Mom and Dad are crazy about the water.

Dad has cooked self-caught salmon on the bar-b, and when he brings it in from the deck, scents of tarragon and lemon follow him. My parents grumble sometimes about the fact that my boyfriend doesn't eat meat, but at least Graeme is fanatical about seafood. This works to my advantage. It's hard for my parents to dislike someone who loves the water as much as they do. Though, over the years, they've tried.

My dad first met Graeme on a drizzly day in Walla Walla, Washington, at 5:07 in the morning. It was Parents' Weekend at college, and Dad, in an effort to bond with the latest heartthrob, was parked outside Graeme's house, probably trying not to think about the likelihood that his nineteen-year-old daughter was upstairs naked in this young man's bed.

I imagine Dad looking at the digital red numbers on the dash and tapping the horn again; he's been waiting nine minutes. Should he go knock? The next moment, the side door opens and Graeme shuffles out, clothes rumpled and shoelaces half-tied, carrying an old fly rod and a tan fishing vest. He stuffs his gear through the lowered window of the tailgate and climbs in.

Dad smiles and shakes Graeme's hand. "Good to finally meet you!" Dad's already had a cup of coffee.

Graeme's requisite "Nice to meet you, too," comes out slow and ragged. His eyes are bloodshot, his voice gravelly from sleep or lack of it.

A few hours later, after their fishing expedition, Dad and Graeme head to DJ's Restaurant, where they've agreed to meet Mom and me for breakfast. Mom and I are chatting in my Jetta when Dad pulls into the space to our right. He rolls down his window, cups his hand to the side of his mouth, and stage-whispers to Mom, "Psst . . . Hey, cutie, wanna screw?"

Mom laughs. I roll my eyes; it's just like Dad to be silly and crass. He's probably trying to impress Graeme. I take it as a sign they've formed some sort of male bond.

But after we've eaten and Graeme's left for his rugby game, I ask Dad how the fishing trip *really* went. He doesn't regurgitate the quip he'd delivered at breakfast: "The fishing was great—just the catching wasn't so good." Instead he runs his fingers lightly across the top of his head and sucks in his breath. "Well, I think it was a bit too early in the morning for Graeme."

"Oh, no," I say. "Graeme's used to getting up early to fish. He's been fishing all his life."

"Yeah, well, you guys must have had quite a party last night."

I blanch.

Then Dad ticks three items off his thumb and two fingers: "He reeked of alcohol. He couldn't cast to save his life. He fumbled for his words like an old man with his fly."

And that would be strikes one, two, and three.

Over ten years later, back in Mom and Dad's dining room, I'm hoping my parents' opinion of Graeme has matured some. Lord knows, he has. He's now a vice president of a small Seattle company and does business deals all over the world. He kind of has his shit together. Except for the fact that he's about to drop everything to sail across the Pacific Ocean with his girlfriend.

Dad's serving up the salmon, Mom's carving off thick slices of bread, and I'm sweating about our Big News. Graeme's "This looks great!" comes off a bit Wally Cleaver–ish, so I can tell he's nervous, too. The serving dishes dance their jig around the table and I wonder how to say it.

"Uh, Mom? Dad?" I begin. "We wanted to talk to you about something."

Mom's eyes flit to my right hand, which is dishing the last of the season's string beans onto my plate. She realizes her mistake and glances at my left.

Still no ring.

She looks at me, arranging her face into a smile. "What's up?"

"Well . . ." I set the beans down. Graeme's plate is heaped with salmon, spuds, and veggies. He's not eating yet. He waits for me to continue.

I take a deep breath and then, "WewannabuyaboatandsailacrossthePacific." I glance from Mom to Dad like a sixteen-year-old announcing she's pregnant. Our news has gone over about as well.

"We sailed out of Tokyo Bay in February, the least likely month for typhoons," Dad says, shaking salt on his potatoes.

Almost seamlessly, we've made the leap from our Big News to an Old Family Legend: how my parents capsized a forty-five-foot sailboat off the coast of Japan thirty years ago—and nearly died. It's long-lost family lore in our household, a story that used to elicit such stern glares from Mom that it stopped getting told. Now it almost feels like a dirty family secret, though it starts out innocently enough: Dad was in the navy, stationed in Yokosuka, and he convinced Mom it'd be fun to sail on a friend's boat to Guam.

I already know they never made it that far.

I haven't heard this story told in years—my memory of it is vague—and it can only be resurfacing now for one reason: Mom and Dad want to scare the crap out of us so we scrap our idea of sailing. But Dad's face is alive with the telling, and Graeme, who's never heard the tale, is fully on board. So I just listen.

"As we left the bay," Dad says, "Mount Fuji rose up over the sea like one of those famous woodblock prints. It seemed an auspicious beginning." He pauses for dramatic effect. "Then it started snowing."

Dad, in signature form, begins with his thumb and ticks off every other setback they encountered that first week at sea: continued snowstorms, broken hydraulic steering, seasickness, and—he clutches his ring finger now—the most severe squall he'd ever seen. "Weather reports had predicted perfect conditions for our passage south to Guam," Dad says. "They were wrong."

Mom's face is empty. She's looking down at the old walnut dinner table we've had for ages, and I wonder if she's examining the tiny half-moon nicks inflicted by a high school game of quarters. Mom and Dad never mentioned them, so my brother and I didn't either. But maybe they're scars you don't see unless you know to look.

Dad continues, his chin dropping to his chest. "Things got really grim on day six. The waves were like mountains, we were skimming down their sides. Our only goal was to avoid the breaking crests." His hand moves to the top of his head—a gesture he's had as long as I can remember—and smooths his thinning hair. Dad describes the salty sting of the sea, the jarring motion of the boat, and the foaming breakers raging white against a black sky. "Your mother and the other three crew were in life jackets in their bunks below. The boat was all battened up. It was just me and the skipper in the cockpit." He and *Misty*'s owner had secured themselves to the boat with tethers and carabineers so they wouldn't be swept off deck.

"Because of the busted hydraulics," Dad says, "we'd attached lines from the wheel to the tiller shaft." Graeme nods, clearly understanding this emergency steering configuration, though it makes little sense to me. "We'd been able to dodge the worst of the breakers so far, but then"—this is when Dad adds the sound effects—"over the screaming of the wind and the roar of those breakers"—he whistles airily and waves his hand like a conductor's—"I heard something even louder." From his throat emerges a sound that is an improbable cross between a pit bull and a semi. "It was a rogue wave, taller and wider and scarier than any wave we'd seen. It completely filled the sky—the top third was white foam—and it was coming straight for us."

I hear the cane seat of Graeme's chair creak as he leans into Dad's story. I'm getting sucked in, too. Mom is expressionless.

"I braced myself as the breaker hit us dead-on," Dad says, his left hand the wave, his right the ship. "It threw our twenty-four-ton vessel sideways down the wave, slammed her through the water, and rolled her a hundred eighty degrees." Dad's hand twists and turns and stops with his fingers pointing into his lap. The mast, cockpit, and cabin were submerged in the sea where the bottom of the boat had been; Mom's ceiling was now her floor.

"As my body entered the freezing water I remember thinking, 'I'm dead. We're all dead,'" Dad says.

I imagine him in the green water, pinned under the boat like in some bad movie, eyes buggy, with bubbles leaking from his mouth. The tether that had once kept him on top of the boat now held him underneath it.

"But after thirty seconds," Dad continues, "the boat righted herself and pulled me and the skipper out of the water with her."

I exhale a breath I didn't know I was holding.

"Besides being really wet," Dad says, "everyone was fine."

Graeme asks for a detailed inventory of all the damage—engine room flooded, batteries flooded, ports stove in, cabin structure shifted sideways—while I imagine Mom in the bucket brigade, expelling the knee-deep water below. As kids, my brother and I begged our parents to tell this story to our friends. Mom and Dad rarely obliged. So I told the story myself, emphasizing what to my child's mind was the most baffling and horrific detail: "They had to throw a ten-speed bike over the side!" Apparently we haven't gotten to that part yet.

"So, what happened next?" I ask, popping a potato wedge into my mouth.

Mom looks at Dad, looks down at the untouched meal on her plate, then looks at me. She shrugs anticlimactically and, for the first time to-night, speaks. "We just huddled in our bunk and waited to die."

I stop chewing. I haven't heard this part of the story before.

"We talked about you and your brother," Mom says.

In 1975, I was four and my brother was six. Mom and Dad left us with navy friends on base while they went on their sailing "vacation."

"We talked about how you would grow up without us," Mom says, turning toward the bank of windows. It's dark now, and instead of the lake our own reflections stare back at us. "I remember afterward, back on base, some lady stopped me in the commissary. She *scolded* me." Mom's index finger wags. "'So *you're* the mother who left her children to risk her life on a sailboat.'"

I guess I'd forgotten this detail.

Then, looking toward the veiled lake, Mom says slowly, deliberately, "The waves just kept crashing and crashing. It seemed impossible for the boat to take the pounding. We kept thinking, *this* wave will be the end."

Her chin begins to quake.

She turns back to Dad, and when she continues, her voice shakes, "We said I love you a thousand times." Dad takes her hand and squeezes it. "We laid in our bunk. We held each other. We cried and cried and cried."

It's a terrible thing imagining your parents waiting to die. Worse is watch-ing your mother cry. So now I'm crying—Dad is, too—and the table is awkward and silent. My finger traces one of the table's tiny nicks, almost imperceptible even though it's been there for years. And it occurs to me that this adventure story I bragged about as a kid may not have been my mother's proudest moment. In fact, I realize, my finger resting in the cres-cent scar, it could well be her worst.

Graeme, meanwhile, doesn't seem exactly sure what to do. He bows his head, as though in prayer, and runs his fork lightly back and forth across his empty plate.

Eventually, Dad lets go of Mom's hand, picks up his blue-and-white-checked napkin, and dabs under his eyeglasses. They bob up and down on his forehead, cockeyed and comical, like the punch line to some slapstick joke. I exhale the inklings of a laugh, and a sling of snot descends to my chin.

"Shitfuck," I say, cupping my hand under my nose.

Dad looks at me, hands still gripping his napkin, and shakes his head slowly—whether in disbelief at my snot or his resuscitated swearword, I'm not sure. Then his shoulders begin to shake. He begins to chuckle.

And now we're laughing, leaning back in our chairs, slapping our thighs. Mom laughs, too, and Graeme, palpably relieved, serves himself another chunk of salmon. As the tension eases, my parents and I blow our noses and shake our heads. We say things like "Damn!" and "Jeez!" and other exclamations that do little to express the tempest of emotion served at dinner tonight.

Soon, with Graeme's prompting, Dad finishes the story. He describes their second capsize, only 120 degrees this time. He ticks off a new list of broken items, including two cracked booms and large fissures in the ferro-cement hull. And, he says, in an effort to prevent another capsize, they towed stuff off the stern of the boat to slow her down—chain, rope, an anchor, even a ten-speed bicycle. I nod, recognizing the bike from my childhood version of the story.

Finally, the weather abated. The crew jury-rigged as much as they could and sailed for a Japanese island about two hundred miles away. Normally they would have covered the distance in forty-eight hours. With their battered rig, it took them six days.

When *Misty* arrived at Chichi Jima they became local celebrities because the boat had been reported missing in Japanese newspapers, radio, even TV. Thanks to gifts of food and booze from local officials, *Misty*'s crew celebrated their survival in style.

"Eventually, after nursing our hangovers"—Dad winks at Mom—"we worked up our sea legs again. We boarded a northbound ferry to Tokyo that returned us, finally, to our kids."

"Thank God," Mom breathes, her shoulders falling with relief.

I, too, feel relieved and thankful—so thankful—to have my parents here with me. They're in their sixties now, healthy and fit with only small signs of age creeping in. They were younger than I am now when they sailed away on *Misty*. Young and stupid, they might say. But they were dreamers and adventurers. I've always loved that about them.

"Wow!" I say, squeezing Graeme's hand. "What a relief."

"And what a great story!" Graeme adds as I kick him under the table.

Strike forty-three.

Mom sits up and rolls her shoulders back. "A great story?" she asks. "Maybe so." She looks at us hard. "But a good experience? No. Definitely not."

Mom turns to Dad for support; he shrugs in mild agreement. She forges ahead. "You waltz in here tonight, a couple who over the past decade has spent more time broken up than together—I'm not being critical, honey, I'm just being honest."

I nod. What she says is true.

"And you tell us you want to quit your jobs, buy a cheap boat, and sail it around the Pacific . . . just the two of you." Now she's ticking things off on her fingers like Dad always does: "No offshore sailing experience. No extra savings to make repairs on the way. Not even a marriage license to hold you together."

Her eyes dart between us. Graeme and I are silent.

"And, to add insult to injury, you plan to cross the very waters that nearly did us in thirty years ago." She lets that sink in, and when she speaks again, she sounds tired. "And *who* will take care of your dog? And *who* will look after your home? And *who* will collect your mail? And *who* will manage your finances?"

Mom pauses to take Dad's hand. She looks at him and back at us. Then says resignedly, "*We* will, honey. Because we love you, and care for you, and that's our job as parents . . . to be supportive."

Dad nods. Mom exhales slowly, like an engine letting off steam.

"But you come in here tonight, drop your 'Big News'"—her left hand crooks out quotation marks—"and expect us to be excited about it? Well now . . ."

I stare at the napkin in my lap.

"Come in here and tell us you're in love, planning a wedding, even eloping. We'll do backflips and jump for joy."

Her pause is pregnant.

"Love is a wonderful thing, honey. But the sea . . . ?" Her voice trails off.

Dad doesn't miss a beat. "The sea is one fickle bitch," he says.

Thereby inspired, Graeme and I begin boat shopping the very next day.

3

The One

for the entirety of my adolescent and adult life I've lived with this
paralyzing fear that I'll choose the wrong One. That I'll fall in love, get
married, and ten years later realize I made a terrible mistake. Even though
you love someone right now, how can you know you'll love them when
you're seventy? And, alternately, if you *aren't* sure you love someone right
now, how can you know that, when you decide you do, it's the real thing?
Because aren't you *just supposed to know*, like, right off the bat?

Well, I didn't. When Graeme waltzed back into my life a decade after
we fell in love in college, my initial thought was that he should turn on
the shiny heel of his wingtip and waltz right back out. Granted, this new
and improved International Business Guy Graeme was clearly focused and
mature, but he wasn't nearly as drooly as the cute, outdoorsy rugby player
I'd dated as a coed. The sun-deprived paleness of his skin, the dishwater
eye-bags from jet lag, and the slight paunch bulging over his suit pants
didn't help. And while I know you're not supposed to choose a mate based
on something as shallow as ill-fitting trousers, I wasn't exactly sure what
criteria *are* acceptable. Or, more important, accurate.

I mean, is it the fairy-tale stuff? Like:

Do you love each other?
Does your heart go pitter-patter?
Do you make each other happy?

Or is it the practical stuff:

Do you get along?
Do you have common interests and values?
Do you have good sex?

Or maybe the best barometer is one of those old adages, like:

Does he treat his mother well?

Problem with that last one is Graeme's mom is so abnormally *normal*, he'd be crazy not to treat her well. (And I'd be crazy not to want her as a mother-in-law.) So that adage didn't really help either.

One of my girlfriends, who had chastised me over the years for being Overly Analytical and Way Too Picky, theorized that a man who keeps coming back is probably meant to stay. But I took logic in college, and the inverse seemed just as likely true: A man who keeps losing his stick is likely not sticky enough.

And yet, despite my early doubts, Graeme *has* stuck. Partly because, in time, I was able to answer yes to all of the questions above. And partly because Graeme intellectually and fundamentally challenged the way I think about relationships. For a nerdy girl like me, that's actually quite sexy.

It happened two winters ago: We'd been rekindling the flame for a few months then, having lots of fun, definitely falling back in love. And yet. I just wasn't sure he was the One. I mean, I'd loved other guys in my life and was certainly glad I hadn't married *them*. So . . .

Graeme and I are spending this serious weekend at his aunt's beach cabin on the Washington coast. It's a tiny one-bedroom place that's so cute it belongs in one of those fabulous flea market makeover magazines. A battered old sign greets you as you enter:

PLEASE REMOVE YOUR CLOTHES!

We're sitting at his aunt's vintage enamel table in red vinyl-padded chairs when I tell Graeme I'm just not sure he's the One.

And instead of being crushed, he tells me he doesn't *believe* in the One. Or soul mates. Or any of that crap.

"You have to make it the One every day," he says. "Through blood, sweat, and tears, laughter, hope, and faith." (I wrote it down, so I remember his exact words.)

What he means is there's no intrinsic, predestined, objectively verifiable match out there for any of us. We *make* this love the One. By nurturing it. And believing in it. And *creating the relationship we want* each and every day.

"But how do you know if it will *last*, Graeme? Like *forever*?" I ask.

"You don't *know*, Janna. You DO. You do the things that will make your relationship good today. And the next day you do that again. And again. And again. The goal isn't simply to have a marriage that *lasts*." Graeme fingers the grooves of a bright red ashtray, now a change holder since his aunt quit smoking.

I cover his hand with my own.

He looks up. "The goal is to create something wonderful, together, every day for the rest of our lives," he says.

And that little speech is enough to convince me that Graeme is, indeed, the One.

Almost Two Years Later . . .

Graeme puts a beer bottle to his lips and spits. He sets it back down, picks up another exactly like it, and takes a swig. I don't know how he tells them apart, but with all the Copenhagen he's chewing these days, he's getting lots of practice. I've just eased into the foyer, which doubles as an office in our small house, and I lean my shoulder against the doorjamb. Graeme's back is to me, arching protectively toward the computer screen like a guy surfing porn. Graeme is searching for a sailboat to take us across the Pacific Ocean. One that's strong, fast, comfortable, and seaworthy. There are plenty of boats like this online. Just none we can afford.

Standing with my arms across my chest, watching my boyfriend obsess over boats, I decide I can live with the mint color I painted on the walls in here. I intended it to be sage, but those little color squares are cruel jokes; they trick you into thinking that you know what you're getting when really you never can tell. In any case, Graeme and I won't be doing any unnecessary house projects before we leave. Only enough to get the house rented. Because Graeme is too busy choosing his—*our*—new boat. And I, well, I'm hopeful that soon I'll be busy planning a wedding . . . though I can't do that until my *grumble grumble* boyfriend pops the question.

Graeme and I have been living together for a year and a half now, and even though last month's B-HAG resolution canceled my plan of buying a new vacuum cleaner, domesticity suits us pretty well. He's gone half the time on business travel anyway, which reduces the mess by 50 percent. And his travel gives me lots of time to work and spend time with my dog and hang out with girlfriends. That's the glass-half-full take on having Graeme gone so much. The reality is that I'd rather live *with* picking up his wet running gear from the floor, and having to remind him to take out the garbage, and integrating two busy lives into one, than the long-distance purgatory caused by his frequent trips to China. Graeme and I have a love/hate relationship with China.

When Graeme graduated from college ten years ago (after dumping the dishy but naggy me), he followed his parents to Taiwan. They'd moved there the year before to teach English; it was Graeme's mom's lifelong dream to teach abroad, and once his dad sold the fishing boat, she made it happen. Graeme, like his parents, started on the ESL gig but soon got a job in a factory doing business. Whatever that means. No one in the factory spoke English. No one in his town spoke English. No one in a twelve-mile radius spoke English. Graeme learned Chinese.

This skill has come in quite handy. And it complements his other business skills—things like supply chain management, and export finance, and enterprise resource planning. Skills, frankly, I never knew existed, let alone knew Graeme possessed. Back in college he was just that cute, outdoorsy rugby player who double majored in philosophy and politics. Who knew he'd grow up to be a successful business guy?

I take a step farther into the foyer, sweep the current sprawl of sweaty socks and running shoes into the corner with my foot, and run my hand down Graeme's back. The blue-and-white screen lights up his face like the glow of a fish tank. He leans back, yawns loudly, and reaches blindly behind his head with both hands, one set of stretching fingers inadvertently brushing my boob, the other almost catching in my hair. "Hiiii," he says. He lowers his hands, leans forward again, and says, "Look at this one." Graeme back-pages a few clicks until there's a small navy blue sailboat on the screen before us. "*She'll* go," he says and turns, smiling.

"*She'll* go" is Graeme's new motto. He says it with such fervor, such intensity, such passion, it sounds like a preacher intoning the faith of Mary or a frat boy assessing the incoming freshman girls. I peer at the Web page and run my eyes over the long list of specs. Graeme, his voice breathy with enthusiasm, interprets the numbers. After a few stats go in one ear and barely reach the other, I interrupt him.

"Click to the interior photos," I say, squeezing his shoulder.

And this bares the Naked Truth: What Graeme and I are looking for in the One is totally and utterly opposite.

Things Graeme Considers
- Hull material (preferably aluminum or fiberglass)
- The rig (mast configuration and types of sails)
- Keel construction and hull shape (affects how sturdy and fast she is)
- How tall the mast is (it's a guy thing)

Things Janna Considers
- Does the boat have luxuries like refrigerator, heater, oven, shower?
- How comfy and how numerous are her bunks?
- How many people can fit around her table to play cards?
- Does she give me the warm fuzzies?

I'm unimpressed by the photos of this blue boat and her cramped, spare interior. "What about that one you showed me with the roomy living area and two sleeping cabins?" I ask. "That would be perfect for when family comes to visit."

Graeme groans. "That boat was so beamy and so slow, it would take us three years just to get to Mexico."

"Oh." I pause for a moment and think. "But aren't wide boats really comfortable and really sturdy and really really safe?"

"Yeah . . ." Graeme sighs, clicking back to the sleek racing yacht he was lusting after when I walked in. I suspect he's spent the majority of his nights drooling over boats like this one: way too sexy, way too technical, way too rich for our budget. "But speed is important, too," he says. "The faster you make your passage, the less chance you have of getting caught in bad weather."

Or a typhoon, I think, taking my hand from my boyfriend's shoulder and hugging my own. My folks' story sobered us, though not enough to get us off our sailing dream. Still, it worries me . . . but Graeme is already clicking to the next sailboat site. He reaches for his beer. He spits.

"OK, back to work for me," I say, envisioning all the papers I have to grade. I peck Graeme on top of his head in an effort to avoid the shoe polish scent of his chew. It gets caught in my nostrils anyway and follows me back to the dining room. Dad's typhoon story follows me, too. What was it he called the sea? One fickle . . . ?

I seat myself before the stacks of student essays covering my white dining room table—let me amend that: *our* white dining room table. Graeme inherited it by moving in with me. He thinks the table is worn and shabby; I think it's shabby chic. As unobtrusively as I can, I nudge my cold feet under my dog—*our* dog—Scout, who's sleeping under the shabby (chic) table. She's bound to move at any moment because, unlike most chocolate Labs, Scout's aloof and persnickety, only giving and receiving affection when she wants to give and receive affection. She's another thing in my life I'm not sure Graeme's thrilled about inheriting.

With my feet warming under Scout's belly, I stare at the piles of papers. It would be very cool if they could grade themselves. I pick up my mechanical pencil and try twirling it on the nest of my fingers; it rattles across the table. Scout jerks up from my feet, casts me a dirty look, and slinks off to her dog bed. *Sigh.* I begin reading. Sophie Miller's opening sentence says: "Shakespeare's tragedies end in death, his comedies end in marriage." I add a semicolon. Then I think, *If death is tragedy and marriage is comedy, what do you call waiting for your boyfriend to propose? Romance?*

No. Horror.

The thing that sucks most about waiting for the man you love to propose is that it makes you feel like every other woman out there waiting for the man she loves to propose. It takes your life (which you consider fabulous), and your relationship (which you consider special), and your sense of self as a strong, independent, self-sufficient woman (which you consider inviolable), and drops them into a pot of cliché stew that's bubbling over with all those needy, naggy, desperate, must-get-married-*now* women with whom you have absolutely nothing in common.

Nothing.

But my mind gerbil-spins around and around, and it says this: We set sail in less than a year. Yes, we need to find a boat. Yes, we need to prepare for the trip. But we need a marriage certificate more. *Because I refuse to sail across the ocean with some One who can't commit.*

"I've found her!" Graeme's voice beams on the other end of the phone. He sounds as happy as a guy calling home, announcing his engagement to his mom.

"Yeah?" I say. "Really?" My voice feels rubbery with the realization that I've come in second to a sailboat, that Graeme's decided on *her* before he's decided on *me*. *Now this is ridiculous*, I think. *Can I possibly be feeling jealous of a boat?* I tap my forehead, trying to rid it of this pettiness. "So, tell me," I say in an overbouncy tone, "how'd you find her?" I'm trying to hide my disappointment.

Turns out Graeme was on his lunch break, walking the docks, "kicking the proverbial tires on used boats" as he likes to say, when he stumbled across a real catch. Graeme actually had an appointment to see a 1994 Sweden 39—way too new, way too fast, way too expensive—but he figured a little peek wouldn't hurt. So he slobbered across the pristine decks of the Sweden, looked into her every modern nook and fancy cranny, and was skulking guiltily down the gangway to leave when his eyes met *Dragonfly* across the dock. She was old. She was small. She was tired. But she had a little je ne sais quoi that piqued Graeme's interest. That je ne sais quoi, Graeme realized as he examined the FOR SALE sign on her rail, was her price.

Dragonfly is a 1973 Hallberg-Rassy Rasmus. Which doesn't mean anything to most people but is kind of like finding a vintage Mercedes Benz in mint condition. The Rasmus (meaning "God of Winds") is the original model that put the Hallberg-Rassy boatyard on the map. A new thirty-five-foot HR would cost as much as five hundred thousand dollars; *Dragonfly*'s listed at just over fifty. But what makes this boat special (besides the price) is the way she fits both Graeme's and my list of Things We Want in the One. Classic, narrow hull design for Graeme. Comfortable, loungeable cockpit for me. Sturdy and versatile ketch rig for Graeme. An extra guests' sleeping cabin for me. Inch-thick fiberglass hull for Graeme. Gorgeous mahogany interior for me. And, for both of us, she's got what's called a hard dodger, which is a sturdy windshield and overhead shelter that covers half the cockpit. *Practical*, thinks Graeme. *Comfortable*, thinks me.

When Graeme stepped aboard *Dragonfly* that first day she barely flinched. *She's capable*, Graeme thought. *Sturdy. Confident.* Later he would say she smelled like a good old boat should: "a whiff of teak oil, a spot of leather, some salt." Her warm wood interior gleamed like a vat of chocolate, and her layout said *Make yourself at home!* She was tidy. She was compact. And she was clean. But not *too* clean, Graeme noted; a bit of her experience showed through, despite her owners' best efforts to spruce her up. *This one'll go*, Graeme thought to himself back in the cockpit, running his hand along her slightly rusted stainless steel wheel. *She's got good lines, she's got solid bones, and she'll go.*

To the broker Graeme said: "I better call my girlfriend. This could be the One."

A month and a half later, and we've just returned from our inaugural weekend cruise on our new boat *Dragonfly*. And despite the fact that I think she's a pretty decent gal, I can't help but notice she gets a lot more attention these days than I do. Which only marginally explains why, when Graeme says in his chipper voice, "Wanna go to the used marine store and see if they have any good deals?" I burst into tears.

We're sitting in Graeme's 4Runner (again), I'm crying (again), and Graeme's being sweet as Jolly Ranchers (again). This seems to be a recurring theme. A few splatters of rain dribble down the windshield like the slimy tear concoction on my upper lip, creating an Impressionist-meets-Cubist view of the marina parking lot. I'm crying so hard and so unexpectedly that I've taken us both by surprise. And I have no idea how to answer Graeme's question—"What's wrong?"—while keeping my strong, independent, self-sufficient dignity intact.

So I don't keep my dignity intact. I snivel. "I thought we were going to talk about marriage this weekend," I say.

Graeme examines the surface of the windshield, as though analyzing the composition of a painting. "You did?"

"Yes, I did. A couple weeks ago I said I would stop bringing the topic up." My sniff sounds more like a slurp. "I said I'd wait for *you* to bring it up."

"You did?"

"Yes, I did. And we talked about *when* might be a good time for you to bring it up. Since I, apparently, always choose *bad* times to bring it up. Since, even though you say you *want* to get married, every time I try to initiate a reasonable discussion about *what that might actually look like*, we fight. So I said, 'Maybe we can talk about it on our inaugural trip aboard *Dragonfly*.' And you said, 'Yeah. OK. Sounds good.'"

"I did?"

"Yes." *Slurp*. "You did." The slimy tear concoction dribbles again. "But you didn't." I honk my nose into a leftover fast-food napkin Graeme's fished out of the glove compartment.

"Oh."

Silence.

"Let's go for a walk," Graeme says.

We pull up the hoods of our rain jackets and walk the cement boardwalk. Past the big boats. Past the little boats. Past the soft-serve shop where we realize the sky's no longer drizzling. We pull back our hoods and walk the paved path along the beach at Golden Gardens. Even with the damp, gray day, couples are holding hands and walking dogs. We don't hold hands. We don't walk our dog. We just argue. About marriage.

The man I want to marry climbs twenty-thousand-foot mountains for fun. The man I want to marry brokers million-dollar business deals for work. The man I want to marry plans to sail across the Pacific Ocean for his *honeymoon*—since he agrees we should tie the knot before we untie the lines. And yet the man I want to marry is scared out of his wits of weddings.

Of course, I've tried to tell Graeme a zillion times that *marriage* and *wedding* are not synonymous. But every time he hears the *M*-word, really he hears: "Will you stand naked before five hundred of your closest friends, relatives, and complete strangers, to tear your heart out, rip your flesh, cry, bawl, sniffle, and basically lose your shit in order to profess your devotion to the woman you love?" And at that point in the conversation, he loses his shit.

The supreme irony, of course, is that I'm not wed to having a wedding. Elope? An option. Just our nuclear families? Interesting. Just our best friends? I'm open. All I want is to *talk* about it. Like we did when we were brainstorming our B-HAG; like we do with all our big dilemmas and decisions; like we do with even the small stuff in our relationship. But when the *M*-word rears its Medusa-like head, Graeme and I are not able to discuss anything anymore because my daring, audacious boyfriend turns completely to stone.

Now, perhaps this is a sign that Graeme does not want to marry me. But—and maybe I'll chow down my words later—I just don't think that's it. For starters, Graeme has spent the past two years convincing me he's the (I-don't-believe-in-the-One) One. Plus, and this actually is more romantic than it sounds, he listed asking me to marry him as one of his New Year's resolutions (though that was eleven months ago now). There was that postcard from Helzberg Jewelers indicating an item put on layaway. And that phone call from Helzberg Jewelers confirming a payment plan put in place. And a phone message from Helzberg Jewelers saying payment was past due (OK, this last one worried me a bit). But in his defense, Graeme's been out of the country a lot.

Graeme has never been squeamish about saying he wants to spend the rest of his life with me. And he agrees we should be married before we set sail. My boyfriend only turns to stone when it comes to the details of *how*.

We reach the end of the beach where the sand runs out and the train tracks bank hard against the water's edge. I choose a damp boulder to sit on and pull my rain jacket down to prevent wet patches on my butt. Graeme picks up a stone from the beach and takes a seat next to me. This, I'm soon to learn, is the setting for our Engagement Story. Where Graeme will have his Glorious Epiphany. And I'll be Gloriously Disappointed.

"I love you," Graeme says, handling the rock like a pitcher on his way to the mound. He turns the black rock round and around, fingering the thick white ring that encircles it.

Since I was a kid I've considered these ringed rocks wishing rocks, as long as the ring is continuous, no breaks. Every time I find one on the beach, I throw it over my shoulder, launching a wish into the sea.

"I want to spend the rest of my life with you," Graeme says. "And I know I want to marry you."

I nod. It's sweet of him to say, but it makes me smile sadly because, really, none of this is new.

Graeme continues, unraveling the jumble of his thoughts by following a single, twisting line. "I've already made the commitment in my heart. I've already made the decision in my head. Nothing's going to change that," he says.

I know, I think. *So why can't we just* talk *about marriage? The nitty-gritty, like what and where and when?*

But here's Graeme, getting all philosophical and poetic, practically talking to himself. "We're already committed." He looks at the waves. "We're already going to spend the rest of our lives together." He rubs the rock. "So the tough part—the searching, the finding, the choosing—is already over. Right?"

I make no reply. He's not expecting one.

"In a way, we're already married." Graeme lets this seep somewhere deep into his brain for a while. "Yeah. The toughest part is over," he says. "Really, we're already married."

I'm thinking, *No, actually we're* not *married. And we can't even talk about how we'll* get *married without you freaking out* . . . when I see that he's looking at me intently. "We're already there," he says, tears brimming his eyes. "So what am I waiting for?"

Graeme's hand reaches for mine. Graeme's gaze holds mine. Graeme says, "Will you marry me, Janna Marie Cawrse?"

And I think: *This cannot be happening.*

And I say, "Are you *serious*?"

And I wish it were in that happy-girl-laughing tone that one envisions for her Engagement Story.

Oh. But it's not.

Graeme is a robin's nest. I am scattered twigs.

Graeme is a shiny penny. I am a bent bottle cap.

Graeme is a blue ribbon. I am bleach.

Graeme is spongy moss. I am fireplace soot.

Graeme is fresh-brewed coffee. I am burnt toast.

Graeme is dew. I am dung.

Graeme is the reflection of landscape in mirrored sunglasses. I am rust on a bullet-holed stop sign.

Graeme is shoulder and cheek and lip and eye. I am that area just behind the ankle bone that crumbles dirt when you scrub hard enough.

In other words, how Graeme and I feel right now, how Graeme and I view this moment, is completely and utterly opposite.

Ten hours later. Midnight. I'm lying on my back in bed, tears leaking into my ears and onto my scalp and down to my pillow. This one's a silent cry, even though it doesn't have to be. Graeme is fast asleep.

Of course, back on the beach, I said yes. We hugged and we kissed and we walked back down the beach, and got in the car, and drove to the mall. Turns out Graeme had canceled the ring from Helzberg Jewelers on principle because they'd ruined his surprise. So we picked out a new ring together and went out to a nice dinner and talked about the nitty-gritty of marriage. Finally. What we didn't talk about, though, was our Engagement Story, whose events I'm playing over and over in my head. I'm trying to figure out if I'm mad at Graeme about today. Or just plain mad at myself. It looks like it's a bit of both.

On the one hand, I'm disappointed in Graeme because his proposal was as much a surprise to him as it was to me. He didn't know, even two minutes before, that he was going to plop the question. No plan. No ring. No knee. No nervous conversation with my father over beers beforehand. And, even though I'm no traditionalist, it would have been nice if just one (1) of those elements had been present in today's proposal. Because Graeme's Glorious Epiphany, which I know was genuine and inspirational and heartfelt for *him*, feels a bit like, "Hey, we're practically married anyway, so what the hell, let's make it official" to *me*.

On the other hand I'm disappointed in myself. Why did I have to cry? Why did I have to nag? Why did we have to fight for the entire hour before he proposed? I think that's the thing that bothers me most: the proximity between our fight and his proposal. And, if I'm honest with myself, it's not just because my red-rimmed eyes and splotchy face must have made for a pretty grim view when he was asking for my hand. Really, it's even more shallow than that. Because what bothers me is how the story will sound— "I cried, we fought, he caved"—when I tell it to friends, to family, to kids someday. Even to you.

Because what does that say about your relationship if the guy you love has to be pushed and prodded to propose? *Warning!* And yet, I'm more sure of my relationship with Graeme than just about anything else. So it's not that I *personally* feel warned and worried. It's that I'm afraid others will feel that way, and sit in judgment upon us. In the same way, I suppose, that I've sat in pews, watching friends and relatives marry, wondering if it's a good match. Doubting if it's really the One. As if there really *is* a One (old ideas die hard) that can be known and judged by bride and groom, let alone by a mere observer.

I reach over to the bedside table and grab my cotton hankie (Mom always said using Kleenex is like putting tiny splinters up one's nose). I blow and wipe, wood-product-free. And I guess that's the thing: I hate the idea of having any splinters, any superstitions, any doubts tickling my nose (or anyone else's for that matter) when I get married. I want it to be certain. Clear. Obvious. That Graeme is the One for me. As if convincing everyone else that my marriage is sound will simply make it so. Forever.

The problem, I've realized, with Graeme's anti-the-One theory is that it creates an incredible burden. Because, instead of having our relationship just magically *be* the One, we have to make it and craft it and invent it and reinvent it. Every day. Which sounds both empowering and terrifying and like a whole lot of work.

My nose tickles again. And even though I thought I was finished, tears well up, too. Lying here, feeling disappointed in Graeme, feeling superstitious about our engagement, feeling daunted by the lifelong task of marriage that lies ahead—it all makes me feel even more disgusted with myself. Because who criticizes a proposal of marriage that comes in such an earnest and honest way? And who worries that her Engagement Story isn't romantic and convincing enough? And who clings to a false belief in the One, when she knows relationships take genuine, constant, hard work?

Only one kind of person does all this: one fickle you-know-what.

The Cost of a Dream

t he thing about (A) preparing to sail across an ocean is that like (B) planning a wedding, it takes (C) a lot of time. We don't have a lot of C. So, being a mature, modern, non-sex-role-stereotyping couple, we're divvying up the work equally and fairly, right down the middle. Guess who's got column A and guess who's got column B?

While it would be sweet to say my fiancé is integral to every wedding decision "we" make—the color of the napkins, the size of the bouquet, the fancy new dog collar around the ring bearer's neck—I have to say: He's not. Nor am I integral to the upgrade of the boat's GPS, the installation of the autopilot, or the subsequent repairs to each when neither system works.

Enter the Royal We. As in:

"Did we get those save-the-dates out, Janna?"
"Have we decided which radar to buy, Graeme?"
"Do we have the caterer booked, Janna?"
"Can we fix the boat's toilet so it doesn't sound like a herniating goose in heat, Graeme?"

A common response to all of the above is: *The Royal We did it.*

When Graeme and I first moved in together, the Royal We was instituted for mutual jobs like sorting the recycling or shopping for groceries. It was a nice way to say: "I haven't gotten around to this task; I know it's as much my responsibility as yours; any chance you've done it?" It was a courtesy, not a nag (at least in the right tone). But it's grown now into a division of labor that suits our separate skills and interests well: Graeme's the Royal We of the boat; I'm the Royal We of the wedding.

Not that I'm wild about weddings. I don't like foof, I abhor pomp, and stringing toile is as high on my list as plucking armpit hairs one by one. But I do like a good ceremony, I am crafty, and I'm good at organizing things. So planning a down-to-earth wedding that feels intimate and personal and meaningful is right up my aisle. And Graeme, well, Graeme's Royal We Job makes him happier than a barnacle on a boat's bottom.

Plus, it's not like planning a wedding and planning a boat trip are *totally* mutually exclusive. They do dovetail every now and then—e.g., in the financing department. Because, by a wacky twist of fate, the Cost of our Dream Wedding has become inextricably linked to the Cost of our Dream. Let me explain: When I was in high school, Dad told me weddings were a waste of money. (Like Graeme, he also didn't want to cry in front of hundreds of people.) So Dad said if I eloped, he'd give me the wedding money to put toward something else: the down payment on a house, a new car, a contribution to my retirement plan. My father can be a very generous, very practical fellow.

But now that Graeme and I have decided we don't want to elope, Dad's changed his offer. He says he'll fund the wedding at the going rate (à la Google), and that whatever we come in underbudget, he'll donate to the cruising kitty. My father can be a very generous, very flexible fellow, too. And it's proof that, after several months, he and Mom have gotten over their initial freak-out about our trip.

So every buck I save on our wedding is a buck earned for our boat. And while Graeme could complain about the *time* I'm spending on wedding preparations, the same is not true of the money. Here's what the next six months of *my* life look like:

- Decide that the best way to save money on your wedding is to serve wine from Trader Joe's known as Two-Buck Chuck. It's definitely cheap and probably tacky; do it anyway.
- Decide that the next best way to save money on your wedding is to host it in a barn on an island far away from Seattle's spendy reception halls. It's definitely cheap and probably tacky; do it anyway.
- Decide that the third best way to save money on your wedding is to forgo a live band in exchange for a karaoke DJ who specializes in disco music and *Grease* songs. You get the picture.

- Buy the perfect wedding dress for under $250 (including tax) by shopping across the street from St. Vincent de Paul's Thrift Store in a low-rent area outside Seattle.
- Buy film for your friend's Nikon 35 mm instead of shelling out the dough for a professional photographer.
- In place of a string quartet or a wedding singer, write a song for your fiancé and convince his aunt and your mother (the latter of whom can't watch AT&T commercials without crying) to sing it during the ceremony.
- Accept your soon-to-be mother-in-law's generous offer to put on a rehearsal dinner barbecue for the *entire guest list* the night before the wedding.
- Accept your father's generous offer to provide self-caught salmon and halibut for the caterer to cook for the reception.
- Craft, sew, steal, and borrow everything you possibly can for the wedding (e.g., the programs, the bridesmaids' gifts, the portable sound system from work, the cigarette-burned veil from your girlfriend's wedding).
- Ask your pregnant friend to be your matron of honor—then tell her the wedding is on her due date. (No, I'm not joking. Yes, I'm ashamed. And while it has nothing to do with being cheap, it certainly fits with the tacky theme.)
- Realize that when you have something you're passionate about and invested in vying for your time, those papers to grade, those lessons to plan, those student plays/poetry readings/sporting events/concerts take far less of it.

I've become one of those teachers who just, well, teaches. Of course, he-who-shall-not-be-named (Graeme) would argue that I've simply traded my perfectionist, plate-too-full teaching for perfectionist, plate-too-full wedding planning. But the wedding is for Us (both Real and Royal), and putting us/me first for once feels good.

Plus it's not like Graeme is sitting at home twiddling his thumbs. Instead, he's twiddling about on *Dragonfly*. Here's what the next six months of *his* life look like:

- Buy a ten-year-old single-sideband radio at the used marine store.
- Brag to your wife about what a deal it was!
- Install single-sideband radio yourself using seaman's intuition.

- Fire the guy who installed single-sideband radio because it doesn't work.
- Repair/reinstall single-sideband radio using a convoluted instruction manual, advice from passersby on the dock, and information gleaned from a brand-new *Marine Electronics Encyclopedia* that was twice the cost of the radio itself.
- Brag to your wife that it works!
- Repeat above steps for every single piece of equipment on board.

Nope, Graeme's not bored at all. In fact, he's happier than I've seen him in a long time. I am, too. And, of course, that's when we get the call.

We're on the road between a wedding errand and a boat chore when Graeme's cell phone rings. Steering with one hand, Graeme picks up, and I punch down the volume on NPR. Things are eerily silent on this end of the phone; all Graeme does is nod. But even so, I'm not certain something's wrong. Until Graeme pulls over to the side of the road, turns the key, and sets the emergency brake.

Graeme says, "How big is it?"

Graeme says, "What do the doctors say?"

Graeme says, "When can they operate?"

And my insides slide from the warmth of my gut into the crunchy gravel beneath the car.

The next morning Graeme has a quarterly board meeting at work. The board members are big shots in the community, higher-ups from Microsoft and other local corporations. When it comes his turn to present, they look at him expectantly. He opens his mouth to deliver his spiel: shipments, inspections, productivity, bottom line. Nothing comes out. He looks from his notes to the window outside. Gray. Rainy. His eyes tear up. "I'm sorry," he says. "My mother has breast cancer."

"Do you think we should postpone the wedding?" I ask, ramming my gloved hands into the pockets of my jacket. We're standing at the edge of the neighborhood ball field; Scout is off leash illegally. She's doing her crazy, circling, nose-to-ground run. Pretty soon she'll bring back a ball.

"I don't know," Graeme says. "Maybe."

"I mean, I'm sure we could reschedule everything. We still have four months. And people . . . people understand this sort of thing. . . ." My voice follows my gaze up a steep berm where tall yellow grass grows. Graeme follows it, too. A red Doritos bag stuck in the grass flashes with each wave of the wind. I turn back toward Graeme and take his bare hand in my gloved one. Finally I ask the other big question, the one I know we've both been thinking about for the past week: "Do you think we should cancel the sailboat trip?"

"I don't know," Graeme says. He lets go of my hand, climbs up the hill, and grabs the offending Doritos bag. He descends diagonally, heading toward the garbage can by the baseball backstop. When he returns I've just thrown the ball for Scout again. He says, "First let's get Mom through this surgery."

The best way to describe Graeme's mom is to describe the way she laughs. Not at clever, funny things (in which case her laughter is joyful and hearty and unabashed), but at tough stuff: like her husband's dangerous addiction to fishing boats, or her two sons' scary obsession with mountain climbing, or her own diagnosis of breast cancer. Her reaction looks like this: an exaggerated rolling of the eyes, a shaking of the head, a drawn bow of the mouth, and an ohhhhh that eventually divides itself—oh-oh-oh—into long, lingering laughter. Her laughter is not denial or subterfuge. It's not naïveté or insincerity. Vickie's laughter is affirmation. It says: We've dealt with tough stuff before; we'll deal with tough stuff again. And we'll do it by way of laughter because it's better than the alternative.

So when we approach Vickie's hospital bed early Friday morning and ask how she's feeling in preparation for her surgery, she shakes her head, rolls her eyes, and emits her ohhhh-oh-oh-ohs. She's nervous, she says, but ready. Optimistic that all will be fine. So pleased and thankful we came.

After the surgery, describing the months of radiation ahead, Vickie scrunches her face like one of those sour-faced panty hose dolls. It's another one of the expressions she employs to forgo crying. "The treatment should be finished by your wedding," she says, "—just."

She does not allow us to change the date of the wedding. She won't hear of canceling the trip. She's already got her own travel plans penciled in for the fall. Life goes on, she says without saying it, and she will show us how. Though, when Graeme and I contemplate leaving family now, the cost of our dream seems steeper. And at the same time, watching Graeme's mom cling to her own dreams, we understand even more why we must go.

Only our dog, Scout, does not. Scout's not sure why anyone with opposable thumbs and the ability to reason would choose to spend a day, let alone months or years, on a sailboat. In Scout's estimation, a sailboat's a seesaw where your partner's a bully who keeps jumping off.

We learn this the first time we take Scout sailing on *Dragonfly*. While we load provisions onto the boat for the weekend, Scout curls up on deck. Lounging in the cool sun, Scout looks comfortable. Happy even. But as soon as the boat starts moving, so does Scout. She paces back and forth along the deck, sniffing the air, her ears cocked back. When we stick *Dragonfly*'s nose out into Puget Sound, Scout retreats to the safety of the cockpit. And as we hoist the sails and the boat starts to tip, Scout weaves between our legs, shaking and whining. We try to soothe her with kind words. "It's OK, Scout. You're going to be all right, Scout."

Scout will not be soothed.

Pretty soon the sails are set and Graeme and I take our seats in the cockpit. Scout chooses her seat, too, snuggled in close to my hip. I put my arm around her and think, *Oh, it's nice to have a cuddly dog for once.* But then Scout crawls on my lap. There's a gust of wind and the boat heels more, and Scout inches her rump a bit higher. She's now sitting on my chest, like in that movie *Alien*, where the creature bursts from Sigourney Weaver's chest. Fur tickles my bottom lip. I giggle. At the next gust, Scout is sitting, no exaggeration, upon my shoulder. She looks like a pirate's parrot.

If you've ever tried to sail with a seventy-five-pound Labrador retriever on your shoulder, you'll know it's not easy. Of course, it's quite a feat for Scout, too, as a bony shoulder on a laughing human isn't such a comfortable spot either.

But, then, parroting parrots is only one of Scout's issues with the boat. The other problem for a well potty-trained dog is where to pee at sea. And Scout, not to brag or anything, is a very well potty-trained dog. When Scout was a pup I craftily decided to teach her to pee on command. For some reason my roommate suggested "Do it up!" as our signal phrase. It stuck. So, like Pavlov's dog, Scout will squat (rather than slobber) just about anywhere you say "Do it up!" Only, as we've recently learned, not on the deck of a boat. Which is a slight problem, as peeing on a boat is a necessity for a dog destined to sail across an ocean.

Ah, but we've heard there's a way around this problem.

I head to my local Crown Hill Hardware and buy a green doormat made of artificial turf. I know it looks a bit odd to our neighbors, walking my dog with a green doormat rolled under my arm, but according to what we've read, it's essential that I get this mat good and sopped before I transfer it to the boat. The idea is to give it enough doggie scent to convince Scout it's OK to pee upon. And once she's used it successfully on board a few times, we'll be able to drag it behind the boat to clean it every now and then. At least that's the plan.

So every morning I'm skulking down the streets, carrying the green mat, urging Scout to "Do it up! Do it up!" When she lowers her haunches to pee, I sneak up and slide the mat underneath her. When she finishes her business, she trots off nonchalantly down the street, dragging me, my poop bags, and my dripping mat, as though all dogs deserve turf service from their so-called masters.

Problem is, when we present Scout with her new potty spot on the boat, she sniffs it once, sniffs it twice, then turns her nose to land and whines. She will not pee on a mat. She will not pee on a hat. She will not pee on a boat. She will not pee on a coat. She does not like our green mat plan. She does not like it, Janna and Graeme.

Graeme, sensing some tough love is required, offers to give some of his own time and attention to the project. He claims he'll turn Scout into a sea dog yet. So one weekend, while I'm busy chaperoning a school dance, Graeme and his brother, Ashley, embark on a quest to give Scout her sea legs.

That first night out, according to Graeme's version of the story, the two brothers feel they need to provide their reluctant pupil with some motivation. They decide to engage Scout in a drinking contest. It's a festive way to mark the occasion, Graeme reasons. Plus, since Scout's beverage of choice is water, the boys will have the beer to themselves.

At first, Scout matches the brothers bowl for beer; after all, sailing is hard work for a shoulder-climbing dog. But after Round Three, Scout slows down. And a worried look appears in her eye. Graeme senses it's time to attempt Scout's first, as he calls it, "boat movement." He and Ashley take Scout on deck to where the moon illumines the green mat.

First Graeme demonstrates that peeing on the mat is Totally Acceptable Behavior on the boat. "Do it up!" he says while pissing on the mat. Scout only paces and whines.

Next Ashley demonstrates that peeing on the mat is, yes, Perfectly Acceptable on the boat. "Do it up!" he sings while adding his scent to the mat.

Only Scout isn't getting into the spirit of things. All through the night, the brothers drink beer, and Scout laps halfheartedly from her bowl. "Do it up, Scout!" rings from one end of the harbor to the other. The boys cajole Scout, they sympathize with Scout, they speak sternly to Scout, they piss. To no avail. Finally, around midnight, they give up and go to sleep. Scout has won the battle.

Unfortunately for Scout, though, a battle is not a war. In the morning, forgoing the usual dogwalk ashore, the brothers set sail for another harbor, four hours away. All day long, even with a further pee-demonstration, Scout refuses to do it up. (Graeme decides that stubbornness is a trait learned from one's mother.) Six miles from their destination, Scout begins to whine insistently. Now she's pissed off. Sensing he's up against more than he can handle, Graeme fires up the sailboat's engine and roars off in the direction of the harbor.

As *Dragonfly* enters the narrow channel between shore and sandy spit, Scout gauges whether or not she can make the jump. She can't. So she paces back and forth, bow to stern, whining louder as the boat nears land. When *Dragonfly* is six feet from the dock, Scout makes her move. She takes a running start, clears the rail, and lands on the dock on all fours. On impact, Scout sprints for the grass onshore. She makes it four or five steps before springing a leak; she poops and pisses the length of the dock. When Scout reaches the authentic green grass, she hunkers down, walks a few steps, hunkers down again. Her pee makes the sound of a dog sighing. Meanwhile, Graeme's got to pick up her poop, step by step by step. *Payback*, Scout must think as she squats again. And again.

In the end, Graeme loses not only the battle and the war, but almost his head.

"Don't you know you can kill a dog by not letting her poop or pee?" I fume.

Graeme, the adoptive dog father, swears he's never heard of this veterinarianal fact. He also swears he'll plan our future weekend sailing trips around places Scout can do it up ashore.

And so for the time being we toss the green mat overboard (proverbially, of course), and embrace our deck-pacing, shoulder-sitting, green-mat-shunning dog, who otherwise is not half bad to sail with.

Only now it's unclear if Scout will ever be a blue water sailor because, alas, there are no beaches to pee on when crossing an ocean. And we begin to wonder if this is yet another cost of this dream of ours. We knew we'd have to say good-bye to friends. We knew we'd have to say good-bye to family. But we didn't know we'd be leaving just when our family needs us most. And we hate the idea of deserting a dog who doesn't understand "We'll be back."

After our allotted (C) time passes, we find that we've successfully (B) planned our wedding, and (A) prepared for our trip. All that's left to do is tie the knot and untie the lines.

So we caravan with close friends and family to the islands north of Seattle, toting kegs, barbecue grills, and sweating coolers of fish. From the broad wooden beams of a big red barn we hang colorful Chinese lanterns, and we clothesline the walls with hundreds of black-and-white photos. The locale may not be couth, but it's a great place for a party.

Graeme's mom has her last radiation treatment on a Thursday morning, gets on a ferry that afternoon, and joins the gang that evening. The next day she and her family prepare a huge barbecue for our entire guest list. When I ask her if she's up to it, she doesn't shake her head and let out her silver-lining laugh. She just says, "You bet I am!"

When the ceremony comes, everyone plays a part. Our brothers, thanks to the power vested by the World Wide Web, officiate. Our friends give advice. Mom and Aunt Crystal raise their voices and sing. And Scout, she bears the rings—cheapo five-dollar bands from Seattle's Pike Place Market—in a tiny drawstring bag around her new collar.

And so, on the summer solstice of 2003, in a seaside barn with family real and chosen, drinking cheap wine and singing Olivia Newton-John's "You're the One That I Want," Graeme and I say I do. To each other. To our sailing dream. To life.

Here's the song Janna wrote for Graeme, the one she made Aunt Crystal and Mom sing at the ceremony because she was too cheap to hire a wedding singer:

The Rock Song

As a girl she was superstitious
Found ringed rocks and made three wishes
Threw them over her shoulder as blind as three mice
When she wished she wished for him

Happiness on a boy was pinned
'Til a voice started whispering you better think twice

And she learned
I found this rock, found it for me
Picked it up by the edge of the sea
Rough edges smoothing with the surf
How can you know
How far a stone can throw
The deeper well, the deeper I grow
Closer to you the more I'm myself

With his dad he oft was fishin'
For a good catch he was wishin'
Why did he let that one get away
Moved his life across the world
Learned of love from other girls
But from his shore kept casting for more her way

And he learned
I hold this rock, hold it for me
Picked it up by the edge of the sea
Rough edges smoother with every wave
How can you know
How far a stone can skip
Bridging borders, bridging lips
Closer to you the more that we change

The charm it comes with the third
Mountains scaled and lessons learned
Tide of life and love it ebbs and it flows
Quicksilver lightning flash
Burns down to embers and ash
But wind fans the flame of love and it glows

And it grows
I bring this rock, bring it for you
Picked it up by the green and the blue

Ocean that's beckoning us to sail
And now we'll know
How far a dream can go
My wish for you, I'm sure you know
Is a life of love and all it entails

(Listen at www.byjanna.com.)

Part 2

The Coast

Shakedown Summer

June 2003—Getting the Kinks Out

Y ou forgot your WHAT?"

"My *mumble mumble* pills."

"Did you say your *birth control* pills?"

"Yyyup."

This is the conversation, the day after our wedding, that begins Graeme's and my married life together. It also kicks off our Practice Honeymoon Cruise, not to be mistaken for our Real Honeymoon Cruise, which won't begin until September. We're doing a practice run now, called a Shakedown Cruise in sailor-speak, to shake out all the kinks before the real voyage begins.

This morning we waved good-bye, amid light raindrops instead of confetti, to two dozen guests at the dock. It should have been closer to a hundred guests but, *oops,* I told people the wrong marina. That was the first snafu in the plan. And now there's this wrinkle: Mom calling to say she found my toiletry kit at the inn and, not to be snoopy or anything, peeked inside on a hunch. Sure enough, my birth control pills were there. Right there. Next to my K-Y jelly. *Thanks, Mom.* Oh, and she discovered, popping the pill pack open, that I forgot to take this morning's pill, too. *Even better.* Graeme's face goes from seagull white to buoy red to kelp green as I tell him all this.

"But don't worry," I say. "We have a plan."

Friends will bring the errant pills to us in La Conner, a waterside town just north of here. From there we can continue on our Shakedown Cruise, sailing the two-thousand miles of coastline around Vancouver Island, shaking out all the kinks we possibly can.

The biggest kink I've wanted to shake out, the main thing I've been obsessing about for the past few months—besides the wedding, of course—is losing my blue water virginity. Because, up until a few days ago, I'd never sailed on the open ocean before. I was the boating equivalent of the girl who'd made it to third base (lakes, bays, sounds) but had never gone all the way (the so-called blue water). Plus, up until tonight I certainly hadn't sailed in the dark. We'd always made a point of being someplace safe—at a dock or on anchor—before the sky got so black it slinked into the water. So taking the plunge like this—standing watch all alone from midnight to 4 A.M. while sailing on the open ocean—is like losing one's virginity, not in the safe, predictable way of missionaries, but in some kinky, upside-down, tantric acrobat position—*the very first time*.

So here I sit, folded into the corner of *Dragonfly*'s cockpit, my neck and nerves and eyes agog, staring into a black sandbox sky of stars. Graeme is sleeping below. Every noise sears my brain and every movement makes me start. Is that normal, the *ch-ch-chreek* sound coming from the mast? What about the *CHAgluck* swing of the mizzen? Did I just see something to my right? I turn my head like the kickback on a sprinkler. Nothing.

Our run is from Tofino, a tiny town on Vancouver Island's stubbled western shore, to the regal and palaced Victoria, B.C. The seas are flat tonight, the winds light, and I haven't had to adjust *Dragonfly*'s sails yet at all. The only tricky part is avoiding shipping traffic as we near the Strait of Juan de Fuca. It's kind of like those eye tests they give you at the optometrist's, where you press your face into darkness and raise a finger every time you see a light. Only, as we get closer to the shipping lanes, there are more and more pinpricks of light. And if I miss one, the consequences could be dire.

Peering through binoculars (a wedding gift) I examine and analyze every faint glow I see. If it's red, it's the other ship's port, or left side. And if it's green, it's the ship's starboard, or right side. (I remember this because "green" and "right" and "starboard" are all longish words, whereas "red," "left," and "port" are shorties.) The only way you can surmise where the heck a ship is going is by identifying these key colors. And that's important to figure out, because a light that looks miles away could be upon you lickety-split. Usually, though, they cross your path at a good distance—no harm, no foul. It's when you see red and green at the same time, getting bigger, that a ship is coming straight for you.

OK, so it's a bit more complicated than those eye tests at the doctor's office.

Pfuh. A noise to starboard startles me. I look and see nothing. But it's strangely familiar. Like the gentle half-snore Graeme makes when he sleeps on his back. *Pfuh. Pfuh.* There it is again. Not Graeme. Not a ship. Nothing on our boat. It's something in the sea.

I peer over *Dragonfly*'s gunnels into the inky ocean. Nothing. *Pfuh.* Now it's on our port. I leap to the other side of the cockpit, stand on the bench seat, and stare into the water.

What I see are streaks of light like swoopy trails of sparklers on Independence Day. Only much bigger. And better. This is what happens when a pod of dolphins meets bioluminescent plankton, aka phosphorescence—tiny organisms that live in the water and glow in the dark when swooshed. So as the dolphins swim along *Dragonfly*'s hull, dolphin-size tubes of light bend and wobble and dip. With every *Pfuh* there's a splash of neon on the water's surface. Like an upside-down fireworks show dazzling the night-sky of water.

Tonight's show lasts an hour. I think, night watches are all right by me.

July 2003—Divorce Docking

Of course, a successful Shakedown Night Watch doesn't mean we've got this sailing thing down pat. When we return to Seattle, amid packing up the house and provisioning the boat, Graeme and I try to sail *Dragonfly* as much as we can. We only have two months until D-day, and we're still not very good at it.

Instead of working together like a well-oiled machine that spins and whirs and hums, we're more a crappy-ass, junkyard, lawn mower engine that hollers and curses and farts. Especially when it comes to stopping the boat before it hits something hard, e.g., the dock at Fisherman's Terminal, the pilings in Port Townsend, the ground in Kingston Harbor.

And so Graeme calls in the big guns: A two-time circumnavigator. A veteran sailor. An expert instructor. A *woman.* Nancy Erley, founder of Tethys Offshore Sailing for Women, agrees to come down to the boat and provide professional consultation about how we might sail successfully—as a couple. Predictably, overbooked, overstressed me, I'm able to chat for only half an hour before rushing off to an appointment I completely forgot.

Which leaves Graeme in the hands of a woman who doesn't shy away from the tough questions. Like: "I'm sure your five-foot-four wife is quite strong but . . . why is she the one running around on deck with boat hooks and fenders? Why is she making five-foot leaps across cold water to slippery docks? Why is she using her small frame to stop the momentum of a ten-ton tub careening toward pilings, boats, and docks, with three knots of current, twenty knots of wind, and a sailboat's notoriously poor maneuverability?"

Er.

Nancy, looking Graeme up and down, goes in for the kill: "Your wife seems astute, able, and intelligent, Graeme. Can't she turn the steering wheel left and right, and move that little gear shift stick back and forth as well as you?"

Graeme gulps. Giving up control of the helm is like giving up control of—everything. But what Nancy suggests fits our Royal We philosophy: Graeme is strong and daredevilish, so let him do the grunt work and leaping; I'm pretty good handling a six-inch stick, so let me shift the gears and drive the boat. And as we continue sailing into the summer, that one little role reversal changes, well, everything.

It used to be that Graeme docked by intuition, sensing the current, feeling the wind, calculating the angles in his head. Sometimes this worked. Sometimes it didn't. But now, with me at the helm, Graeme and I analyze the elements and verbalize a plan beforehand—together. And for the first time, there's something important *I'm* in charge of on the boat. And slowly, very slowly, *Dragonfly* and I are getting to know each other a bit better.

The other new development is that Graeme and I have adopted SILENT HAND SIGNALS when docking *Dragonfly*. The opposite method (aka divorce docking) involves shouting instructions, shouting retorts, and generally pissing each other off. Stroll within earshot of any marina on any summer's day, and you'll see divorce docking is by and large the method of choice among boating couples. But our method, in contrast, has this single benefit: Motioning one's hand in a reverse direction vigorously (urgently! madly!) is far less damaging to the relationship than yelling, "Reverse. *Reverse!* GODDAMMIT I SAID RE-VERSE!!!"

Of course, we can only pat ourselves (silently) on the back so much. Because none of this skill in stopping the boat actually helps us *sail* her any better. And that's still a problem. Though we're hoping we can sort of figure that out, you know, on the fly.

August 2003—Perfectionist Provisioning

On the bright side, while I may not be an excellent seaman, I am becoming a Provisioning Diva. I've always been obsessed with containers—colorful baskets, tin bins, wooden boxes, cloth sacks; I usually have more containers than stuff to contain. Now, though, on a rocky and rolly boat where *everything* needs containment, I'm like Martha Stewart meets Sanford and Son. Organizing bliss.

I've got mesh bags for dirty laundry, hammocks for clean, collapsible buckets for water, milk crates for linens, tiny boxes for nuts and bolts, Ziplocs for medications, and woven baskets for just about everything else. Plus, I've measured every inch of cupboard space aboard *Dragonfly* and have systematically installed stackable, plastic, covered bins for all our foodstuff. Each box has a label, and each has its place. I call it custom design. Graeme, having to pull out two bins of granola bars to access the bin of pasta, calls it a pain in the ass.

I've also made half a dozen trips to Costco to buy canned goods, dried goods, snacks, pop, and beer. I read one book about a sailing family who filled an entire cupboard with Jiffy peanut butter alone. There was a photo of all those plastic jars lined up, *J* to *Y*, *J* to *Y*, on custom-size Jiffy shelves. After my sixth trip to warehouse food land, however, Graeme puts a cap on bulk groceries. He claims people eat, and hence buy food, everywhere.

I guess he's right.

One thing he's not right about, though, is that my latest project, creating small wedding photo albums for our parents and grandparents, is a waste of time.

Sweating at a green plastic table in front of a taco truck, Graeme wonders aloud why I'm spending hours choosing, ordering, printing, assembling, and labeling six different photo albums when there's still so much to do on the boat.

"Well, for one, none of my grandparents could attend our wedding, so I want to make them feel like they were there." I spoon a dollop of salsa on the last of my fish taco. "And your grandparents are old enough that they probably wouldn't mind a reminder of our big day." I take a bite, chew, and swallow way too soon. "Plus, it's important to me. It's my project. I want to do it."

"But *Dragonfly* is your project, too," Graeme says. "And we only have one month left."

"*Dragonfly* will be fine. Believe me." I take another bite and swallow it almost whole. "And, as you've pointed out, it's not like we're leaving civilization immediately. There are plenty of stores—and we'll have plenty of time—all down the coast." I wipe the corner of my mouth with a wadded-up napkin. "We can do stuff along the way."

Graeme stands up, gathers his paper plate and empty Diet Coke can, and says, "Well, we better get back to work."

I pick up my half-full pop, stuff the last bit of taco into my mouth, and chew as we walk across the gravel lot back to the car. I'm annoyed he doesn't get why I'm doing this; the albums are gifts for his family, too. And yet he's right that I tend to bite off more than I can chew.

Never enough time in the day, I think, shading my eyes from the sun.

And I wonder if time passes differently on the ocean.

Of course, the cars get sold. The house gets rented. The boat work gets (mostly) done. Summer draws to a close. On our last visit with family before we leave, Graeme watches his eighty-something-year-old grandmothers thumb through the prints from our wedding. They get tears in their eyes.

Graeme gets teary, too. And now I know he gets it.

At the end of the party, we leave instructions with Graeme's folks about our itinerary; they'll meet us in a couple spots along the coast. And then Graeme's grandmothers shush us out the door, as though we're a young couple late for a moving pictures show.

"Have a good time, you lovebirds!" they say. "Hurry back!"

September 2003—The Voyage Begins

Pulling away from the dock on the first morning of our Real Honeymoon Cruise feels exhilarating and momentous. Standing behind the wheel in my snappy white sneakers, my hair blowing in the breeze, I'm the model in the tampon ad—*Carefree!* Except that we've got to stop at the communal dock for a couple last chores before we leave the marina. We've got to fill up our water tank and, most important of all, pump out our head.

First, a little terminology: The "head" on a sailboat is not the top of the mast or the nose of the boat or some Starship *Enterprise*–like command center. The head on a sailboat is its bathroom or, more specifically, its toilet—a linguistic connection you can take as ominous. The head leads to the holding tank, which is where, in the United States at least, boats are required to store sewage until either (A) they travel three miles from land to dump it overboard, or (B) they dock at a marine-grade Porta Potti where they can pump it out.

As an aside, travelers in search of turquoise waters should be warned that not a single country between the United States and Hong Kong requires sailors to use pump-out stations. In fact, most countries outside the United States don't *have* pump-out stations. That brown floatie thing you encountered while snorkeling among the pretty boats in Cabo last year? Not a candy bar.

But as I was saying, today our holding tank is chockablock full, and it'll be a while before we're far enough away from land to dump. So our first step is to suck that shit out.

The water is as gray as the weather. The harbor is quiet except for the occasional seagull's squawk. And at 6 A.M., the live-aboard community in the marina is still snug in their bunks. So Graeme and I use our SILENT HAND SIGNALS as we ghost wordlessly toward the Shilshole Bay pump-out station. We're good enough at docking by now that I don't have to use the most expressive SILENT HAND SIGNAL I know, the one named after the *bird* sitting on the piling nearby. We secure the dock lines and I don my heavy-duty orange rubber gloves with a snap. I clamber on deck, unscrew the cap to the holding tank, and peer into the bowels of the boat.

Now you may wonder why I, the blushing bride in the tidy tank top and bright white Keds, is the one hovering over the tank of poo, while my captainly husband cowers on the dock as far away from the anus-like opening as possible. Graeme, a man who will wear the same boxer shorts for days at a time, a man who has tested various forms of foliage for their ass-wiping qualities on long morning jogs (dare I say runs?), and a man who once even caught in his bare hands his drunken friend's fresh turd tossed to him while swimming in the ocean (the only warning being, "Here! Catch!"), has an intense aversion to shit. Perhaps it's this last incident that scarred him. Anyway, I long ago learned that any job involving feces (cleaning the household toilet, picking up dog poop, fixing the herniating goose sound emanating from the boat's toilet) results in melodramatic nose-pinching, reflexive gagging, and incessant bitching from my then-boyfriend-now-husband. So it is I who must take this job, as it were, head-on.

Standing on the dock, his nose turned away in disgust, Graeme dangles toward me a long gray hose of variegated plastic that is attached to the poop-sucking machine. He holds it at arm's length, like one would a dirty rag, or a dead rat, or a long gray hose of variegated plastic that is frequently dipped in shit. I grab it and stuff the end in our holding tank. He retreats to the poop-sucker and puts his hand on the switch. It's time to start pumping.

Graeme flips the switch, and the hose in my hands begins to vibrate. It makes a sound much akin to that which your household vacuum cleaner would make if, instead of flushing, you decided to vacuum out your soiled toilet bowl. *SSSHLLEEEEWK!* Now pretend your vacuum hose is blessed with a clear plastic section through which you can observe the flow of the brown effluent. Well, I'm watching this see-through section with the same morbid fascination with which one pops a zit, when I realize that the dang thing is no longer working. Not only has the brown stuff slowed to a trickle, but the pump is making an angry whining sound. I push the hose into the hole harder. No good. I wiggle it back and forth. Still no poop. Yet I know the tank can't be empty.

With one hand holding the hose firmly in place, I run my orange glove across my neck—cut it. Graeme turns off the machine. Graeme scratches his head. Graeme taps his foot. Then he suggests that we flush some fresh water *into* the tank while we're sucking the poo *out* of the tank—kind of like a sailboat enema! Unable in that brief moment to conjure any logical objections, I stick a green garden hose into the water hole of the holding tank. The water hole lies, logically, just in front of the poop hole. Then I return my hands to the gray variegated plastic hose, which is still inserted in the poop hole. I look expectantly at Graeme.

"Ready?" he asks.

I nod.

Now. Have you ever taken a good long swig of Coca-Cola right before your friend makes you laugh? Have you witnessed the force of a fire hose let loose on a burning building? Have you visited the geysers at Yellowstone National Park? We're talking Old Faithful here.

That shit shoots sky high and lands *everywhere*—on the boat, on the dock, on Graeme, on the seagull sitting on the piling, and most particularly on ME. My tank top is no longer tidy, my shoes no longer white. My shrieks rise like a siren, waking every sleeping sailor in this marina and the next. Shit drips from my hair. Shit slithers down my cleavage. Shit plasters my eyeglasses. In darkness, I use my index fingers like windshield wipers across my spectacles—back and forth, back and forth—until I can finally see again. And there before me stands Graeme, clutching his belly with one hand, cupping his gagging mouth with the other, staring in horror at his newly betrothed bride. Graeme's threatening to lose his cookies while I've already lost my hygiene, my sex appeal, my pride.

Therefore, slowly, deliberately, valiantly, I rotate and raise the middle finger of my right orange glove, now dripping brown, and direct it squarely at my queasy husband. He has no right to barf. He's not the one with poo trickling between his boobs.

And then, Graeme starts to smile. "Is that a red pepper flake from the other night's dinner?" he sniggers, pointing to a bright red fleck on my forehead. "And there on your shoulder, that's got to be corn."

I can see a few kernels sticking in his hair, too. And, since the only other option is to cry, I start giggling as well. Until we're both doubled over laughing because it's better than the alternative.

Soon Graeme's got me stripped half-naked on the pump-out station dock with fresh water splashing over me. As he sprays me down he muses, "Some sort of pressure must have built up when we added water to the tank."

I shrug, not caring so much how it happened, as how I'm going to get this stuff out of my hair, my nostrils, my ear canals. Once he's washed the thick off, I slosh down to the head to shower. I open the cupboard where we keep our toiletries, the same cupboard that houses the large white holding tank of poo. And here I notice a distressing new development—the shampoo, the conditioner, and all our Ziplocs of medications are floating.

Shitfuck! I think. *We've overflowed down here, too!*

But on closer inspection, I realize the cabinet is filled, not with sewage, but with water. I stick my head half-in the cabinet and look up. There's the thick hose that connects the tank to the deck where I sucked (and blew) all our effluent out. But, lo and behold, the water hole in the deck is not connected to the holding tank at all; it's just an empty hole leading into the cabinet. So the water we *thought* we'd been putting into the tank to produce the sailboat enema *really* splashed straight down—no harm, no foul.

Hmph.

This puts a kink in Graeme's theory. Because if there was no pressure built up by adding water to the tank, then what made her blow?

Returning to the cockpit after my shower, I explain this perplexing new discovery to Graeme. He scratches his head. He rubs his chin. Then he grows grave and philosophical. "As you know, Janna, shit happens."

I roll my eyes.

"And when shit happens," he says, "I want to be as far away from it as possible."

I smirk. "Is that your Yoda way of saying 'Let's get the crap outta here'?"

"That's my way of saying, 'Anchors aweigh, my wife, anchors aweigh.'"

Water, Water, Everywhere

*P*ut your right hand in a fist. Cock your thumb out just slightly. And hold it up so you're looking at the back of your hand. This is your map of Washington State. Everything to the left of your arm is the Pacific Ocean. That airy V between your thumb and fist is Puget Sound (imagine lots of little islands in there). And the open, top part of that V is the Strait of Juan de Fuca (rhymes with Puke-uh). Seattle sits on the left side of your knuckles.

Graeme and I left your knuckles amid a fountain of sewage about a week ago, and I'm still wondering what it portends that our trip began in the shits. But close friends joined us in those airy islands for a final send-off, which was a nice distraction, and then we traveled up your opposable digit, fighting our way out the Strait of Juan de Puke-uh, alone. Every day or two we've stopped in a new port; every day or two we've left for another. Heading, like young salmon, to the ocean. Tonight we'll reach the tip of your thumb, where we'll turn the corner, enter the Pacific, and go south down your forearm. Only it's hard to imagine what the open ocean will be like when this V of only semiopen water is already kicking my butt. At least I haven't puke-uhd yet.

But I do have an underlying feeling of malaise. I'm not nauseated *per se*, but I have that prenauseated sensation of having to burp all the time, and I'm always worried that instead of a belch, I'll get a barf. If it weren't for my year-long supply of birth control pills, I might think I was pregnant. Or traveling up a stretch of water that's trying to warn me about something.

The other problem is Graeme's already driving me nuts. For starters, without an office to go to and clients to woo, he no longer changes his clothes or wears deodorant or shaves his face or brushes his teeth regularly. Not that I do all those things as religiously as I used to either, and I've never been one to quibble about hygiene. So perhaps the problem is that, without papers to grade, a wedding to plan, and a boat organization system to custom design, I'm actually paying attention to Graeme's grooming habits for once. Then again, maybe the real issue is that I'm below in the stuffy cabin of our sailboat right now, which is acting like a pinball machine on tilt (I'm the pinball). Graeme, on the other hand, stands behind the wheel in the fresh air of the cockpit, purposefully plowing the boat into the worst of these monstrous waves.

And he's got a smile on his face.

I'm below sucking stale, propane-filled air for a reason though. My left hand steadies a pot of boiling water. My right hand grips the table behind me. And my legs are spread in a surfer's crouch. I'm the dutiful new wife attempting to cook.

I'm a horrible cook.

The first job I landed out of college was cooking for guests on a dude ranch, though I didn't know it at the time. I applied to a cowboy school in Wyoming to lead horse trips into the wilderness and was rejected; they said they didn't accept girls into their *cowboy* school. But, they added optimistically, they wanted to hire me as a "general ranch hand." I asked if this was a euphemism for cooking and cleaning. They assured me no more cooking and cleaning than the cowboys had to do themselves; ranch chores were split up evenly. So one long road trip later, I moseyed up to a roaring campfire that lit the cute faces of cowboys-in-training.

A yell went up, "Yee-haw! The cook is here!"

I stopped. Looked behind me. Looked left. Looked right. Then looked at the cute cowboys around the fire. "I'm not a cook," I said.

"Oh, yes, you are," they said in unison.

And they were right. I was a girl, hence, I was a cook. My only consolation was that I had to have been the worst goddamned cook that dude ranch ever saw. (Though I turned out to be an OK cowgirl; bowleggedness has its benefits.)

And now. Ten years later. I'm still a horrible cook. And there are no cute cowboys or pretty horses to distract me from this fact. Unless you count the white horses galloping outside my window. "White horses" is the name for waves that crest white and frothy like this. The waves' throaty rumble reminds me of horse snorts, and the froth reminds me of horse sweat. Which, instead of bringing to mind valiant galloping horses like Seabiscuit, makes me want to blow biscuits instead. Because cooking on a boat in galloping seas, in a word, sucks.

If you want to know what it's like to cook on a boat in rough seas, try this: First, rename your kitchen "galley." Then cut it to a fifth its regular size (unless you live in Manhattan, in which case cut it in half). Then say good-bye to everything you might expect or want or need in a kitchen, and say hello to this: A shallow, leak-prone sink whose moldy caulk sticks out around the edges. A small, rusty oven that has no chance of fitting a full-size salmon, let alone a turkey. Say hello to a three-burner, manually-lit propane stove whose knobs refuse to turn without the full-court press of your right palm pushing while your left hand trembles with its damp match that—damn!—blows out in the slightest breeze. Say howdy to a refrigerator (sans freezer) that makes its home under a seat under a cushion under someone's ass, which isn't very convenient but doesn't really matter because the fridge rarely works. And when it does, it fills up with a gallon of moldy, food-debris-strewn water so that you're not willing to eat anything from it anyway.

Don't offer your greetings to a garbage disposal. A dishwasher. Or countertops. But, hey, what you lose there, you make up for in faucets! You have three: One saltwater foot pump that draws directly from the frigid and, depending on where you are, polluted water beneath the boat, and smells sulfury, like millions of tiny organisms have crawled into the pipes and died (they have). One freshwater hand pump that's made of brass, and therefore looks very nauti-cool, but that loses its prime, i.e., its ability to pump water, in between each use. And one normal freshwater faucet that has hot water if the engine's been running long enough, but which your evil husband forbids you to use because it draws off the batteries and Rule of Rules: On a boat, where you're unplugged from the grid, you *must! conserve! batteries!*

Now take your new galley, stock it with crappy cooking gear you used car camping, and place it in the small, stuffy, mildew-prone box that is a fiberglass sailboat hull. Now tilt, or "heel," the whole thing thirty degrees—that's right, make your floor as steep as a hillside—and bash the whole thing into waves as hard as brick walls. Over and over and over.

OK. Now. Cook!

• • •

Before Graeme and I got married, I read (OK, skimmed) a book called *Marriage Shock* by Dalma Heyn. It's one of those self-helpy books about how marriage can change women, not just for better, but for worse. It was sobering and not a little distressing, but I thought it important to pull my head from the clouds for a brief prenuptial moment and think about the real changes ahead. Predictably, the only passage I now recall from the book was about sex.

It went something like this: Antonia and Jonathan had a fiery, passionate, healthy sex life before getting married. It was even a bit kinky; Jonathan was the first lover with whom Antonia felt totally uninhibited. But then, as soon as this happily sexed couple wed, they lost the spark in bed. It seems that, along with the new china place settings crowding their house, some big, bulky Wife Baggage had moved in, too. And poor Antonia was no longer able to talk dirty to her (gulp) husband.

The book went on to describe other bits of Wife Baggage—those subconscious but powerful expectations women have about being The Perfect Wife—that plague perfectly reasonable, independent, even feminist women when they tie the knot. And while I don't recall any of the other examples in the book, I'm fairly certain my obsessive desire to cook this hot meal for my new husband while our boat is trying to murder me is my personal Wife Baggage to bear, the result of watching *Leave It to Beaver* reruns every day after school for seven years.

I hate June Cleaver.

But apparently I still want to cook like her.

With one burner boiling pasta water and the other burner warming pasta sauce, I notice that one of the pot-clamps is losing its grip. Our stove is not gimbaled, meaning it does not stay horizontal; it tilts along with the boat. So I have to lock all the pots into place on the stove. Only sometimes they unlock. Unexpectedly.

I brace myself against the table behind me and begin screwing the pot-clamp back into place. At that moment, one of the Strait's big rollers heels *Dragonfly* a few degrees past her already precarious tilt. Pasta water leaps out and stings my hand; the stove's blue flames hiss red. I run my hand under frigid seawater to cool the burn, and now the cabin reeks of sulfur. Another wave plows into us, slamming my hip into the table. This time the entire pot of boiling water threatens to fly kamikaze-like off the stove. It has merciful second thoughts. But still.

"Gra-eme!" I yell toward the cockpit. "Gra-eme? Do we have to bash into it so hard?"

No response.

And it's then, looking out the companionway, that I see my husband haul on the main sheet in an effort to make the boat go even faster. The jerk. I clang the reddened ladle into the sink and storm up the steps to where I'm standing on Scout's green pee mat, right there in the cockpit. Graeme, hair riffling in the wind, broad smile on his face, is oblivious. Looking out to sea, he sucks in the salty air like the guy in the Old Spice commercial. "Ahhh . . . ," he says. "It sure is rough, but we're making seven knots. At this speed we'll get there before dark." Then he looks down at me. His smile falters. "Uh. How's it going?" he asks.

Clearly, my rational mind tells me, *it is THIS MAN'S FAULT that we're heeled thirty degrees, that we have twenty knots of wind on the nose, and that the ride is as rough as a washing machine on heavy-duty.* "This isn't a race, Graeme!" I roar. "I'm trying to cook down here, and the heel is making it impossible." I glare at the red mizzen sail and see that it's unfurled to its full height. "How much sail do you have up anyway?!"

My husband's eyes flicker to the full canvas hoisted before him, just about every stitch of sail we own. His smile vanishes. He clamps his jaw.

"Look," Graeme says stonily, "if you think *this* is bad, then we're in *real* trouble. We haven't even reached the ocean yet." His blue eyes turn back to the whitecapped sea. "So you better get used to it."

And there's a crash below.

It's long been suggested that men and women are essentially, undeniably different. I'm no sociologist, and I don't care to speculate on nature vs. nurture and other chicken-and-egg schemes, but I must say that nowhere have the differences between my new husband and me been so palpable as in this last week of sailing, or "cruising" as it's called.

Now, I cannot say that these differences are necessarily determined by sex. Surely there are lots of men who, scoffing at chips and salsa, venture below during high winds and rough seas to spend hours with sharp knives and a hot stove creating a meal for their partner that, by the time it's finished, they're too nauseated to eat. And certainly there are plenty of women who do everything in their power to maximize speed under sail—hoisting every stitch of canvas, maintaining the rhumb line despite a contrary swell—even if it means a less comfortable ride for their partner trying to cook.

Sure, these people exist. I just haven't met them.

Of course, we're only a week in, and I haven't met *any* of my fellow cruisers yet. And what I may later shrug off as a classic example of male/female differences at sea, right now feels like cause for mutiny.

I rush below to survey the damage. Two pot-clamps have indeed kamikazed off the stove, and the sauce pot has slid sideways off its burner. It's tilted at a precarious angle against the pasta water, but neither pot has actually spilled. *Phew!* So I reposition the sauce, screw the clamps back on, and—what did my therapist tell me?—*breathe*. I sit down at the settee to think.

From Graeme's perspective, the goal is to get out of these rough conditions as quickly as possible. As he explained back when "we" were boat shopping: fast boat = less storm exposure. With all the sail tweaking he's doing and the excellent time we're making, he probably thinks he deserves a medal for expert seamanship.

I, on the other hand, in an effort to provide my partner with a nourishing meal, am pretty damn certain I deserve a *Ladies' Home Journal* Award for cooking under duress. The nausea, the bumps, the burns—it's treacherous down here. So why, with a request to reduce sail and fall off a bit, am I made to feel like such a chicken?

When I emerge into the cockpit a few minutes later with two steaming plates of spaghetti, I'm in that teeter-totter space of relationship spats: halfway still pissed off; halfway ready to make up. Graeme gives me a cringing smile. "Looks great," he says, his voice a white flag. I notice he's changed course and put reefs in the sails—a more comfortable but slower ride.

I hand him his plate of spaghetti without making eye contact. "I'll help you take out the reefs after we've eaten," I say quietly. I sit down and take a bite of pasta, and my mind momentarily brightens with: *Tastes pretty good!* But as I twirl the noodles round and round my fork, my mind continues to teeter:

He married me. He loves me.
He didn't take my needs into consideration. He loves me not.
He put reefs in. He loves me.
He had too much sail up in the first place. He loves me not.
He changed course. He loves me.
He told me to DEAL with it. He loves me not.

He quit chewing tobacco for this trip. He loves me.
But I drive him nuts . . .

And that's when I realize that I'm not the only one craving a little distance these days. Because, let's face it, I'm getting on Graeme's nerves, too. And I don't think I can just blame a week's worth of nicotine withdrawal. Too much time together? Maybe. But—I twirl and slurp my spaghetti as I think about how counterintuitive this sounds—I don't think togetherness is really the problem. I think it's not enough *otherness.*

See, it used to be that a dozen different people met the emotional, social, and intellectual needs of our everyday lives: Appreciation from a co-worker. Reality check from a boss. Sympathy from a friend. Laughs with an acquaintance. Conversation with a brother. Help from a parent. A wag from Scout.

Now it's just the two of us, on the edge of a big ocean, and the only people we've got are each other. No more girlfriends to lean on or buddies to vent with. Whatever I need, from here on out, I need to get from Graeme.

Or myself.

There was this wedding Graeme and I attended back when we were still fighting about weddings. It was a lovely affair, very personal and spiritual, each part of the ceremony imbued with meaning. I remember how the bride and groom did this interesting ritual where they each had a pretty pitcher of wine, and throughout the ceremony they would pour from their pitchers into a communal glass, say a few words, and each drink from it. You know, to symbolize their union, their interdependence, and their commitment to seek sustenance from each other.

And maybe that's what marriage is about: Committing to fill your cup solely from your relationship's well, and being satisfied with whatever (frigid, sulfury) sustenance splashes out. But if that's true, then our well is tasting pretty brackish these days—I look at Graeme, who's looking out to sea again—and I can't really say it's quenching my thirst.

Turning the Corner

i open my eyes to the sound of rain and close them again. Rain. Again. We're anchored in Neah Bay, still in the drizzly Pacific Northwest; I knew there was a reason we were heading south. Last night was howly with wind, and Graeme must not have tied the lines running down *Dragonfly*'s metal mast properly because they slapped all night long. *Blang! Blang! Blang!* I dreamed of fleas. And how Scout's dog tags jangle when she scratches. And how she paws and flips her empty metal water bowl over and over and over when she's thirsty. Multiple times I woke and thought about venturing outside to tighten the lines, but Graeme's the one who left them loose. Petty, I know, but it was cold and rainy and dark, and I was tired. So tired. So I cursed him regularly and drifted in and out of flea-ridden sleep.

I open my eyes again and look to his side of the bed. Empty. Unless you count the human-size pile of clothes taking up half (of his half) of our triangular bunk. The mesh laundry bag I installed for him back in my Martha Stewart days hangs empty on its hooks. My husband is not very tidy. Of course, this is something I knew about him from living together. But back then he used our second bedroom as his closet, and its permanently closed door successfully hid the mountain of dirty/clean clothes (you never really knew) that cascaded from hangers to hamper to floor, into foothills around the room. There are no permanently closed doors on a thirty-five-foot sailboat.

I close my eyes again and listen to the rain and the clangs of Graeme making coffee and the crackling of the weather station on the VHF radio.

I am usually a morning person, an out-of-bed-bounder, a let's-solve-the-world's-problems-before-the-first-cup-of-coffee sort of gal. But for the past few days I haven't wanted to get out of bed. At all. Graeme starts to whistle, and I wonder if he puts on these extra-good moods in an effort to cheer me up. Or annoy me to hell.

The Andy Griffith imitation stops midchorus, which signals that the forecast for Cape Flattery must be starting. Weather forecasts are a morning ritual now. Everything on marine weather radio is spit out from a computer in a prerecorded, subhuman, monotone loop. They've updated the computerized voices over the years, so what used to sound like a drunk Arnold Schwarzenegger, and later turned into Fargo-ese, is now a female voice that's not so bad. Only she puts weird emPHASis on her sylLABles and runs certainwordstogether. I strain to listen: "Cape Flattery to Cape Look-OUT . . . gale warning. ToNIGHT: north winds thirty-five to forty-five KNOTS, becomINGnorthwest and diminishINGto fifteen to twenty-five KNOTS by midNIGHT. Seas fifteen to nineteen feet. ShOWers . . ."

The forecast for today is not good. Neither is the computer's understanding that words ending in *ing* can stand on their own. Donna, as the voice is called, continues droning out numbers, but I've already stopped listening because they roll out so fast I can't make sense of them. I know Graeme is scribbling the numbers on a piece of paper. He'll give me a slow, sober, human report as soon as it's over.

Eyes still closed, I'm starting to drift off to Scout dreams again when Graeme calls, "Did you hear that?" There's a pause and a shuffling sound. Then his voice is closer. "Sounds like we can go tomorrow," he says, kissing my forehead. "The weather's finally going to clear."

Yes! my heart surges, *we can finally leave after three days of purgatory waiting in this godforsaken place!* And then, just as quickly, my heart constricts. *Shit-fuck. We're actually going to Turn the Corner.*

Turning the Corner is the phrase Graeme and I use to describe how we'll leave Washington's semiprotected thumb and head south into the open-armed Pacific. My girlfriends, on the other hand, employ Turning the Corner to describe falling in love. It was coined by my friend who was dating, at her mother's suggestion, her mother's financial adviser; my friend only e-mailed the guy to get her mom off her back. Turned out he was actually pretty decent. Though, after a few dates, my girlfriend told him she wasn't sure they had that Spark.

Well, turns out he wasn't feeling the Spark either, but he had an explanation; he'd been closet-quitting his closet-smoking habit since he met her, and it had made him a seriously unfunny guy. Luckily, he hung in there. He told my friend—no joke—"I'm going to grow on you like mold." And, sure enough, a few months later she announced that she'd Turned the Corner—she was in love! I was hired on as a bridesmaid by the end of the year.

But if Turning the Corner in love is the moment you fall for someone—a moment that is pretty much out of your control—then Turning the Corner in sailing is more like marriage: You have complete control over *if* and *when* it happens, but once it happens, you're committed. Whatever the weather gods bring, whatever tricks Neptune plays, whatever equipment troubles you have, you just have to ride out. Because, like divorce, trying to sail back from whence you came—in contrary winds, waves, and current—is often far worse than any storm you're already in. So when you Turn the Corner, you have to choose your moment wisely. And have an oceanful of good luck.

With these thoughts percolating in my brain, I'm no longer sleepy. And I can feel Graeme waiting for a response to his exciting news about the weather. Yet I'm not ready to be fully here with him, so eyes squeezed shut, I mumble in a fake half-asleep voice, "OK, Graeme. Give me the full report."

Graeme climbs over me into our serviette-shaped bed and crawls under the comforter between me and the laundry pile. He puts his arm across my hips. I can tell he's worried about me.

"Well," he says, "no surprise, the weather is still bad today. But tomorrow we've got a forecast of ten to twenty knots, decreasing throughout the day. The sea should lie down, too. And it should last the two days we'll need to make the hundred-mile run to Westport."

I keep my eyes closed. Thinking. Graeme and I have agreed to be conservative about choosing our weather windows, a fact for which I am supremely grateful. From his commercial fishing days, Graeme already knows how miserable it is to be at sea in snotty weather (you don't catch any fish tied to the dock). And while there's a difference between forecasts that bring Discomfort vs. Danger vs. Disaster, things can change quickly on the ocean. Plus, Graeme's pretty certain he'd rather avoid all *D* words in our honeymoon cruise; so we've agreed to wait for a wind forecast no higher than twenty knots.

Not all cruisers do this. A little white sloop named *Twixt* and a larger boat with eyes painted on its stern (Graeme spied on them through the binoculars) have come and gone in the past few days. Both times the forecast was for twenty-five knots. Maybe these boats scooted south fast enough to avoid the current gale. Then again, maybe they're caught in it right now. I'm glad we stayed put.

I'm also glad we've been able to avoid, thus far, Turning the Corner. This decision, like choosing a life partner, feels hefty to me. Scary. And I wonder if this is how Graeme felt when contemplating asking me to marry him. Because, even though I *know* I want to head south in our little boat, I have to admit that postponing our Turn around the Corner has been a bit of a relief.

On the other hand, we've been stuck in Neah Bay for three days. Three long, dreary, cold, rainy days that have given me plenty of time to churn over Graeme's and my many Wrong Turns in our past. So what makes us think—an overly analytical and slightly-grumpy-right-now person like me must ask—that we'll be able to make the Right Turns moving ahead? Whether in love *or* in sailing?

The answer is: I have no clue. And that's why I keep my eyes shut. And try to focus on Graeme's body heat next to me while fear descends around me like a fog.

Neah Bay is a one-road Indian reservation town that clings like a hangnail to the thumb tip of Washington State. Graeme, in other attempts to cheer me this morning, tells colorful tales of his fishing days here as a kid. Like the time he and his brother, Ashley, wandered up to Washburn's General Store and came face-to-face with the local bully and his cronies. After a few choice words were exchanged ("Get off our land, White Boys" and "OK"), Graeme and his brother hightailed it, under a rain of rocks, to the marina. Once there, the docks were so old and rickety, Graeme says, it was like Frogger, jumping from dock to log to float, to get back on board.

Then there was that time the boys rowed their family's leaky Avon rubber raft over to nearby Waadah Island to check out the goats. The place was teeming with them, Graeme says. He and Ashley walked around the island, wielding sticks like swords, scrambling over boulders, skipping rocks, and "hunting" goats, only to find when they returned to their dinghy that the wind had picked up; they'd have a heck of a time rowing back to the fishing boat. Being sea-savvy and inventive kids—and knowing their mom would give them a tongue-lashing if they didn't return before dark—the boys ended up dragging the raft along the adjacent breakwater until they had a better angle on their fishing boat. With the wind still blowing, but more at their backs, they clambered in and rowed like hell away from the *baa*-ing goats.

These days, there are no goats left to gawk at on Waadah Island. And even if there were, we'd have a hard time seeing them through this veil of rain. The most curious attraction here now is a gray cement structure the size of a highway floating in the bay. In an effort to figure out what it is, Graeme and I don our foulies (aka yellow bibbed foul weather pants and rain jackets) and putt-putt-putt around it in our dinghy. As we circle in closer, yellow and white lane markers give it away; it is indeed a highway, an old section of the Interstate 90 floating bridge, we'll later learn, purchased by the local Makah tribe as makeshift building material for a marina. When the Makah finally got the funds to build the marina properly, the highway didn't have to be used. So there, like a gray, hulking whale carcass, it floats.

After a lunch of tuna fish sandwiches, Graeme and I head to the local Makah Museum. Walking through town, Graeme says the rest of Neah Bay is looking better than he remembers it, even in this nasty weather. The cement docks in the marina are brand-new, there are several fishing charter operations, and an espresso stand at the top of the dock does brisk business. Plus, Washburn's General Store is packed floor to ceiling with everything from Wiffleball bats to cottage cheese to marine supplies to panty hose. Still, Neah Bay is far from booming. The unemployment rate here hovers around 50 percent, and almost half the Makah people live below the poverty line. And yet it feels different, Graeme says. There's something in the air—besides wind and rain. Call it, I don't know, pride.

In the past decade, the Makah nation has experienced a cultural renaissance of sorts. When the gray whale was taken off the endangered species list in 1994, the tribe decided to pursue their long lost tradition of whaling, a subsistence and spiritual activity that was guaranteed them in the 1855 Treaty of Neah Bay. In 1999, under approval of the International Whaling Commission (IWC), the Makah held their first hunt in some seventy years. They maintained certain aspects of their traditional hunting methods, e.g., the hand-paddled dugout canoe made from a cedar tree. But they also complied with the IWC's modern strictures by posting a rifleman in a motorized chase-boat so they could kill the animal as swiftly and, hence, humanely as possible after harpooning.

I remember, recalling the news coverage of the event, how the animal rights activists raged. For them it signaled a serious threat to a once-endangered species, the murder of a highly intelligent mammal, and the legal crack in the door that might allow commercial whaling to recommence in countries like Japan and Norway. Since then, activists have taken the Makah nation to court, and the battle's still raging. So now the Makah are not able to hunt whales until (and unless) the legal issues are straightened out. At least they can't hunt whales lawfully.

Graeme and I reach the museum and shed our raincoats in the lobby. We walk through the place like it's a cathedral. Awed. Hushed. Reverent. Reading the saga of smallpox and oppression and assimilation, I have to wipe my eyes. I always do at exhibits like these. But by the time we circle back to the entrance, I see more clearly the Makah and their specific history. And this place makes more sense now. I grab my still-dripping coat and walk up to Graeme, who's standing in front of an exquisitely carved wooden mask in the lobby.

"Hey," he says, turning to me. "Check this out. Ashley's friend Micah made this."

"Wow." I peer up into the eyes of a white face, chilling and intent. The placard says it's a Pook Mask, the face of a drowned whaler who was "re-animated to bring a message of change." The mask is minimalist but commanding.

Graeme and his brother went to school with Micah McCarty, who's now running for the Makah Tribal Council. That's the Makah's elected governing body, Graeme explains. Graeme wasn't close friends with Micah, but Ashley was; they were in the same grade, and they still keep in touch.

"Damn. If we weren't leaving tomorrow, I'd get Micah's number from Ashley and give him a call," Graeme says. "I wish I'd thought of it sooner."

"Well, tell me more about him," I say as we head back outside. We've got a long, wet walk back to the boat.

Micah grew up in Olympia, off the reservation, but he spent summers here with his dad. After high school he moved to Neah Bay and got into art—actually makes a good living at it. But his involvement with the whaling controversy piqued his interest in politics. Though Micah didn't paddle in the hunt, Graeme says, he worked on behind-the-scenes stuff—even went to Monaco for the 1997 meeting of the International Whaling Commission. Micah's pretty adamant about the Makah's right to hunt whales.

Graeme agrees. "Whaling is totally part of their culture," he says, "and not just as food or a resource, but as part of their religion. Plus, there doesn't seem to be much threat of endangerment anymore."

I can see his point. I just read at the museum that the Makah's quota is only four whales per year. This from a whale population that has rebounded, many say, to its original size before overhunting (about 20,000 whales). Plus, I worry that cultures can go extinct, too. And while the museum shows that the Makah have certainly survived without whaling, it's very clear they're an oceangoing people at the core; they derive their livelihood and spirit from the sea.

Graeme's been reading a lot about salmon lately, too, and he says pollution and dams and global warming affect the Makah's reliance on salmon—just like his dad's commercial fishing buddies are feeling pinched. So why not let them hunt four whales a year? Graeme says. The hunt in 1999 made such a difference for this town.

And yet I still feel just a touch ambivalent. Which seems odd in a woman who, in her twenties, had an iron-clad opinion on just about everything. (On things I didn't have an iron-clad opinion about, I made one up on the spot.) But as I've gotten older I've found myself becoming slightly less vociferous about my beliefs, not because I'm getting shy or wimpy or wishy-washy (*puh-lease*), but because my beliefs are becoming less black-and-white. It occurs to me now that people who stand on the other side of an issue are often just as adamantly and passionately convinced of their beliefs as I am of mine. This totally freaks me out. On the upside, though, it encourages me to give my thoughts a bit more thought, and my views are becoming more nuanced, perhaps more mature this way. Definitely more gray.

My ambivalence at this moment, however, is not due to mature, measured reason. My brain feels addled and foggy, as though someone's put a smoke bomb to my ear. *Shhhiiissssss.* My throat is phlegmy and tight. Keeping my head down, clomping through the rain, I worry that I couldn't make an intelligent decision right now if my life depended on it.

Which isn't great timing.

Because we Turn the Corner.

Tomorrow.

Actually, we don't Turn the Corner. We *cut* the corner instead. We forgo the extra miles out and around Tatoosh Island, a nail clipping, if you will, of the peninsula's thumb, and we cut the corner between the mainland and Tatoosh lighthouse. It's a narrow strip of water called "the gut" by fishermen, and Graeme says he's taken this shortcut dozens of times.

It's beautiful, if a bit eerie. We slide past gnarled bonsailike trees clinging to sea stacks with a bird-talon grip. Sea lions roll like brown cigars on rocky ledges, their body heat rising above them in wisps. And the ivory lighthouse floats above a low-lying mist that clouds the water in irregular patches. Weather conditions have changed completely from when we were in the Puke-uh Strait. No more white horses. No more steep waves. No sign of the ocean swell I was fearing. Like that creepy movie, it's dead calm—only there's no psycho guy plotting to kill us. (I checked.)

A few nautical miles later and the world really has been reduced to us alone. Because—and here's the irony of waiting for a mild weather window—we're now trapped in fog. Dense fog, wet fog, white fog. The kind of fog that makes you feel like you've sprouted gills and are breathing underwater. Or drowning.

The universe is silent except for the grumble of *Dragonfly*'s engine and the slap of our mainsail as it flops back and forth. There's no wind. So we're motoring along at our usual five knots (a tad less than 6 mph). Graeme and I don't say a word. We're taut, listening above the puttering of our motor for a radio transmission, or a ship's horn, or the whining of a tanker's massive engine. Since we're blind in this fog, and following our GPS course trustingly, noise is our primary defense against a collision with a freighter. Which would surely shipwreck *Dragonfly*, and most likely kill us.

When the fog first started wisping in, Graeme told me a story his father used to tell him. It's that old fisherman's fable about the tanker that traveled from Seattle to Japan, only to pull into Tokyo Harbor and find a thirty-some-foot sailboat mangled and pinned to its bow. "We don't want to *be* that sailboat," Graeme delivered as his punch line.

Only I didn't find it funny.

So Graeme tried another of his dad's jokes. "You know, it can get so foggy out here sometimes," Graeme said, "that you need a map just to scratch your ass."

I gave that a snort, just to make Graeme think I hadn't *totally* lost my sense of humor. But, really, that didn't seem so funny either.

And now that it really *is* that foggy, neither of us is laughing. Or scratching anything. We're just silent and still and listening.

Another defense ships have against fog is radar. That said, other ships' radars are no help to us, as we're too small to make even a blip on their screens. So we have to rely on our own. And while the big guys show up blaringly on our screen, Graeme says we can only keep the radar on when we're running the engine (we are). *And* when the engine is charging the batteries properly (it isn't). Something's wrong with the alternator, Graeme says, after checking the battery bank once, twice, three times. No juice. So we only flip the radar on every fifteen minutes.

And we listen.

I sit on the thin pad in the cockpit, huddled in yellow foulies, staring earnestly into the gray. It's like some optical illusion the way the fog erases all perspective; how far you're actually seeing into the distance is impossible to tell. Every few minutes I clap the clapper on our ship's old brass bell to warn other vessels of our whereabouts. *Ding! Ding! Ding!* It rings clear and sharp and true. Like the jangle of Scout's dog tags. Or the chime of a girlfriend's laugh. Or the sound of the phone ringing, my mom's voice on the other end.

I miss my family. I miss my friends. I miss the perfectly potty-trained dog who begged off our boat trip. My folks agreed to take Scout while we sail, which is yet another one of their generous gifts to our B-HAG. But the problem with dogs is they don't understand B-HAGs or extended honeymoons or "See you soon." And I've heard they can harbor grudges the size of freighters. So Scout's new living arrangement sits heavily on my lap like a brown rump of guilt. And the guilt of leaving Graeme's family just when his mom is overcoming breast cancer presses on my body with the same silent weight.

But, really, guilt is just part of it. It's more than guilt I'm feeling. It's foreboding about a trip that started off with crap. It's dread that Graeme and I won't be able to meet all each other's needs. It's fear about having Turned the Corner into the great wide Pacific Ocean.

And one other thing. A simple emotion, but worst of all. The way I least expected to feel as we begin our adventure, our honeymoon, our life:

Unhappy.

"What's that?" Graeme says, "Do you hear that?"

I rise to my feet and stare even harder into the mist. "I don't see anything," I say.

"OK, but do you *hear* anything?" Graeme is reaching toward the radar's ON button.

"No," I say. "What do you see on the radar?"

"Nothing yet. It's still warming up." He pauses. "Just listen."

I nod. I listen. I stare.

And just when I think Graeme's crying wolf, I hear it. A low, almost imperceptible rumble. It waxes and wanes like a snore. But it's there. Drifting in from my right.

I begin to say something to Graeme—

And then the ship is upon us. Just off our starboard bow. Rising in the sky as gray and massive as a building.

"Oh my God." I breathe. "Turn port. Port! *PORT!*" I say, abandoning our usual SILENT HAND SIGNALS. Graeme reaches back from the still-warming radar and spins the wheel. Hard.

Dragonfly careens like a double-decker bus as she swerves left. The freighter, like the winner in a backroads game of chicken, doesn't flinch. Its bow wake churns by like a massive steamroller. We raise our eyes to the ship's deck high above us, stacks of red and blue containers looming out of the fog like an imaginary Lego city. The wall of the ship continues past, slowly, slowly until eventually we rise and fall, rise and fall in the freighter's wake. It misses us.

I look to Graeme, hungry in this cold moment for a spark of reassurance. He's got his eyes cast on the stern of the freighter, a contemplative look on his face. Then he steps up out of the cockpit, sidles to the rail, and unzips his zipper.

"Well, that was close," he says, looking down.

The sound of water hitting water whittles through the fog.

And we pass, as they say, like ships in the night.

Step Up

O ne month and 750 miles later, our near miss with the freighter is but a foggy memory. We've made our way south in skips and hops, stopping in Oregon to visit Graeme's old fishing ports, and in Northern California to visit salty, blue-collar towns. And, of course, we've sailed under the Golden Gate Bridge (!), eaten Ghirardelli chocolate (!!), and sailed back out into the Pacific. As promised, we've only traveled when the wind forecast was twenty knots or below. So far.

The amazing thing is we're not the only ones who've quit our jobs, bought a boat, and are out here doing this; we've met scores of other sailing couples along the way. And our sense of alone-ness during that first month has evaporated into a social schedule that makes our college days look downright geriatric. Now that we're surrounded by other "cruisers," there's a happy hour every night, hosted aboard a different boat, and attended by practically everyone anchored in the harbor.

Emphasis on *practically*. Because I have to admit that, once or twice now, Graeme and I have been royally snubbed. See, there's this boat called *North Wind*, with two fun-loving Canadians aboard, who seem to invite everyone to their happy hours but us. Rumor has it they think we're too young. Which is ironic, because they remind us of the popular kids in high school around whom everything revolves, the prom court equivalent of cruisers. And while the king and queen are just two pleasantly plump, retired folks in their fifties, they've got some super-magic charisma. They're the first to tell a joke, the first to share a harrowing story, the first to be hailed when happy hour is brewing.

Now *that's* something you should know about cruising: hailing. Instead of calling each other on phones like landlubbers do, we cruisers hail each other with short-distance VHF radios. Imagine a trucker's CB where you press a button and speak into a mic—only our "handles" are our boat names, and we don't say "breaker breaker one nine." Instead, everyone tunes in to channel "one six" because that's the Coast Guard's frequency for communicating distress. So if your boat is sinking you can call "Mayday, Mayday," and just about every boat in the vicinity will hear you—and hopefully help you. All other calls (e.g., social organizing, chitchatting, exchanging weather info) initiate on channel sixteen but immediately switch to another frequency so emergency calls can get through. A typical transmission between cruisers goes like this:

Channel 16

NORTH WIND: Twixt, Twixt, Twixt, this is *North Wind*.

TWIXT: North Wind, this is *Twixt*. Six nine?

NORTH WIND: Six nine.

[*North Wind* and *Twixt* both switch their radios to Channel 69. Incidentally, so does every other cruiser within earshot; eavesdropping is an accepted, if unspoken, practice among boaters.]

Channel 69

NORTH WIND: Twixt, Twixt, Twixt, this is *North Wind*.

TWIXT: North Wind, this is *Twixt*. What's up? Over.

NORTH WIND: We're thinking happy hour. Our boat. Five P.M. Want to bring your accordion and play a couple tunes? Over.

TWIXT: Accordion? An accordion's a car engine played by a stripy-shirted Frenchman whining about lost love and hubris! I play a concertina! The size of a hungry man's soup bowl! Good for songs of lust and hard sailing! Ha ha ha ha ha. Over.

[long pause]

NORTH WIND: Um. OK. Bring that. Over.

TWIXT: See you tonight! *Twixt* clear and back to sixteen.

NORTH WIND: North Wind clear and back to sixteen.

[And everyone, including all the eavesdroppers, switches back to 16.]

Channel 16
NORTH WIND: Azimut, Azimut, Azimut, this is *North Wind.*

And so it goes until practically every boat in the anchorage has been called. Except us.

But not tonight. Because here we sit among eight other cruisers, crowded into *North Wind*'s cockpit, sharing stories and drinking warm beer (it's always BYOB, and *Dragonfly*'s refrigerator is busted). For some reason, here in Monterey Bay, where half a dozen boats have been waiting for a weather window for three days, *North Wind* finally deigned to invite us to one of their happy hours. Maybe it was the free haircut I gave the queen on the dock the other day. Or Graeme's assistance fixing the king's water pump. Or their realization—once they actually took the time to talk to us—that we're not the young, snobby Microsoft millionaires they imagined. But either way, it's nice that they've deemed us worthy. We even went for a walk with them down Cannery Row today.

Cannery Row, with its aquarium and shops, is the main draw for tourists to Monterey Bay. Cruisers also like Monterey for its snug marina. As an official literature geek, though, I was curious to see what drew John Steinbeck here so many years ago. Back in 1945, he opened his novel *Cannery Row* saying:

> Cannery Row is the gathered and scattered, tin and iron and rust and splintered wood, chipped pavement and weedy lots and junk heaps, sardine canneries of corrugated iron, honky tonks, restaurants and whore houses, and little crowded groceries, and laboratories and flophouses.

Of course, the squalor that inspired Steinbeck's novel is nowhere to be seen anymore. If Steinbeck strolled down Monterey's busy boardwalk today he might instead write:

> Cannery Row is the collectible and delectable, taffy and ceramic figurines and As Seen On TV, groomed pavement and parking lots and T-shirt shops, sardine-packed sidewalks of corrugating baby strollers, wine bars, restaurants and old-fashioned ice cream parlors, and big crowded art galleries, and an aquarium and tourists.

In other words, the only squalor left in Monterey is back here in the harbor, just beyond *North Wind*'s cockpit, where juvenile sea lions averaging 250 pounds are waging war on sailboats.

Normally, Monterey Bay has about 150 resident sea lions sunning themselves on the distant breakwater. But this year, an El Niño year, about 1,500 sea lions have moved in, overrunning docks, boat ramps, city sidewalks, and the decks of boats. These cute, cuddly creatures have jumped upon, spat upon, shit, pissed, and puked upon, and even sunk several moored boats already. They break stanchions, bust tillers, topple booms, and shatter windows. And they leave a stench of dung and vomit behind. Just yesterday Graeme snapped a photo of a sea lion in midair, making its leap to a pretty boat called *Cinnamon Girl*. There were a dozen sea lions aboard her already. And they must have kept coming. Because today, rumor has it, she sunk, too.

Jean, a woman with graying hair under a turquoise visor, says you can only use garden hoses and Super Soakers to shoo the sea lions away because they're protected under the Marine Mammal Protection Act. But now, with this burgeoning population, there's not enough food to go around. "One guy said they remove ten carcasses a day from the floats and beaches," she says.

As leavening, Graeme tells the story of his father's confrontation with a 1,500-pound bull sea lion on the back of his fishing boat. Graeme's dad walked out one morning, coffee cup in hand, only to find the beast lounging on the back deck. It took a wooden boat hook and a whole lot of arm waving and hollering to coax it off. Graeme's dad returned to the cabin to get a second cup of coffee. When he came back out, the damn thing was aboard again, drooling over the scent of salmon coming from the ship's hold. Graeme's dad spent another half hour chasing the thing off, and once it flopped back in the water, Graeme's dad started up the engine and skedaddled.

It's an animated story, complete with hand gestures, and it goes over well. So does Graeme's disgusting-sounding but actually-quite-tasty sardine dip (the skin, bones, eyeballs, and fins sort of blend in when mashed up enough). The king scrapes the bottom of the bowl with his cracker. "Good dip," he says, looking at me. "Tuna?"

I shake my head and point to Graeme, the real chef.

"Sardines," Graeme says.

The king's lower lip turns down slightly. He takes a long swig of beer,

wipes his mouth with the back of his hand, and looks back and forth sus-
piciously between Graeme and me. I'm not sure if he's scowling at the
sardine vertebrae he's inadvertently swallowed, or the fact that, in his book,
real men don't make chip-dip.

Seeking more comfortable terrain, the king shifts the conversation
toward standard sailor fare: weather observations, weather predictions,
weather laments. This subject, small talk among landlubbers, requires
constant checking, double-checking, interpretation, and analysis among
sailors. Because when you live on the sea and travel by the wind, understanding, preparing for, and dealing with bad weather can mean life . . . or
its alternative.

As if to illustrate this point, the king launches into a story that's sure to
be a crowd pleaser. "Hey, did you guys hear about *Fast Lane*," he asks, "the
boat that abandoned ship on the way south?" Despite the king's holding-
court demeanor, his fuzzy brown beard and stocky frame remind me of an
overgrown Fozzie Bear.

"Yeah," Graeme says. "We met *Fast Lane* in San Francisco." People go
by boat names these days. "But we never heard the details, so tell us the
story."

Other heads around the cockpit nod. Graeme puts an arm around my
back and settles in for a good story. Meanwhile, I wipe the sardine bowl
with a cocktail napkin, crinkle open a bag of peanuts I brought just in case,
and pour them in. These happy hours always require lots of munchies because they usually end up lasting through dinner. We've been here, I glance
at my watch, about three hours now. I'm hungry for something more than
grazings but not quite ready to abandon ship yet.

"Well," the king begins, leaning forward and rubbing his bare kneecaps,
"*Fast Lane* hired two crew members to help them sail down the coast. The
skipper was pretty experienced, but his wife, you know, wasn't." He makes
a face that says *typical!* and elbows the guy sitting next to him.

The queen peers into her beer can, as if looking for the ON/OFF switch
to her husband's antics. She says, "They just wanted a few extra hands to
help." She looks up and smiles ironically. "Turns out they got one with an
itchy trigger finger."

"Right," the king says and clears his throat. "So anyway, they're out at
precisely the wrong time, just when that nasty storm hit off Fort Bragg in
September. And, the way *Fast Lane* describes it, the waves are taller than
the mast, the wind is blowing like a mother, and you can't hear yourself
fart, let alone think." The king's audience chuckles nervously. "It's got to

be downright scary out there. Then one of the hired crew starts freaking out, saying he has family at home and doesn't want to die at sea." The king pops a few peanuts in his mouth and looks around the cockpit. Everyone can relate.

"So the skipper tries to calm the guy down," the king says, swallowing. "But he's got his hands full with the storm. The boat is hauling ass down these waves, pretty much out of control, and he's afraid she's going to capsize if they don't slow her down. So he goes to the bow to release the anchor and chain."

This is exactly what my folks did in that typhoon off Japan. When you don't have a drogue or a sea anchor (a huge parachutelike thing to slow you down), you drag whatever you can: anchor, rope, or, like my parents, a ten-speed bike.

The king continues. "So when the skipper gets back to the cockpit, after practically risking his life on the bow, he finds out his hired crew has sent out a Mayday call behind his back."

"Low blow," Bob from *Twixt* says, his concertina resting on his lap.

We murmur in agreement. Calling Mayday when you're not in imminent danger (i.e., sinking) is a major faux pas because you're basically asking the Coast Guard to endanger their lives in order to save your unendangered one. Plus, not to sound old-fashioned but, in this case, the crew member is committing mutiny.

The king shakes his head in mild protest. "Now, it's all fine and good to blame the crew," he says, "but what people don't realize is that the skipper could still have called the Mayday off at that point. Just called the Coast Guard back and said, 'Whoops! Sorry! No Mayday here!'" The king holds his palms high, as if in a stickup. "But for whatever reason—I mean, it was nastier than a humpback whore out there—the skip lets the Coast Guard take over. And so a helicopter flies out, lowers a harness, and hauls them up, one by one. The skipper said that was the scariest part of the whole debacle. The boat was miserable, sure, but safe. But trying to do a rescue in those kinds of conditions? Anything but safe and sound."

Comments fly around the cockpit of all the things that could have gone wrong, and a triptych of images flashes through my mind: Body swinging into rigging. Helicopter hitting mast. Rogue wave breaking over everything. The king's story reminds me of my parents' typhoon, and I consider telling that story when the king is done. But no, my mom wouldn't appreciate that. The true weight of her terrifying experience would be lost over peanuts and beer.

The king is silent for a spell, turning the empty bottle in his hands. When I reach next to me into *North Wind*'s cooler to offer him another, he waves me off.

"The bugger of it," he says, picking at the tattered beer label, "is that the Mayday call cost them thousands of dollars. Because once the weather subsided a day or two later, *Fast Lane* had to pay a salvage crew to recover their boat. See, there's this antiquated maritime law that says anyone who finds something at sea—be it a drifting tennis shoe or a drifting $200,000 sailboat—can claim ownership, free and clear. So the recovery fees are exorbitant, since realistically, the crew you send out could just reclaim your boat for themselves. Anyway, they found her bobbing about fifty miles offshore. And the kicker is she was in almost perfect condition. The dinghy was ripped off. The weather canvas torn. A few stanchions bent. But nothing of consequence to her safety."

I'm skeptical of the king's interpretation of maritime law here, but I won't quibble over details. I'm more interested in the last thing he said, so I ask him, "Do you think if they'd stayed on the boat they would have been fine?"

"Oh yeah. More than fine," the king says. "A lot less poor and a hell of a lot safer. Trying to harness in to a helicopter while your boat is kicking like a mare in heat just isn't something you do if you can avoid it."

Graeme adds, looking at me, "That's why they say you should only abandon ship when you have to step up to your life raft."

A strange look must flash across my face because Graeme clarifies. "You know. If your boat is actually *sinking*. And your life raft is floating higher in the water than your boat is. That's when you abandon ship. Only if it's a step *up*."

"Right." I nod, though I understood the first time. I was actually screwing up my face in response to a slight wind shift. *North Wind* is now directly downwind of sea lions. *Pee-ew.* It's time to abandon ship.

It seems everyone has a story about a storm to share. A year ago it was my parents' capsize. Last night on *North Wind* it was a helicopter evacuation. For most sailors it's a tale of enduring high winds and seas. But for everyone, a story inevitably leaks out about a different kind of storm we cruisers encounter: The kind that erupts when living in a confined space with someone you love.

Take this morning's squall aboard *Dragonfly* for example. I'm lying like a gigantic insect in bed (again), half-listening to Graeme listen to the weather (again), when he hollers out, "What's on your to-do list today?"

I hear him switch off the radio; the forecast must be over. I answer, "What's the weather look like?"

"Can't leave yet," he says. "Maybe tomorrow. Or the next." There's a short pause. "So what's on your list for today?" he says again.

"Um. Work on our wedding album maybe?"

Silence.

"I thought you made a bunch of those albums before we left," he says after a few moments.

With a look that says *duh*, because he can't see my face when it's facing his monstrous pile of laundry, I say, "Those were mini albums for our families. Not the big, mondo, official album for us to keep and cherish forever."

"Right," says Graeme. I hear the *shlewk*-ing slurp he makes when sipping really hot coffee. "Haven't you been working on that thing for the past month or something?"

"Well. Yeah," I say, wondering why he asked about the minis if he already understands I'm working on the biggie.

"How long is a wedding album supposed to take anyway?" he asks.

"I don't know. You know. However long it takes."

"Well, what about the weather canvas for the cockpit? Or the organizer for the hanging locker? Or the sunshade we were talking about?" He *shlewks* again. "Any interest in pulling out the sewing machine to get those projects going?"

"Well, it's not like we can't travel from point A to point B without those things," I say. "And Mom said she'd help me with the sewing when they visit us in San Diego." I run my finger along the bug screen I sewed and Velcroed to the hatch above our bunk last week; at least *that's* something Graeme approves of. "Plus, if I get the photo album done by San Diego," I say, "I can send it home with my folks so we don't have to carry it back out to sea."

"Yeah, OK," he says. "But San Diego's still a couple weeks away. And, you know, a photo album doesn't get us from point A to point B either." *Shlewk.* "And it's taking so much of your time." I can hear him getting up from the table, probably ready to start on his day's first project. "I don't know. Maybe you could focus on something a bit more useful to the trip."

They say relationship issues are really recycled issues, that today's problem is yesterday's in disguise. Well, the photo album fight hasn't bothered to change its sheep's clothing this time; we've fought about photo albums (of all things) before. But the wolf that underlies it is this: Graeme and I have hugely different approaches to time.

Graeme is one of those superefficient so-called humans who gets twice as much done in half as much time. (Though don't look too close, because there's likely something shoved in the rug, swept under the closet, jury-assed, half-rigged, or forgotten.) I, on the other hand, estimate a day for a project and end up spending nine. Things *always* take longer than I expect because I do them with painstaking precision. And while I'm usually happy enough doing them, and proud of how my projects turn out, I often regret or resent, later, the time I spent.

But that's just part of Graeme's and my problem. Because underlying this time issue there's another, deeper one that stretches like sinew under the wolf's skin. It's this: Besides how (and how long) we do things, Graeme and I also disagree about the stuff we actually do. And *my* stuff, according to Graeme, isn't quite up to snuff.

For instance, virtually everything Graeme does these days is useful and necessary to this boat trip. A fact for which I can't deny being thankful. Each day he wakes with a project in mind: He oils and caulks and fills and empties and cuts and connects and tightens and loosens and gaskets and scrapes and solders and screws and maintains and repairs and installs and diagrams and designs and consults and buys. These are often deal-breaker tasks; if they don't get done, *Dragonfly* won't be shipshape enough to continue to the next port. So Graeme has each day's work cut out for him. And he's inspired by it.

My work, however, is not cut out or dried. Each morning I wake to a blank slate of a day, a smooth, gray, sixteen-hour sheet of time. In it, I might cook a few meals, or if Graeme's cooking, do a few dishes. I might read a book. I might write in my journal. I might arrange canned goods into plastic storage bins. I might clean the toilet or work on our photo album or plait my hair into two swinging braids. I might procrastinate the boat's sewing projects by taking a walk around whatever port we're in. Usually to an Internet café where I e-mail my girlfriends about how lucky I am to have all this free time.

Of course, I don't mention that I'm not getting half the things done I'd said I'd get done "if I only had the time."

And it's not just that I'm lazy. Part of the problem is that any task I undertake (see previous list) always balloons to whatever time I have to give it. Which, right now, is endless—because we're unemployed, on our hon-eymoon, and floating. If there was ever a time to go slow, this is it, right? The other reason I'm so unproductive, though, is that none of the tasks on my list are all that inspiring. Or essential. Or pressing—either to this ship or to this trip. Which means, in essence, that Graeme could be doing this voyage alone. Without me. Because, at least when it comes to the boat, I'm totally and utterly unnecessary.

Another day later, still in Monterey, still in my PJs, I'm flipping lazily through our still incomplete wedding album. Graeme bounds down the companionway, full of energy. I'd heard him listening to the weather report earlier this morning, but by the time I scrabbled out of bed, he was gone. My guess is he's been out walking the dock, checking in with other boats about that age-old question: Should we stay or should we go?

Though that's not what he mentions first. He peers into the sink, which is filled with cold water and soap scum and greasy Ziploc bags. "I'm not sure this antibacterial bath is working," he says.

I look up from a picture of Scout bearing our wedding rings. "Antibac-terial bath?"

"Yeah, I'm not sure these bags are getting very clean." He swipes a fin-ger into the sink and holds it up for me to see. It's orangey-red with pasta sauce residue.

I close the album, stand, and sidle up to Graeme's chest, smiling. He wraps one arm around me, but keeps the other arm, the one with the dirty finger, waving in the air next to us. He looks like a groom threatening to wipe wedding cake on his bride.

"That's not an antibacterial bath, silly," I say. "That's the project I started yesterday and never finished." I lean back, dodging his finger as it threatens my nose. "Sorry. Are you in dire need of a Ziploc bag or something?"

"No. I'm in dire need of a mate," he says. "Because—I think we should go. Pronto. Everyone else is."

"Oh *reeeally*?" I say, drawing out the word goofily like the Best Man from our wedding would. I slip out from under Graeme's arm and move to the sink. "What does the forecast say?"

"Fifteen to twenty-five knots." Graeme wipes his reddish finger on a dishrag. "But it should decrease by tomorrow," he adds.

"Twenty-five knots? But that's against our rule."

Graeme nods. "I think we can handle it."

I squirt some antibacterial dish soap in to the sink, knowing I shouldn't waste this water, and begin scrubbing. We *have* gotten better at sailing together. A lot better. He no longer minds that I don't super-tweak the sails, and I don't mind that he does—as long as it's not on my watch. Plus we've unexpectedly had twenty-five knots before, and it actually makes for a pretty fun sail. This forecast will probably be just fine.

"You're that sick of watching me fiddle with photographs and glue and silver metallic pens, huh?" I keep my eyes on the sink.

"Naw," Graeme says, "I'm that sick of the sea lions."

I turn my head toward the cockpit and sniff the ever-present stench of our brown, cuddly neighbors. Graeme went head-to-head with one on the dock the other day, waving a plastic dinghy paddle to shoo it out of his path.

I rinse my hands, dry them on a blue dish towel, and wipe them on my PJ pants for good measure. Then I put my hands on my hips and say, "OK. I'll get dressed so we can go. These bags can soak a bit longer in their 'anti-bacterial bath.'" I use a fake British accent for the last part. "I'll be ready in fifteen minutes."

In actuality, it takes me thirty.

Six hours later and we're racing around Big Sur. Literally. Five boats left together this morning, and despite the fact that we call ourselves cruis-ers—and cruising boats are notoriously slow—today we're in a serious race to reach Hearst Castle in San Simeon Bay, our finish line. Graeme, for his part, is giddy. This is the first chance we've had at head-to-head combat, and he's pleasantly surprised at *Dragonfly's* performance. She's an old boat with traditional lines, built long before any of our friends' boats, and still, despite her old technology, she's holding her own. Beating some even.

"I'm starting to wonder if *Dragonfly's* a bit of a sandbagger," Graeme says, grinning wickedly. He's standing under the dodger, facing aft, watch-ing me as I sit behind the wheel. He scans the horizon for the umpteenth time. "You ladies are doing great," he says, referring to me and *Dragonfly.* "I can barely see *North Wind's* sails back there anymore." He picks up the binoculars for a closer look.

I've got our autopilot Willie driving, but I'm tweaking the sails a tad more than usual—and am starting to think this racing thing is not so bad. Until something odd happens.

"Uh, Graeme?" I say. "I think we have a problem."

He lowers the binoculars and pulls his baseball cap down on his forehead. "What's up?" he says, setting the glasses down on the chart table.

Dragonfly is turning increasingly toward port, turning, it seems, of her own accord. I've disengaged Willie and have the wheel in my hands, and I'm turning it to starboard. All the way to starboard. "Willie lost it," I say. "And now the steering's weird. Here, feel this."

Graeme takes a quick glance at the instruments—wind direction, wind speed, boat speed, compass heading—and climbs behind the wheel to take my place. *Dragonfly* is still moving at a nice pace, and she's not turning in circles or anything, but she's definitely off course. Heading slightly to port, which is where—with the wind, current, and waves as they are—she'd naturally like to go. Graeme swishes the wheel back and forth like that old *Saturday Night Live* skit of Toonces the Driving Cat. Nothing.

"Shit," Graeme says.

"Shit?" I say.

"I think we've lost our steering."

So much for the accuracy of weather forecasts. The wind has picked up to thirty knots. The waves have grown steeper. And I'm perched on the back deck of *Dragonfly*, steering her with a tiller.

You may recall *Dragonfly* steers with a wheel.

Graeme's diagnosis was right. We've lost our hydraulic steering, and so, like a ship's wheel on a kid's jungle gym, the wheel no longer turns anything but the imagination. Graeme is down below trying to fix it. He's been trying to fix it for four hours now.

Meanwhile, someone's got to control *Dragonfly*. She's moving stiffly and stubbornly, like a horse tossing her head at a bridle. So I'm bundled in foulies and life jacket, sitting sidesaddle on the roof of the aft cabin, well outside the protection of her cockpit. A line is clipped from my life jacket to *Dragonfly*'s steering pulpit just in case she tries to buck me off.

My right arm is hooked around a massive, wooden emergency tiller that extends like a polished phallus from *Dragonfly*'s back deck. I'm embracing that thing like one would a lover, or the single device that stands between our lives and the lee shore (that's what sailors call those rocks on our port side that will shipwreck *Dragonfly* if she's allowed to follow her own course). We hauled out the emergency tiller and attached it directly to the rudder post, which turns the rudder, which turns the sea. This means I've got the most direct form of steering possible. Reassuring. Except it's like trying to parallel park a semi with eighteen flat tires and the power steering gone out.

It's getting dark now. I ate two granola bars two hours ago when Graeme spelled me so I could pee. But I have to pee again. And every now and then I think I hear the sound of the waves crashing onto the rocks. Realistically, though, I know the rocks are farther away than my imagination thinks because if I squint, I can see the little black triangle that is our boat on the video screen of our GPS. The yellow blob on the screen is land. The yellow blob is still, thankfully, a ways away.

But so is morning.

I thunk on the rooftop of the aft cabin. "How's it going?" I shout down to Graeme. Wind socks me in the mouth and splashes a burst of saliva onto my left cheek. I lean my face down, not willing to unlock my sleeper-hold on the tiller, and wipe my face across my yellow sleeve.

"Still working on it," Graeme says, poking his head up through the hatch. He's holding a wrench, his knuckles gooped with grease, red nicks of blood bite his hands. But Graeme undertakes boat work like he approaches love: with pure, dogged persistence. "We'll see if this next trick works," he says optimistically. His head disappears again.

So I continue to steer as dusk pulls its shade, *Dragonfly* bucking her way through the sea. My temples are crusty with dried salt. My right butt cheek is numb. And I sniff my nose every few seconds. When I look back at the waves, only outlines appear, white horses galloping in thin white lines. The wind whips moisture from my eyes, but I'm not crying. Far from it. I'm alert. I'm on. I'm doing it. And I pull against *Dragonfly* like one nudges a sore tooth, relishing the dull ache in my limbs.

After another hour, Graeme emerges from the depths of the boat, worn, weary, and satisfied. "I think I finally got it," he says and turns *Dragonfly*'s wheel.

The tiller under my arm pushes against my ribs then pulls sharply away, flopping my tired body like a rag doll.

"Yep, you got it," I say, releasing my grip and stretching creaky arms and hands into the black release of sky. Letting go feels like freedom. "Well done, Skipper," I say wearily, climbing back into the safety of the cockpit.

"Well done, yourself," he says, tossing his head toward the awkward spot I just spent the past too-many hours. Then he holds up greasy hands. "Here, take the wheel while I clean this gunk off. Then you can take a break." He smiles. "You and the old girl have had quite a ride."

He's right. We have. But I'm actually feeling a bit peeved at the old girl right now. She let us down. I rest my hands on her wheel and stand and squat, stand and squat, trying to get my blood circulating again. I watch Graeme disappear down the companionway, then lift my gaze back to *Dragonfly* to glare at her hard. The wind has eased, she's no longer tugging at me, but I curse her nonetheless. She's the only thing that stands between us and the elements. I want to know I can trust her.

I don't.

Graeme returns a few minutes later and erases my scowl with a quick kiss on my cheek. He smells citrusy from the orange pumice scrub he cleaned up with.

"Really, you did a great job," he says, watching me crawl to the corner of the cockpit and sink into myself with a sigh.

He's right. He would have had a tough time fixing anything without me here, corralling *Dragonfly*. And finally I smile, realizing I'm something that I haven't felt since we left: necessary.

Part 3

South of the Border

The Pink and the Blue

a few important stats to keep in mind about cruisers:

- 85 percent[1] of cruising boats are commandeered by couples.
- 95 percent[2] of these couples are male-female partnerships.
- And 90 percent[3] of these male-female partnerships follow a division of labor called the Pink and the Blue.

Now, ask any cruiser out there about these two particular colors and they'll tell you what you already guessed: Women do Pink tasks (cooking, cleaning, laundry, sewing), and men do Blue tasks (electronics, mechanics, installing, fixing).

Up until now I have been a Pink-and-Blue denier, figuring if I didn't acknowledge our old-fashioned division of labor, it wouldn't exist. But it does. Well, kind of. Because, in keeping with the stereotype, Graeme does do most of the Blue tasks on board. But the Pink tasks—cooking, dishes, laundry—we're still dividing. Which leaves things a bit lopsided. Because if

---

1. This number is a figment of my imagination. As one cruising industry expert put it, "Trying to quantify cruisers is like herding cockroaches." But as far as I can tell, the vast majority of sailors cruise as couples.
2. I made this number up, too. While I'm sure there are some same-sex couples cruising, we haven't met any.
3. Again, complete fabrication. But we've only met one (1) male-female couple where the woman is the boat's mechanic.

I'm not stepping up to the Blue plate on board, then how can I still expect him to step up to the Pink?

Now, for the record, I have successfully done puh-lenty of Blue *house* jobs in my time. I'm a regular jill-of-all-trades. I've tiled floors, mowed lawns, hung shelves, and sledgehammered walls. I've hauled crap to the dump, cleaned rat shit out of the basement, and unscrewed the P trap under the kitchen sink. I've even painted, with an industrial sprayer rented from Handy Andy, the interiors of two full houses. So I'm neither lazy nor wimpy nor totally inept at Blue tasks on land.

But I am on the boat.

In my meager defense I submit the following: I know nothing about engines, electronics, the mechanics of in-mast furlers, et cetera. I care nothing about engines, electronics, the mechanics of in-mast furlers, et cetera. And, while I've got an OK vocabulary, can explain Kantian philosophy, and have an amazing capacity for recalling song lyrics off the top of my head, I have a difficult time even *learning* about engines, electronics, the mechanics of in-mast furlers, etcetera. To me a single paragraph from *Boat Electronics for Dummies* makes Faulkner read like Dr. Seuss in comparison.

On the flip side, I can offer a bevy of reasons, ranging from the logical to the subconscious to the wholly and utterly irrational, why I've refused to Think Pink thus far on our cruise. For example:

1. I (still) suck at cooking.
2. I don't find any particular joy or stimulation in most Pink tasks. (Exceptions: I like cooking crêpes and I love sewing baby quilts.)
3. Unlike many of my fellow cruisers, for whom Pink Is the Way Things Are and Always Have Been, I was born after the women's liberation movement they helped create.
4. When I was a kid, Carol Channing railed against house chores on Free to Be You and Me. In high school, I was horrified by "Mother's Little Helper" on my parents' Rolling Stones album. And in college, I wrote a paper on The Feminine Mystique. Don't ask me how, but I got the impression somewhere that domesticity = bad.

In summary, I've avoided Thinking Pink because it reinforces the stereotype that women cannot understand engines, electronics, the mechanics of in-mast furlers, et cetera. And therefore should stick to mindless, insipid, inconsequential drudgery.

God, I hate it when my particular skills (or lack thereof) align utterly with a female stereotype.

A pink and blue sunset roils across the sky of Bahía Tortugas, an isolated spot about halfway down the leg of Mexico's Baja peninsula, just below the kneecap. Tonight is my big night: girls' night out. Or rather *on*. I've invited four cruising friends to hang out on *Dragonfly* for some much-needed girl time. These "girls" range in age from late forties to late sixties; I'm the only early thirties in the fleet right now. It's a little weird. I've never spent so much time socializing (i.e., drinking) with people my parents' age. Though it's more odd for them than for me, I think, because there's a motherly instinct that kicks in, like you're not supposed to get drunk or tell dirty jokes or talk about sex with someone who could be your daughter—even if you don't have one. Tonight, though, this doesn't seem to be a problem.

We're theoretically playing a game of hearts—there's a poker tourney for the boys on another boat—but the game's not moving very fast. Each hand is punctuated by stories and laughter, long questions and longer answers. And wine. Lots of wine. When I ask the ladies about the Pink and the Blue, it's unanimous. Everyone divides the work this way.

"But doesn't it remind you of June Cleaver?" I ask.

"Cleaver Schmeaver," Ruthie, a white-blonde, overly tan retiree, responds as though waving an imaginary fly from her face. "That's the problem with being young. You worry what people think. The point is to make the cruising thing work." She lays down a diamond. "Clay does that by tinkering with the rigging. I do that by baking bread. What's the difference?"

"Well . . . for one, the boat won't sail if the rigging's not maintained," I say. "But you can certainly travel from point A to point B without—no offense—freshly baked bread. Or any bread for that matter."

"Come on, you have to eat!" says Jean, laughing and tugging at the bill of her turquoise visor, which she sports even though it's nighttime.

"But wait," the queen interjects. "I know what you're talking about. That's how I felt when I quit my accounting job to stay home with the kids. That nothing I did really, truly mattered." She nods toward me. "But after raising three kids, I got over it. My work at home was just as important as my husband's paycheck—not that he realized it."

"Oh, but it is!" the rest of us chorus in unison. We look around then and realize in amazement that the queen is the only one here with children.

"Yeah, yeah, I know," the queen says, waving her wineglass like a censer. "Everyone says raising kids is important. But it's all lip service. I mean, cooking, cleaning, teaching . . . they're some of the lowest-paid jobs on the planet. A housewife does it all. For free." While none of us is sober, the queen is sounding surprisingly sobering tonight.

"Right," Ruthie says. "But I think your point is: Who cares who does what, as long as it all gets done!" She swipes a strand of hair from her face. "Because, even if you don't iron the bedsheets, like my mother used to, it all does, at a certain level, need to get done. And in this day and age, if a woman wants to tinker with the rigging, she can. And if her *husband* wants to bake—or buy— the bread, he can! I, for one, prefer the smell of rising dough to WD-40 any day," Ruthie says. "So I've made my choice." Ruthie's short but shipshape fingernails tap on the table with a dull sound; she motions that it's my turn.

I lay down a nine of diamonds. "But don't you think it's a bit weird, if we really *can* make whatever choices we want, that we're all choosing Pink jobs and the guys are choosing Blue? And, plus, what if I don't *enjoy* baking bread, like you do, Ruthie? *Or* tinkering with the rigging, like Graeme does?" I ask.

Ursula, to my left, plays her jack. In her gurgling German accent she says, "But that's just the work, Janna. Eckhardt and I have been sailing for three years, and, yes, parts of each day are spent cooking and cleaning. But most days I also get to do what I love. My art." She nods curtly.

"That's right," Jean says. "If you don't enjoy the chores, Pink *or* Blue, who cares. It's actually a bit unusual that Graeme does; Don hates all the boat work. But, hey, it's just work after all." She picks a crumb from the edge of the table and puts it on her green cocktail napkin. "You need to speed through all that and get to the good stuff." She cocks her eyebrow questioningly. "You *do* have a hobby on board, don't you?"

"You've *got* to have a hobby on board," Ruthie says.

Ursula murmurs agreement.

I tilt my head noncommittally and get up to uncork another bottle of wine. Meanwhile, the queen launches into a story about earning her ham radio operator's license. Apparently that's her passion these days. I'm too embarrassed to tell anyone what mine is.

A couple hours later and the conversation has gotten decidedly more intimate. Ruthie has revealed that she tried to have children but couldn't. Jean has said she never wanted kids because, frankly, she doesn't like them. And the queen has confided about one of her sons who's in rehab. Ursula avoids the kid conversation altogether by asking to use the toilet, which is the moment I dread most when entertaining guests because our head smells like a thirty-year-old outhouse. Our toilet bowl has calcified scum that no amount of scraping will get out. And the toilet still honks like a herniating goose when flushed.

"Um, sure, Ursula. You can use the head," I say, scooting closer to the table on my folding stool so she can get past. "But excuse the stench. Excuse the stained bowl. And, if you don't mind, will you put your used toilet paper in the wastebasket? Oh, and if you leave the lever in the up position, the seawater will seep in and overflow. I speak from experience."

"*Kein problem*," Ursula says as she squeezes past.

And so I take this opportunity to launch into my treatise on the blatant and inherent sexism of sailboat toilets. "They're so small, they're not made to be sat on regularly," I say. "It's like perching on a goddamn spittoon." I take a healthy sip of wine. "Plus, the stench. The endless manual pumping—"

"And that biodegradable toilet paper is about as smooth as an emery board," adds Ruthie, rubbing her thumb across her fingertips.

"And worst of all," I say standing up, "are the calisthenics you have to go through while pissing on the tilt." I charade the words I say next. "Trying to predict the next swell"—I squat, as if on a toilet—"the slosh of the bowl"—I rock back and forth uncertainly—"and WHOOPS! The douche!" I jump up and grab my ass. The ladies laugh.

It is for these reasons and others too unsavory to mention that men, instead of pissing *on* a boat, choose to piss *off* a boat. Over the side. Standing up. (Though sometimes, admittedly, they miscalculate wind direction and get a *whoops* of their own.)

A *gasp-honk-gasp-honk* comes from the bathroom. Ursula is pumping. I put my hand to my forehead and grimace. And the queen, above the noise, says in her late-night infomercial voice, "This is precisely why I've learned to pee standing up."

"First," the queen says, "you must have impeccable control of your sphincter."

Ursula has returned from the bathroom just in time for a lesson on peeing over the side. She'd ask how this all came about except the walls are so thin on a boat that she was privy to the entire conversation even while in the privy.

The queen sits at the table, clasping her hands in front of her chest like the matron of a girls' finishing school. She does not laugh. She does not crack a smile. Nor do we. If I handed out pen and paper right now, the ladies would practically take notes.

"Without sphincter control," the queen explains, "you can't aim your pee stream away from your shorts. Or"—she offers air quotes—"'hold on' to the man you love." Wink. "So let's start by everyone doing a few Kegels." She switches to the voice of an aerobics instructor. "OK, and one and two and—"

"Kegels?" Ursula interjects.

"What are Kegels?" asks Jean, shuffling the card deck over and over like a form of meditation.

"Oh God." The Queen laughs. "They're the only thing that keeps mothers from perpetually peeing their pants." Her laughter sounds like a garden sprinkler, and her pink fingers lift her glass of wine. She swigs. Then she launches into a detailed explanation of Kegels, including their urinary, natal, and, of course, sexual benefits.

Within minutes, five ladies who've known each other all of six weeks are clenching their eyes shut, throwing their heads back, and singing that old '70s tune about a mama and her squeeze box. Their vaginas are humming along, too. Lip-synching if you will.

As the noise and silliness subside, the queen draws us back to our lesson. "OK, ladies. Let's apply this skill to peeing standing up." Then, as though imparting a tasty tuna recipe or a trick for getting out wine stains, the queen describes the art of pissing upright. She leaves nothing to the imagination.

"The most important thing you have to master is the stance," the queen says, sliding out of her seat into the boat's narrow aisle. She plants her feet wide and grips the edge of the table. Then she leans back, like a kid on a merry-go-round or a stripper on a pole. "It's all about the pelvic tilt," she says. *Bump* goes her butt on the oven door behind her. The queen squeals and adjusts. Then adds, "Now, watch my pelvis. This is how you aim the pee away from your legs."

It's true that as the queen bends her knees, rocks back on her heels, and tucks in her buns, her pelvis tilts skyward. But, from my vantage point, sitting on a stool in the aisle next to where she is standing, all my mind can register are her butt cheeks clenching, her snug jean shorts puckering, her underwear climbing her crack. The queen's blue ass now resembles the top lip of an old lady's pursed mouth.

And it's at this unfortunate moment that the queen tosses her head back and crows, "My hubby thinks it's *amazing* I can piss over the side. He says it turns him *on!*"

At this, the dam of women's voices breaks. Shrieks of laughter and shouts of disbelief flood *Dragonfly*'s cabin and overflow the bay. The queen tries to stand her ground, still gripping the edge of the table, saying that learning the skill is a boon to one's sex life.

Our bosoms heave, our heads shake, our eyes water.

Seeing that she's losing credibility, the queen tries to restore order with a sensible discussion of attire—"Skirts are best," she says, "but panties and loose shorts can be hitched over to one side to make way for the urinary stream." The queen's audience, however, is distracted with laughing.

The queen takes drastic measures: "Now for the real-life demonstration!" She points outside. "Who wants to try? Come on! Who wants to?"

No one except Ursula can deny her need for a bathroom break—we've consumed enough wine to piss an ocean—so ladies begin weaving toward the cockpit, nervous and giggling like girls at cheerleader tryouts. The queen has already started unbuttoning her body-hugging shorts. The underwear peeking out between her fingers is hot pink.

But just then a sound familiar and ominous crashes our consciousness: dinghies full of drunken husbands. It's well past midnight, and the boys have thoroughly redistributed their wealth gambling. They're ready to fold. We ladies try to shoo them away with shrieks and admonitions, but the dinghies bump against *Dragonfly*'s hull insistently.

It's unclear, as the ladies gather their things and climb into the dinghies, whether they're sad to miss the practicum part of the pissing lesson, or relieved. But the queen sees that she's lost her audience, so she buttons her shorts, grabs the plastic wineglass she brought, and stumbles into her awaiting chariot.

As the dinghies pull away I call out in a voice high and watery and drunk, "It's not fair! We weren't finished! This is premature evacuation!"

Then I go below to sit my Pink butt down on my stinky, stained toilet. And pee.

I wasn't planning on tipping overboard, but here I am the very next day, dragging myself like a young Brooke Shields from the sea. Only I'm fully clothed (she was half), I'm tepid (she looked hot), and the sand beneath me is not on a desert isle with a pristine Blue Lagoon, but a brown beach lined with cement homes, thatch-roofed *palapas*, and gawking onlookers. Since there's no marina in Turtle Bay, we cruisers anchor our sailboats in the bay and then have to run our dinghies up on the beach to get ashore. If the surf is low, this is no big deal. Today's surf is not low.

Standing in the shallows, I look for Graeme. He's on the other side of our now upside-down dinghy, which is wallowing in the waves. We grab the dinghy and we flip it back over. Then we haul the soggy mass onshore.

"Oops," I say, resting my hand on the gray inflated tube of our hard-bottom skiff.

"Oops," says Graeme.

I walk over to him and give his arm a squeeze. Flipping one's dinghy, especially in front of an audience of locals and sailors, is never a proud moment. I pick a piece of seaweed from his shoulder and say, "Bound to happen sometime!"

He nods his head, laughing. "If you say so."

Chris, a nineteen-year-old who's sailing with his dad on *Twixt*, the boat famous for its accordion, walks over to us. "You guys OK?" he asks, trying to look concerned. But when he sees we're laughing, he blows on his knuckles and rubs them on his chest. "Need a lesson from an expert, eh?"

We'd followed Chris through the surf. He, in his red, half-deflated dinghy with only mismatched oars for propulsion, had made it look easy. He'd timed it right. We hadn't.

When you're trying to get through the surf onto the beach, you have to watch the waves as they come in and choose the right one to ride. The *littlest* one. And then sneak in sort of on the back of it. But we'd been too slow and had gotten a bit sideways and a big wave had come up behind us, picked up our dinghy's starboard stern and, like a fried egg, laid us over easy. We're, of course, fine. The brand-new digital camera hanging around Graeme's neck is not.

While Graeme and Chris debate whether or not the doused outboard engine will still start, I reach into our dinghy—we call her *Firefly*—and unclip three bulky bags of now-soggy laundry. At least they were destined for the washing machine anyway. I also unclip the dry-bag, which has my dry purse, my dry book, and my dry nondigital camera; Graeme practically ground his teeth flat waiting for me to get everything properly loaded to come ashore. Apparently, being slow and meticulous sometimes pays.

"Hey guys, I'm off to the *lavandería*," I say, handing Graeme a dirty but semidry shirt pulled from the center of his laundry. "You guys'll deal with the motor?" I glance from Graeme to Chris. They nod.

Graeme strips off his wet T-shirt and presses it into my hands. He gives me a quick kiss.

"OK, come find me when you have a prognosis," I say.

And I turn away from the boys and their latest Blue job, and slosh up the beach. I've got one backpack on my back, one backpack on my belly, and another laundry bag slung over my shoulder. Graeme's wet T-shirt is in my left hand; my dry-bag, which carries a book on freelance writing, is in my right. I'll have plenty of time in between loads to dry out. And read about my new hobby.

As I walk through the Mexican morning streets, I inhale the fresh scent of corn tortillas and line-drying laundry. I smile at the two young moms with plump babies on their hips. I wave to the muumuu-clad grandmother clipping orange blossoms from the bush overflowing her patio. And I think to myself, *Maybe the Pink and Blue is not so bad.*

The Net

We've officially been jobless and drifting (OK, sailing) for four and a half months now, and there's one question every landlubber wants to know: How can anyone afford to do this? The answer is, of course, it depends. On how much money you've got.

Just like people living on shore, there are two types of people at sea: the Rich and the Rest of Us. Among the Rich are the Filthy Rich, with their megayachts and hired crew; we haven't rubbed elbows with any of them. Yet. And then there are the Slightly Soiled Rich, who have fancy fifty- to sixty-foot boats and own all the latest techy gadgets. But, unlike the Filthy Rich boaters, the Slightly Soileds are going it alone, cruising as couples like the Rest of Us, so we don't hold their wealth against them. In fact, the Rest of Us appreciate how generously they share their satellite phones, their ice cold microbrews, and the professional weather routing services they pay for along the way.

Graeme and I, not surprisingly, fall into the Rest of Us crew. We're the Normal kind, aka the Average Joe kind, aka the Poor kind of cruisers. Now don't get me wrong. I'm talking hyperbolic Normal and Average and Poor here. Because how can anyone with a waterfront view of shimmering sand and swaying palm trees be considered any of those things? I just mean that we have a small, old boat; we have only basic equipment; and we pinch our pennies as carefully as Graeme used to pinch my posterior. (The rascal.) In other words, we're Cheap.

Which is why *Dragonfly* ends up anchored, not near Mazatlán's world-famous Gold Coast sunbathing beaches, but at Mazatlán's less famous attraction, the Most Beautiful Sewage Treatment Plant on Earth. This happens after an overnight crossing of the Sea of Cortez, from Baja to Mexico's mainland. . . .

> GRAEME: Well, we're almost there. Should we head for an anchorage or splurge for a marina?
> ME: What marina?
> GRAEME: You tell me. You're the one looking at the chart.
> ME: My point exactly. *What* marina?

Graeme climbs down from the battered Igloo cooler that acts as the captain's chair behind *Dragonfly*'s wheel. He hooks his chin over my shoulder and scans the wrinkled, tan-and-white, coffee-ring-stained chart laid out in front of me.

> ME: Do *you* see a marina anywhere?

Graeme is silent for a long time. So I place my finger on a cartoon bubble of a bay south of the city and say, "Let's go there."

Turns out I've chosen a snug little harbor in biking distance of Mazatlán's vibrant Old Town. Perfect! And above our harbor rises the Highest Natural Operational Lighthouse in the World. Cool! And at the base of that, tucked against the lush green hillside, nestled on the shore just upwind of us, resides the Most Beautiful Sewage Treatment Plant on Earth. *Great.*

Now, you'll notice that we did not choose this fragrant location because we were purposely trying to avoid marina costs. (Though, truth be told, we probably would have.) The choice-that-was-not-a-choice was made by our charts. Our very *old* charts. Our very old charts that Graeme bought *used*. Our very old charts that Graeme bought used out of the back of a guy's pickup truck at the Seattle Sailors' Swap Meet, which didn't officially begin until daybreak but where Graeme was shopping at 4 A.M., in the dark, in order to get the Very Best Deal. Apparently, it was hard to see what kind of deal he was *really* getting. Shopping by headlamp has its perils.

Nonetheless, here we sit happily in a well-protected bay, the late evening sun tinting the lighthouse (above) and sewage tanks (below) a brilliant, beautiful orange. There's no wind and, hence, no stench. Yet. And we're thrilled to be bobbing beside two boats that are unlike most we meet cruising—not in their shape, not in their size. But in the fact that the people onboard look strangely familiar. They're young.

In cruiser speak, *young* means under fifty, because the vast majority of cruisers out here are retired. This makes sense, because Retireds have fixed monthly incomes that will float them for several years. So if you're under fifty, people assume you're either Tech Boom Money or Trust Fund Kids. And they look at you askance. Until, that is, you prove you're sufficiently cheap to be considered one of the Rest of Us. But still, there is that nagging question of how Average Joe cruisers, especially at our young age, can afford to quit their jobs, buy boats, and sail for years around the globe. Well, here are three cases in point:

Jenny and J on *Gitane* are the youngest in the anchorage. They're in their twenties, unmarried, both aspiring actors. They have some time off between grad school and real life, so they bought an older, tired-er boat than even *Dragonfly*, and they're sailing her through the Panama Canal and the Caribbean. When they reach Manhattan, they'll pursue their acting careers—and enjoy the low rent of living aboard a boat in New York Harbor. At least that's the plan. All cruisers' plans are made in Jell-O.

Jed and Monica are next. They're married. Early thirties. She's an optometrist; he's a filmmaker (add his movie *North Beach* to your Netflix queue now). They're sailing on Jed's late grandfather's boat *Mary Ann II*, the same boat that carried Jed and his brothers to Hawaii when he was a kid. So Jed's continuing a family tradition, and he didn't have to buy a boat to do it. They, too, will transit the Panama Canal and sail the Caribbean for a year or so before returning to real life.

Finally, there's Graeme and me. We're also in our early thirties, and unlike our mates, we do have an anchor of a mortgage back home. Though, through dumb luck, it happens to be an old house that was split into a duplex in the '70s; its double rents now make us a little extra cash each month. Plus, our embarrassingly cheap wedding and our own scrimping and saving put some money in the bank before we left. And, if we run low on funds, Graeme could get a consulting gig (we hope). In other words, we're patching things together as best we can. And making up the route as we go.

Our B-HAG of B-HAGs is to sail the Ring of Fire:

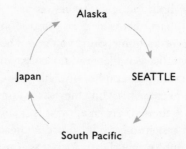

But that trip, following the natural line of volcanoes around the Pacific, takes at least two years. We've only got year-long sabbaticals from our jobs. The jobs are our safety net; we figured we could always return to our old lives if we didn't like our life at sea.

"What if you love sailing and I don't?" I remember asking Graeme when we were first planning the trip.

"It's a law of marriage," he said. "We each need to be happy for our relationship to be happy. So if you don't like cruising, we'll go home. And if *I* don't like cruising, we'll go home." He held out his hand. "Deal?"

I shook. "Deal."

So the question is: Do we keep cruising? Or do we return to the safety net of jobs and family and home? We need to decide now, because where we go next depends on it.

Plan A: We keep heading south, through the nasty stretch of water between Mexico and Guatemala. Past the volcanoes and burning sugarcane fields of Central America. Beyond the Galápagos Islands into the Deep Blue Sea—where there's no mechanic to hire, no expert to call, no defense against bad weather, and no land or humans or security for hundreds and hundreds of miles. If we choose that, we're totally committed.

Plan B: Hang out here in Mexico, eat fish tacos, drink margaritas, and immerse ourselves in mañana time. There are lots of pretty places to see in the protected Sea of Cortez just north of us, and some say Mexico is the best cruising in the world. By the end of the year, we'd head home.

I'm lounging in the cockpit. Palm trees are waving lazily on shore. And the fridge is half-working again, so I've even got a semicold Pacífico in hand.

Plan B sounds pretty painless.

The appealing thing about this anchorage, even if it is downwind of sewage, is that it's free. In fact, that's the great thing about cruising in general: There aren't all the costs of home. Sure, you've got boat maintenance costs and you have to buy food. But there are no car payments, no latté stands, no heating bills, no fashion boutiques, no cable costs, no sports tickets, no shoes-you-*must-have* at sea. And while they say cruisers are in port 80 percent of the time, as long as you're in a low-cost nation like Mexico—and can resist the sale on cast-iron patio furniture at Gigante, Mexico's version of Wal-Mart—life can be pretty cheap. Even if you aren't.

But, of course, we are. Every day we unfold our folding bikes, forgoing taxicab and bus fare, and we pedal pedal pedal toward Mazatlán's Old Town. The handlebars on our folding bikes are tall and erect, the teensy tires the size of dinner plates, so the effect is: *Properly Postured Circus Clown Rides Trike!* As we pedal pedal pedal through the neighborhoods of Mazatlán, yellow-smocked ladies freeze midsweep. Grease-shirted men pull their heads from car hoods. And children wielding bean pods lay their brown swords down. So they can stop. Point. And laugh as we pedal pedal pedal past. Even the dogs chase us with grins.

But no matter. We arrive in Old Mazatlán, pedal pedal pedaling down narrow streets, beneath wrought-iron balconies, past pastel buildings with arched porticos. From a street vendor at Plaza Revolución, we buy what must be the original (and superior) *cóctel des camarónes,* which is not a cocktail glass of shrimp drowned in kitschy ketchup sauce, but a cocktail glass of shrimp drowned in lime juice, tomatoes, cilantro, and chilies. Yum. We fish the shrimp out with golden tortilla chips and slurp the lime juice when we're done. Then, under the jaundiced eye of Mazatlán's yellow-tinted cathedral, we eat mangos-on-a-stick with lime and chili spice for dessert.

Across the busy street and down from Plaza Revolución is the town's main *mercado.* Graeme and I wander the stalls, getting lost and finding each other and getting lost again. We buy aluminum lemon presses, and colorful woven baskets, and fabric I'll sew into napkins for Christmas gifts. Total spent on the six family members meeting us in Puerto Vallarta next week: 500 pesos, or fifty bucks. That's how much we might spend per person at home.

Later that evening we meet our four new cruising friends—Jed and Monica, Jenny and J—at a place called Mariscos Lucía. It's cheap, loud, and crowded, a neighborhood eatery we pedal pedal pedaled past on our way into town. The restaurant's name suggests seafood is the specialty, but in the corner of the patio drips a barbecue with all manner of meat. Graeme orders an app of ceviche and then the spicy *camarónes del diablo* for dinner. I order *carne asada*. Above us crisscross strings of yellow flags advertising Mazatlán's favorite brew, Pacífico, and J comments that you can tour the local brewery here for free.

"We're suckers for free," I say, dipping a chip into one of the three types of salsa provided on each table.

"Is the beer free, too?" Monica asks, smiling broadly. She's got a dark green piece of cilantro stuck in her teeth, but her husband, Jed, who's staring right at it, doesn't say anything.

"That's what I've heard," says J. "Free tour. Free beer."

And so it's unanimously decided that we'll go mañana. Which gets us talking about how cheap cruisers are in general and the six of us are in particular—like keeping up with the Joneses but in reverse. Cheapness is a badge of courage among cruisers. Frugality the stuff of legend.

"Talk about cheap," I say, rubbing a miniature lime across the lip of my beer, "have you guys seen that red pile of rubber that passes for a dinghy on *Twixt*? They call it their"—I palm the lime and raise my fingers in air quotes—"'limp dink'." I shake my head, laughing. "Bob and Chris are great. Their chronically deflated dinghy, however, is not."

"I don't know," Graeme says. "The limp dink got Chris through some pretty big surf in Turtle Bay." Our friends laugh. We told them our dinghy-flipping story the other night. Turns out we're not the only ones at this table who've flipped a dinghy.

"Yeah, we know *Twixt*," Jed says. "Nice guys. Bob plays an accordion?"

"Concertina," Monica says. "They're smaller. Harder to play I think."

Jed nods. "Anyway. They're not planning on using that dinghy as their *life raft*, are they?"

I nod silently, mimicking that expression in horror movies where the nonbeliever sees the Creature of the Deep for the first time. Monica shakes her head. Jenny groans. And it's not clear if they're horrified so much by *Twixt*'s choice of life raft, or by the fact that the life raft debate has now officially been launched.

See, when you sail offshore, it's advisable to carry a life raft as your last-ditch safety net, so you have something to step up to in case your boat sinks. Life rafts are durable, self-inflating pods, specially engineered to survive ocean conditions. But the problem is they cost thousands of dollars, and every few years they cost *another* few hundred for reinspecting, restocking, and recertifying. Plus it's the one piece of equipment on board you will likely (knock wood) never use. So many penny-pinching cruisers have opted for an alternative: carrying a dinghy instead. Now, of course, *everyone* carries a dinghy; there'd be no way to get ashore otherwise. But dinghies are not specially designed for ocean survival. Plus, as evidenced by *Twixt*'s dinghy—and our own, which also leaks air slowly but persistently—dinghies are perhaps not the most reliable of rafts. Would you really want to entrust your life to one?

I'm pressing my finger into the salt in the empty chip dish. Lick. Salt. Lick. Monica's probing her teeth with her pinky nail (I gave her the SILENT HAND SIGNAL). And Jenny is tracing leaves on the plastic, jungle-print tablecloth with her fork. Meanwhile the boys debate dinghies. *Sigh.*

"I'm just saying," J concludes, "I wouldn't head out across the Pacific Ocean thinking my dinghy could double as my life raft. It's crazy. It's irresponsible. It's practically suicide."

I look at Graeme. He smiles at me and downs the rest of his beer. Then he says, his Pacífico bottle hanging in the air like a reverse toast, "I guess that makes Janna and me crazy, irresponsible, and suicidal." He sets the bottle down with a *clunk*. "And undeniably cheap."

After a few pleasant days hanging with our young friends in Old Mazatlán, and a few unpleasant days smelling the scent of rotting shit in the air, we decide to splurge and move north to New Mazatlán's storied marina. Storied because this is the infamous Black Hole Marina, the place where would-be world cruisers tie up, and hole up, and never leave.

Within five minutes of securing the lines to the dock, a brisk woman sporting shorts, T-shirt, and skin as brown as football leather, hustles up to our boat. She flips open the visor on her purple moped helmet and begins: "Hi, I'm Debbie! I'm here to welcome you to Marina Mazatlán! Here is a list of the week's events." She puts a green sheet of paper in my hands. "Don't miss the bocci ball every evening at five! And here's a map of the Gold Coast." She puts a gold Xerox in my hands. "Great restaurants and a movie theater!" She hands me a blue sheet. "And here are the rules for the morning Net. If you're selling something, be sure to say you're 'trading for coconuts'"—she winks—"because we don't want to get in trouble with *la policía*"—she accents the second syllable instead of the third—"for earning money in Mexico!" Debbie puts her hands on her hips. "Now if you have any questions, I'm over on B dock on *Jaaam-borEE!* It's a fifty-foot power boat about halfway down. Don't be shy! And enjoy your stay!" And with that she flips down her visor and hustles back up the dock to her waiting moped. In a few moments we hear her *rut-tut-tutting* the hundred yards back to B dock.

"So that's *Jaaam-borEE!*" I singsong to Graeme and fan his face with the green, gold, and blue flyers. He's still looking stunned by Debbie and her song-and-dance. *Jamboree* is one of those distinctive voices on the radio, one of the most active participants in the cruisers' radio networks, or "Nets" as they're called. And every time she says her boat's name on the Net, she says it in that same tambourine-slapping way—"*Jaaam-borEE!*" I've heard she's been at Marina Mazatlán for years. She's an icon.

Now, I should explain that cruisers' Nets are quite different from the casual conversations and eavesdropping that occur on the regular VHF radio. Because, on a Net, everyone's actually expected to tune in and eavesdrop at a particular time. Which is not to say that Nets are chaotic and chatty and fun. Actually, Nets are official and orderly and intimidating. They follow strict protocol, kind of like Robert's Rules, and boats get lambasted for not sticking with the program. Graeme and I *always* stick with the program.

Here's how the Nets work. Each Net covers a certain area, e.g., the Blue Water Net for the U.S. West Coast, the Amigo Net for Mexico, Tony's Net in the South Pacific, etc.—and there are a couple Nets for each area so you can choose your time, radio frequency, and, often, overall attitude and style. Each Net has a volunteer host who runs the program for the day. They usually begin with the weather, and then take check-ins from boats throughout the area. It goes something like this:

HOST: OK, this is Derek on the Amigo Net, who's ready to check in?
ME [yelling into our mic]: *Dragonfly.*
[At this point a bunch of boats might say their names at the same time, but the host calls back only the name of the boat s/he hears best. This usually is not ours. Our radio is weak. We're usually called upon last.]
HOST: Go ahead, *Dragonfly.*
ME: This is the thirty-five-foot ketch *Dragonfly,* Whiskey-Delta-Bravo-5-6-7-9er. Janna and Graeme aboard. We're twenty miles east of Los Frailes, headed toward Mazatlán, making five knots. We've got fifteen knots from the NW. Low seas. And no traffic. Over.
HOST: So we've got *Dragonfly,* twenty miles east of Los Frailes, on their

way to Mazatlán, making five knots. They've got fifteen knots of NW wind. Low seas. No traffic. [Then, if he's a chummy sort:] Sounds like you're in for a nice ride, *Dragonfly*. See any dolphins yet? [Or, if he's all-business:] Is that it, *Dragonfly*?

ME: Roger. *Dragonfly* clear and standing by.

HOST: OK, this is Derek on the Amigo Net. Who else is ready to check in?

Then other boats jump in.

Now the tricky thing about all this is that you have to remember to state everything, and all in the correct order: your boat name, your call sign (that was the Whiskey stuff), your people names, your location, your destination, your speed, your wind velocity and direction, your sea state, and your "traffic" (or messages) for other boats. And, at the proper time, you *must* SIGN OFF. If you miss any of these steps, the host will actually call you back, often in an annoyed voice, and ask for the missing information. It can be quite stressful.

But it's fun to hear where other boats are and, even better, to get "traffic" from one of your friends. This is when a boat you haven't seen since, say, San Diego calls you from Oaxaca while you're on your way to Mazatlán. They can tell you about a great seafood restaurant or warn you of a front heading your way or make a plan to meet up in El Salvador two months from now. It's very cool. Though, very unbusinesslike. So if someone does call your name for traffic, you're obliged to switch radio channels so everyone else doesn't have to listen to your chatter. (Though you can be sure other boats you know are following and listening, too; it's the best way to keep track of friends.)

Now I should also mention that these Nets take place on high-frequency single-sideband radios, called SSBs among cruisers. SSBs reach, depending on timing and weather and reception, halfway around the world, and with a special modem you can even send e-mail through them. Amazing. They're a huge safety net, as well as a much-needed social outlet, on a long passage. Though we wouldn't know about that. Yet. The route we choose—the Deep Blue Sea Plan or the Margarita Plan—will determine if we experience that firsthand.

What we do know is that tomorrow morning there will be a similarly structured, though more lighthearted, Net on the short-distance VHF radio right here in Marina Mazatlán. And Debbie, of *Jaaam-borEE!*, will preside.

"Well thanks for checking in, everybody! What an exciting Net this morning! And, again, welcome to *Dragonfly* and *Mary Ann II*, our newest arrivals! Now as for the week's activities, those who want to go to the murr-cado together should meet at ten A.M. by the laundry room! And at noon, Dick from *Breezin'* will be hosting a checkers tournament on C dock! This evening, of course, there's bocci ball on the lawn and, since it's Friday, be sure to wear your favorite Hawaiian shirt! And tonight we have a special—"

I turn Debbie off midsentence. I look at Graeme. "Are you thinking what I'm thinking?"

"If you're thinking Debbie's true calling was to be Julie on *The Love Boat*, then I'd say yes," Graeme says. He's sitting across the settee from me, his back leaning against a big yellow pillow in the corner, his nose in a book about storm tactics.

"That's pretty close," I say with a laugh. And then, more slowly, "But I was also thinking how little we have in common with her." I swivel the lid on my travel coffee mug back and forth. "I mean, she's a cruiser, too, right?"

"Well, for one, you don't have to like every cruiser you meet—"

"—I know, I know. But it seems like we often do; now we have more friends our parents' age than our parents have. Which is actually pretty cool." I glance up at Graeme. His book is still open. "I mean, it's not like we're great friends with *every*one, but it just feels like, regardless of age or whatever, we're all sort of in the same boat. You know?"

"Yeah, I know. But we're *not* in the same boat as *Jamboree*—"

"*Jaaam-borEE!*" I sing under my breath.

"—they've been here for like five years," Graeme says. "They're not cruisers anymore. They're moorers. Moochers. Gringos in paradise." His voice is as calm as a lake.

"Do you fault them for it?" I ask.

"Naw. They're still living a dream, even if it's not the cruising dream." His eyes hold mine for a moment. He closes his book. "But staying here's not *my* dream."

I take a sip of coffee. "So you want to officially quit our jobs and keep going south, huh?"

"What do *you* want to do?" he says.

"Welp," I say matter-of-factly, "we know we're heading south to P.V. for Christmas. And lots of our cruising friends are going even farther south than that. Plus, some are jumping straight from Mexico to the Marquesas, which means we won't see them again unless we head to the South Pacific." A smile has snuck into my voice.

I laugh.

"We have met some pretty neat people out here, haven't we?" Graeme says, nodding with one of those I-told-you-so fake frowns.

He's right. Not that those friendships alone would convince me to keep sailing. But it does make a difference. Because in addition to crossing a large ocean on a small boat—the thought of which still freaks me out—loneliness has been another big fear of mine. I think I need close, intimate friendships more than Graeme does. As one of my girlfriends said when she moved to a small town, "All my husband's social needs are met by his brand-new ski buddies. But I need girlfriends, *close* girlfriends, and making those deeper connections takes time."

Now I'm not saying Graeme doesn't need close friends at all, but I doubt, even with his *best* friends back home, that he spends a quarter of the time hashing out issues and analyzing feelings and baring secrets the way my girlfriends and I do. *God, I miss that.*

Fortunately, though, this seafaring life has not been a total friendship desert. I mean, you'd think that close relationships would be hard to create, leapfrogging from place to place to place. But in some ways, travel can act as a high-speed incubator for friendship: mutual passion, common purpose, teamed resources, and intensity (if not longevity) of time. Plus, sometimes you just click with people. And that's how cruising south has been for us. We definitely enjoy most of the people we meet sailing. And we truly connect—on a deeper level—with just enough friends to keep me afloat. (OK, and I still e-mail my girlfriends back home a lot, too.)

"Yes, we have made some good friends," I say to Graeme. "And I like it. I mean, I like cruising."

"You do?"

"I do." I hug my knees to my chest. "I think it's been good for us. Good for me. I feel like I've Turned the Corner with it."

Graeme smiles.

"And, hell, it's our big, hairy, audacious goal, right? We can't chicken out now." Then I add, just to keep my husband's visions of conquering the world by sailboat in check, "Hey, but after we make that Big Right Turn into the Deep Blue Sea . . . all plans are made in Jell-O, right?"

"Sure. OK," he says, holding up his hands in innocence. Then he picks up his *Storm Tactics* book again and starts reading its advice in earnest. Where we're going now, we'll definitely need it.

Men Are from Starboard, Women Are from Port

You think I was *depressed*?" I ask, the end of that awful word flying up toward the canopy of twist-curvy vines overhead.

"Um. Yeah," Graeme says. He's walking behind me, but I can sense the tentative expression on his face.

"Depressed." My tone stays eye level. I continue along the jungle path a few more steps. Then I stop.

He stops.

"De*PRESSED*." The word sinks from my mouth into the mud beneath my rubbery sandals and lies there, pressing to the center of the earth. My newlywed husband is telling me I was depressed for the first month—or two, he says—of our honeymoon. Fine. Perfect. *Fantastic.*

"Um. OK. Maybe a bit blue?" Graeme offers.

I turn round to face him. The rain forested bank creeps steep to his right. Green foliage scribbles down to the river to his left. Above us, the highest trees are in mist. This place smells fetid and fecund at the same time, as if everything is dying and being born all at once.

"You know. It was a transitionary time. You were just a bit blue," he says. His hand alights on my bare shoulder, which is wet with sweat and tropical heat and the whispers of cloud.

I turn and walk again. We move in silence except for the *slurruck* of our Tevas. I extend my fingers toward the overgrown bank and slide them along a leaf as big as an elephant's ear. It's smooth and waxy like the indoor plants my mom grows at home. The definition of green.

"OK. I'll give you 'a bit blue,'" I say, trudging upward. Then, after a few more feet, I add, "But what's the difference?"

"Between 'depressed' and 'blue'?" Graeme asks. This time it's he who stops. "I don't know," he says.

I turn.

His eyebrows lift. "It sounds better?" His voice is a question mark.

We're hiking to the waterfall on Isla del Coco, a volcanic island about 350 miles off Costa Rica. Not that there's only *one* waterfall here. There are over two hundred. But this is the main waterfall feeding the main river running into the main anchorage of Wafer Bay. That's where *Dragonfly* waits, staring up at cliffs splashing wet spindles into the sea around her. She's still going strong after six months' cruising. We are, too. Though our dinghy had to brave some Turtle Bay–size waves to get ashore for this hike. And now I'm worried about the waves for our way back. Oh, but the surf's sure to lay down, Graeme says.

Isla del Coco, once called "the most beautiful island in the world" by Jacques Cousteau, rises from the sea into mist. The almost constant cloud cover earns this verdant rock the title of "cloud forest," a lush ecosystem borne of the island's misty meteorology. And below the mossy cliffs, Isla del Coco is a scuba diver's paradise. The waters here teem with manta rays, dolphins, three hundred species of fish, and a large population of hammerhead sharks. Declared a World Heritage Site in 1997, Cocos Island (as it's called in English) is managed by the Costa Rican government with a team of rangers posted here year-round. The only way for tourists to actually stay *on* the island is as volunteers in a month-long (at minimum) program through the Costa Rican National Park Service. Otherwise, you can stay aboard a full-accommodations tour boat that's geared toward scuba divers. Or, of course, come on your own boat (thank you, *Dragonfly*).

We spent our first couple days on Isla del Coco at Chatham Bay, a thumbprint of a cove on the northeast side of the island. That's where whalers and slave traders and pirates have chiseled their names in boulders on the beach. The oldest graffiti says 1797. Which makes it feel not like graffiti at all, but history. This place feels old. *Treasure Island* old. *Robinson Crusoe* old. More than that—primordial old. Some say Michael Crichton based his novel *Jurassic Park* on this island. And seeing how Isla del Coco lies off the west coast of Costa Rica (like Crichton's imaginary Isla Nublar) and Isla del Coco is the only island in the eastern Pacific with a cloud forest (*nublar* in Spanish means "to cloud"), I'm willing to buy it. At least it *looks* like dinosaurs could live here.

Of course, some say Stevenson's *Treasure Island* and Defoe's *Robinson Crusoe* were based on Isla del Coco, too. I'm not sure I buy *that*; people make that claim about every beautiful, remote, mysterious island they encounter. But since I am a dorky former English teacher and a literary nut, just the thought of this allusive history makes me breathe this place differently. Like a ghost story. Or a treasure map. Or an old friend.

Now I know Graeme is just trying to be a good friend by telling me he thinks I was depressed when we first set sail on this trip. And, anyway, it's my own fault for bringing it up.

I had said: "Dag I love cruising! How else could we ever get to a place like *this*?" (At that point I'd Vanna-Whited my bare arm toward massive palm fronds and wild orchids and whispering river water.) Then I'd said: "I was crazy not to love cruising from the very beginning. Don't you think?"

To which Graeme had said: "Um. Not crazy. Maybe just a bit depressed."

And while this is his way of saying *You had me worried* and *Glad to have you back* and *Reality check, please*—something I've expressed to good friends when I've seen them blue, too—it's still hard to hear. And a shock. Because the person who's depressed is often the last to know.

Of course, I should have known. I mean, I knew I wasn't my usual self those first weeks (months?). And I knew things weren't always peachy. And, duh, not wanting to get out of bed back in Neah Bay was a sure sign of the blues. But depression for me seeps in sneakily like a fog until the only thing I can see is dead in front of me. Like that fear of Turning the Corner. Or worrying that I don't know enough about sailing. Or the biggest question: Is Graeme enough to be my Everything? Whatever issue lies before me looms so large that I can't see anything else. Not the problem's actual size— where it starts and where it ends—or the support I've got to get past it. Or even the solutions bobbing there, right there, just beyond my socked-in vision. It's this lack of perspective, in my experience, that distinguishes the D-word from your run-of-the-mill sadness. It paralyzes me, and crouches on my chest, and presses the fog in deeper.

Now, Turning the Corner into this honeymoon is certainly not the first time I've been depressed. I've always felt the ups and downs of life acutely.

And, like many women, my blues have often fit into that tidy little category called PMS. For me, this started in high school. Back then, Julie Burr, one of the popular girls in my grade, coined the term "Elsie" for her monthly period, as in "Elsie's visiting this week" or "Elsie's kicking my butt today." The name Elsie was not random; it came from another Julie Burrism: L.C. for Leak Check. So, just in case a cheerleader's period showed up unexpectedly at lunch, she could say, "L.C., please!" and her girlfriends would check her rear for spots as she walked away from the cafeteria table. I don't think the football players ever figured that one out.

But I was not a cheerleader. And for me the initials L.C. seemed to signify something more ominous than a stained miniskirt. Like: Lows Coming. Or: Losing Control. Or: Life (soft *c*) Cucks. And it became predictable that, if I was feeling the world more intensely and, hence, more weepily than usual, I could check my bright red school assignments calendar and, sure enough, Elsie would be scheduled for her next visit soon. Only, as I grew older, the Lows Coming sometimes arrived *too* soon. Or the Losing Control sometimes stayed too late.

Or both.

Until, at times, Life (soft *c*) Cucks didn't coincide with Elsie's visit at all.

Across the river, dense loops of jungle unravel and knit themselves back up as thrashing rips the ravine. The animal's wake is a V, undulating through stalks, leaves, and tree limbs. Then all is still.

"Pig?" Graeme says. "Or goat?"

"Not sure," I say. "But one of those. It was too big for a feral cat, and I think we would have seen it if it were a deer."

The ranger told us there are only five types of mammals on the island, all nonnative species introduced, intentionally or accidentally, by humans. Apparently the pigs and rats are a real problem, wreaking havoc on the natural biodiversity of the place. The rangers hunt and trap to try to curb these harmful populations, but, they say, it's a tough battle.

Still leading the way up the trail, I stop to take a swig from my water bottle. The white noise of the waterfall is getting louder, the air even more wet. "We're almost there," I say, handing Graeme the bottle. Then I ask, all nonchalance, "Hey, do *you* ever get depressed?" Of course, I already know the answer.

Graeme shakes his head.

I eye him as he tilts his head back and drinks. This trip has been good for him; he's lost his Business Guy belly, and despite the sunblock we slather on daily, his skin is tan and taut, his hair a cleaner shade of dirty blond. "OK. How about 'a bit blue'?" I ask. "Do you ever get that?"

"Mm . . ." Graeme pretends to consider the question seriously. Then says, "Nope. Not really." He screws the blue cap back on. "I mean, life's hard sometimes. And it's not like I don't get sad or irritable or dissatisfied. But I don't get depressed, you know, like you do."

He lifts his right knee and flicks a dollop of mud from it toward the river. The mud clot veers wildly and lands on my shorts.

"Oops," I say, looking down. His mud has joined my mud; several spots and hand smears are gathered there already.

Graeme is not distracted. "But. *So.* You feel the world deeply. That's one of the things I love about you." He waits till I look up from my muddy shorts. Then he holds my gaze as a sort of underline.

"I knooow," I say, my voice starting normal and then dropping low like a foghorn. A rivulet of sweat trickles down my back. I look away. Why is it so hard to have my husband know that I get depressed sometimes? Probably because, even though we've talked about "my moods" before, and even though I've never been clinically depressed, this is the first we've called my blues by their official name.

Graeme puts the water bottle in my hands, places his hands on my shoulders, then spins me around so I face up the trail again. Then he pats me on the butt. I take this as another sign of reassurance. Or at least a sign that he's ready to move on.

My worst bout with the *D*-word occurred in my midtwenties, the year after I did a program called Teach For America. TFA is a national nonprofit that strives to eliminate educational inequity, which is a fancy way of saying I taught in a depressed area of New Orleans for two years. It kicked my butt. Each day I tried. Each day I failed.

At first, I failed because I had no discipline system and the kids knew it. By the end, having learned to spare the stick and favor the carrot, I *still* failed. Because no matter how energetically my students mimed their vocab words, no matter how vigorously they karate-chopped their punctuation marks (comma "Hi-YA!", period "Kick!", semicolon "Hi-YA kick!"), I never got *every* kid reading at the right level. I never motivated *every* student to do his or her best work. And I never learned to handle adversity with the same grace, the same bulletproof skin, the same perseverance as those kids did. They were astounding.

The irony, of course, is that it wasn't those two arduous years of teaching that made me most blue. It was the year *after*, when I was home in Seattle with my family and friends and had my happy old life back. Only my happy old life wasn't happy anymore. I no longer blithely sang the why-can't-we-all-just-get-along song. Because now I'd seen poverty. I'd seen perseverance. I'd seen the craters gaping in the level playing field of American education, health care, and economic opportunity. And I'd been humbled, inspired, angered, and most important, changed by all this. Who I'd been before was no longer me.

I think my post-TFA blues provide a clue to my bout with the *D*-word on the boat. Because embarking on this honeymoon has also been a time of immense change in the ole identity department. I went from Ms. to married. Employed to unemployed. Landlubber to sailor. And useful, productive, can-do teacher on a mission to help the world . . . to useless, drifting, don't-know neophyte with no job, no passion, no purpose.

I've spent the past six months trying to figure out who I am all over again.

Graeme strips off his T-shirt and enters the pool beneath the waterfall in a sort of half-wade, half–belly flop. The water splashing from him and the falls is cold, too cold for me to swim in; the rain forest clouds are seeping lower through the trees now and the temperature has dropped. Plus, the pool is murky green with floatie things, a little too Creature-from-the-Deep-ish for me.

I watch Graeme swim and splash and scrub his armpits like he hasn't showered in a week (he hasn't). I envy him his love of the water in the same way I envy people at the beach who don't mind the grit of sand between their toes and under their fingernails and sticking to their wet skin (I do). I'm not much of a swimmer myself, or a beach frolicker or a sun worshipper. Or, as has already been established, a hard-core sailor. And so, yes, it still seems a bit strange that I chose this sailing dream—and am actually enjoying it now.

Starting tomorrow, though, all that could change. We're already three hundred miles from the closest continent, and over the next month that distance will only increase. Pretty soon, there won't be anything but water for over a thousand miles. Yikes. And yet, barring any change of heart that the upcoming crossing might bring, I've realized that being an unemployed, country-hopping, culture-imbibing traveler (via sailboat) is actually quite terrific. Especially since I've found my capital-*P* Purpose.

See, back at the beginning of our trip when I was depressed, I started doing what every self-absorbed, pseudopoetic, semineurotic, melancholy former English teacher does: write. First about the fog. Then about the sea. Then about the ports we visited and the people we met. By the time we reached San Diego, I was pecking away on my laptop pretty regularly. By the time we entered Mexico, I'd sent an article to a little sailing magazine in Seattle called *48° North*. And by the time we reached the foot of the Baja, I'd learned I was going to be published!

Since then, I've been writing like a maniac. By finding the new me—the writer me I'd always dreamed about—I rediscovered the old me. Now I'm back to bounding out of bed every morning. To write.

"I'm starting to worry about the surf," I say while perched upon a large gray boulder by the edge of the pool. I toss a small rock into the water, and it makes the sound a fountain penny makes when you miss the bronzed statue's outstretched hand. *Pluck*.

"*Starting* to worry?" Graeme jokes.

"OK, so I *have* been worrying. But those waves were pretty big when we came in. What if they're bigger when we get back?"

"We'll use our stellar dinghy-embarkation skills to get through them," Graeme says and leans his head back into the water to float on his back.

I open a peanut butter granola bar and munch. I bought three Costco-size cartons of these things before we left Seattle, then another two in Acapulco's Costco (cruisers live for good provisioning stops), though now I'm wondering why I didn't prize variety over volume. Take anything six months straight and you'll start to wonder why you liked it in the first place.

I watch Graeme swimming toward the edge of the pool. Something hits my shoulder. "Oi! Did you feel that, Graeme?"

"What?" he asks. He's finally picking his way over mossy rocks toward me.

"That," I say, pointing at the surface of the water now pockmarked with fat, lazy raindrops.

"Uh-oh. We better git," Graeme says, hastily pulling his T-shirt over his wet chest. The ranger warned us that the trail becomes a river when it rains.

So Graeme and I git. The urgency of our departure adds to it a little thrill; we hoop and holler and high-step across the river back to the trail in an effort to beat the rain. And I rejoice that, despite the waterfall's vapor, despite the trees' mist, despite the gray clouds threatening to dump at any moment on this Nublar-esque island, I can see clearly now. The fog is gone.

Only, when we emerge from the damp mountain onto the pebbly beach an hour later, the waves are *not* gone. They're bigger than ever. The size of vans. Bulldozers. My father-in-law's truck. And now we must ford them to get back to our home hobby-horsing on the bay.

My hands grip the port side of the dinghy as I watch wall after wall build, crash, and crumble. Seething white swirls over our ankles, our knees and, on big swells, our thighs. We're waiting, unlike the last time we faced a gnarly surf, for the exact right moment. Only it's not coming.

I glare at Graeme, who's holding the starboard side of our flimsy raft. He grins and gives a cocky, Hollywood two-finger salute. My knuckles tighten around the dinghy's grab line as though it were his neck. And I realize this is not the first time I've been standing just a few feet from my husband and felt an ocean of distance between us.

If there's anything Graeme and I have learned so far about traveling as a couple, it's that being near each other does not translate to nearness in thought, emotion, or experience. Though we've spent almost every moment together for the past half year, our perceptions of and reactions to things are often so vastly different that we could be on different boats. Or, as that marriage guru says, different planets.

Case in point: Here we stand on the same beach, grasping the same dinghy, staring into the same breakers. My jaw is hard-bitten steel. Graeme is grinning maniacally.

"Why are you smiling?" I spit.

"Because this is exciting," he says.

"This isn't exciting, it's terrifying," I say. "Why didn't we come earlier when the surf was lower?"

"Because we didn't know the surf would get so big. And, really, it's not so big. And besides, we were enjoying the waterfall."

"*I* thought the surf might get big." Anger thins my voice. "If you'd paid attention to me, we wouldn't be in this predicament."

"This isn't a predicament," Graeme says. "We've dinghied through surf a hundred times."

"Yeah, and in Turtle Bay we flipped our dinghy and almost busted our engine and totally ruined our camera and had to pay way too much money for a new one. And in Turtle Bay we were near civilization and could buy supplies and get help from other cruisers. But now we're on a nature reserve hundreds of miles offshore, we're the only sailboat here, and we're supposed to be ready to make our longest passage yet." I pause. "Tomorrow." Then I punch my finger at the rollers plowing the beach in regular sweeps. "Plus, that swell back in Turtle Bay? It wasn't nearly as big as this one."

Graeme turns back to the surf. "Turtle Bay was a long time ago," he says. But he's no longer smiling. I can tell he sees what I see now. Yet he doesn't look scared, just determined. "We'll be fine," he says, meeting my eyes. "We'll just wait for a lull in the surf."

"OK." I square my shoulders. "We'll wait for a lull in the surf."

We wait.

And as we wait this thought washes over me: *If Graeme didn't pretend like everything was smooth sailing all the time, then maybe I wouldn't have to get so worked up about stuff.*

And, a few moments later, the reverse: *If I didn't get so worked up about stuff, then maybe Graeme wouldn't feel the need to act like everything's perpetually hunky-dory.*

I look at him, his eyes scanning the sea, arms tensed and ready, a spot of spittle on his chin. Here I am with the same goal, the same stance—I wipe my hand across my mouth—minus the spittle. Maybe his courage and my caution are a balancing act. I wonder if those roles can ever be reversed.

There's a lull in the surf.

"Go!" Graeme shouts. We run, pushing the dinghy between us, the molasses of the water slowing our strides. "Get in!" he yells. "Paddle!"

I clamber in. I grab the paddle and plunge it into the swell, searching for forward momentum. Graeme fumbles with the engine. The next breaker is already building ahead of us.

"Come on!" it's my turn to yell. My paddle is digging up the sea with the insistence of a dog burying a bone. The engine coughs to life and Graeme opens the throttle. Full. He's gambling that we can beat the break. The motor claws at the water. I bring my wet paddle in and hug it to me. Then I lean out over the bow as we shoot forward like some Road Runner cartoon, the spinning propeller finally meeting the laws of traction. The oncoming wave rises into a wall of green.

Past the point of no return, bodies tensed, we ramp up, up, up the face of the wave, through fingers of white, out of the water, into the wild gray yonder. The wave releases its grip on the pontoons. The hull. The propeller. And the engine squeals, *Suuuuu-EEEEEEE*. We cling, airborne, to the sky. When we finally land with the slap of gravity, the engine stutters, finds its footing, then impels us over the long, blue swells beyond the break.

I turn to see Graeme. His face is drained and sweaty, a changed man. The engine almost didn't start. The wave we launched off was much bigger than he'd expected. And it's the first time we've ever been completely airborne in our dinghy. Perhaps watching his wife hang ten in that weightless space above earth hadn't been as much fun as he'd thought. No doubt he anticipates a tidal wave of my haranguing as his next obstacle.

But somewhere during the ride my weight shifted, too. I actually enjoyed the speed, the adrenaline, the feeling of flying. The fear squeezing my chest wasn't so bad either.

And that's the thing about change. Sometimes it happens over days . . . months . . . years. And sometimes it happens in that no-time between air and sea, between him and me, between now. And now.

"We did it!" I yell with a gnat-grabbing grin.

And I lean my upper body out, way out, over the bow of the boat, like one of those exquisitely carved women on the bowsprits of tall ships. Now Graeme is no longer clinging to starboard; I'm no longer clinging to port. We're just two sailors, in the same boat, heading home.

The Spark

it's amazing, though, how two sailors cooped up constantly in the same boat can not find time to, you know, *do it.* (Yes, Dad, I'm talking about sex here, so plug your ears.) But here are two things I'm learning about being on passage: (1) You don't sleep (literally) together because someone's always in the cockpit on watch while the other's down below (literally) sleeping. And therefore (2) it's very easy to not sleep (figuratively) together either. For example, it was a four-day crossing to Isla del Coco. No sex. And then we were at anchor for another three days; we somehow didn't do it then. And now we're embarking on the longest passage we've done thus far—450 miles to the Galápagos—which could take us as few as four days or, since we're truly heading offshore now, as many as you-never-know. Out here, where it's so wet, our sex life is looking pretty dry.

Though at least I have dolphins to flirt with. A dozen of them, reminiscent of Flipper-faster-than-lightning, leaping and frolicking and riding our bow wake like we're the traveling circus coming through town. If dolphins can be happy, which, anthropomorphism be damned, I believe they can, then these particular dolphins are high on endorphins or something. They're making eye contact with me and *smiling*. I'm sitting on *Dragonfly*'s bowsprit in tank top and shorts, rising up and down, up and down, with a clean tinny breeze on my face. These guys are so close I can see every scar and scrape on their gray Play-Doh skin. They have what are called rake marks, made by scraping their teeth along each other's hides in battle and play. The older a dolphin is, the more scars he has. One of these old rakes, who must be as old as King Tut, gives me a wink. I blush.

An hour later what we encounter, however, isn't so chipper as Flipper. I spy an ominous gray metal shipping container, not sitting high up on the deck of a passing freighter where it belongs, but floating, mostly submerged, in the water off our bow. My first endorphin-doped thought is *Here are the missing left-footed Nikes!*—a brain spasm prompted by having found several right-footed Nikes while beachcombing on our Shakedown Cruise around Vancouver Island. Back then, Graeme had theorized that they came from an overboard shipping container full of righties-only—packed separately perhaps to deter theft, since unmatched shoes are no good to anyone. But turns out the real story's much more scientific. Apparently, cargo containers go overboard more often than you'd like to think, and back in the 1990s, a bunch were lost in a nasty Northern Pacific storm. Six months later, people started finding washed up Nikes on beaches stretching from Canada to Oregon, only the shoes' distribution wasn't random. Flotsamists (scientists who study flotsam and jetsam) discovered it was the shoes' slight left and right curvatures that sent the righties floating north on the Alaska current and the lefties south with the California stream. Mother Ocean's own style of natural selection.

But I digress. My second, more sober thought upon seeing that cargo container just fifty feet off our starboard bow, floating like a land mine at sea, expresses itself aloud: "Shitfuck, Graeme, we could have just hit that thing!" Graeme nods curtly behind black binoculars. He doesn't take his eyes off the buoying metal. Only its corner is bobbing above water; its other thirty-five feet are an iceberg below. My toes curl under, gripping the deck. My neck hairs prickle as though I'm cold. In the black of night even the best lookout wouldn't have seen it. If we were to run into something like that, we would very likely sink.

To complicate matters, on the night of Day Five (so much for a four-day crossing) we're almost out of fuel—with still another day's distance to go. See, there was no wind on the way to Isla del Coco, so we motored a good chunk of *that* passage, gambling we'd have wind on *this* leg to the Galápagos. We don't. In fact, instead of wind, there's thunderandlightning with no room for 1-Mississippi 2-Miss in between. And since there's no wind and we have very little fuel left, we're not able to beeline (that is, motor-sail) out of this storm pronto. So we're just drifting. And watching.

And praying—in that curious way nonreligious folks pray—that *Dragonfly*'s tall, metal mast doesn't play lightning rod on us.

Since neither of us can figure out how, exactly, agnostic prayers work, we've put our laptop, our GPS, and all the other electronic equipment we can cram into our oven for insurance. This will supposedly protect them from frying in a lightning strike, Graeme's *Storm Tactics* book says. Who knows how to protect our*selves* from frying, though.

"Do you think it's safe to touch the steering wheel?" I ask, looking down at Graeme's hands wrapped around its half-shiny, half-rust-bitten sheen. "Maybe you should wear gloves." It's hot. The air is dry and static. I feel like I could make sparks fly from snapping my fingers.

"Gloves?" Graeme says. "I'm hot enough as it is."

"Yeah, but I don't want you to be a lightning rod," I say. Every few minutes lightning cracks the black shell of the sky, sometimes illuminating clouds in a glowy nova, other times needling down to the gunmetal water. Since, as far as the eye can see, there's nothing between ocean and sky but us, you could say we've got the best view of a lightning storm ever.

"I don't know, Janna. I think if we get hit by lightning, we're pretty much screwed."

Then again, you could just say a few more agnostic prayers.

Nervous about using electronics during the storm, but wanting to ensure someone knows where we are (you know, just in case), we turn on the SSB radio for a quick check with the Net. Since pushing off from the continent, we've been checking in twice a day, a very reassuring habit. Tonight, however, we learn that thunderandlightning is the least of our worries. Pirates have struck.

Piracy is something people asked about constantly before we left, something that seemed to worry everyone else far more than it did Pollyanna-wanna-cracker me. Depending on the way the concern was framed, I'd respond with one of the following:

(A) *The serious response:* "Most piracy is perpetrated against commercial vessels and cargo ships, not against small, private sailboats."

(B) *The half-serious response:* "No, we're not taking a gun to protect ourselves from pirates. I'm afraid I'd want to use it on Graeme."

(C) *The trivial response:* "Pirates? Pirates are rad . . . Did you know they used to wear gold earrings to cover the cost of burial if their corpses ever washed ashore? And they wore eye patches so one pupil would always stay adjusted to the dark for night raids? How cool is that?"

Apparently not as cool as Johnny Depp has led me to believe. Because a small, private sailboat has been attacked and robbed and left to drift off the coast of Ecuador in the Pacific. *We're* a small, private sailboat off the coast of Ecuador in the Pacific. And this frightening coincidence feels even more freaky right now than the storm squawking and bellowing overhead.

The official details of the incident, according to the International Maritime Bureau's piracy report, go like this:

> 05 April 2004 at 1500 LT [local time] in position: 03:20 N, 084:44 W, Pacific Ocean—five masked pirates armed with pistols & knives boarded sailing vessel under way—tied up skipper & another crew & stripped vessel of all electronic equipment, documents, charts & crew possessions. Pirates came in unmarked fishing wooden vessel, fifteen to twenty meters long, red bottom paint, black topsides & white cabin. They had rammed the sailing vessel at port quarter causing damage to radar post.
> (Fri. April 23 2004)

Granted, neither person aboard was killed. And they were able to get help. But still. We were at their latitude just the day before yesterday, a couple hundred miles east of them but on the same course. The same course, that is, until they got attacked.

And that's when I realize that, if that trip around Vancouver Island was our Shakedown Cruise, then this passage to the Galápagos is our Shakedown Crossing. Only, at 450 miles, it's a mere fraction of the titanic-size crossing to come. And if this is what's in store for us—shipping containers, fuel shortages, thunderandlightning, pirate attacks, and, to top it off, no sex—well, it's hard to get fired up about crossing my Ts, let alone the Pacific Ocean.

Approaching the desertlike Galápagos Islands while surrounded by the sea is the exact inverse (I imagine) of approaching a watery mirage while surrounded by the desert. Only, unlike the mirage, the Galápagos actually exist. Thank God. Because, even though we bypassed the pirates and survived the lightning, the other crummy thing that happened on our Shakedown Crossing is that Graeme and I experienced some serious power struggles—both mechanical and marital.

The first power struggle is that which ensues when you're too far from land for an extension cord. Though on a boat, just like in a car, the engine can charge the batteries. But on a *sail*boat the idea is to sail, not motor. Plus, our alternator—the engine part that charges the battery—is busted. So we're left, happily, with these green options:

(A) Solar panels—but they only work when it's sunny.
(B) Wind generator—but it only works when it's windy.
(C) Towing generator—but it only works when you're moving over four knots.

On *Dragonfly*, we've checked the box that says (D) All of the above.

Well, kind of. We've been relying mostly on solar panels, and they work great, except that sometimes, like on cloudy days, they don't provide quite enough juice—particularly since *someone* on board has decided that writing incessantly on her laptop is no longer a want but a *need*. (That's when the power struggle aboard *Dragonfly* becomes both mechanical *and* marital.) So we've decided to fork over the dough for a combo wind/towing generator once we reach Tahiti. We would have done it sooner, but we're cheap, and the thing costs as much as a life raft. (Actually, we've decided to fork over the dough for that, too.) And, yes, we see the ~~idiocy~~ irony that we won't have either for the Real Crossing, which is where we (gulp) need them most.

In the meantime, though, it's become clear that the Royal We has to fix the alternator—the thingamajig that generates electricity—as our backup power for the crossing. So here we sit in Puerto Ayora (aka Academy Bay), likely the most sought-after eco-tourism destination on the planet, doing boat repairs.

Puerto Ayora is one of the many places where Charles Darwin, on his five-year voyage around the world in the 1830s, collected specimens and made observations that he later used as evidence for his theory of evolution. These days, important work in biology, biodiversity, and conservation continues at the Charles Darwin Research Station here on Santa Cruz Island. And visitors from all over the world spend small fortunes to fly in, tour the islands, and ogle the species: giant turtles, iguanas, penguins, seals, and birds too numerous to count.

The only ogling we seem to be doing lately, though, is of that mysterious species called the alternator. Graeme lies in the cockpit like a surfer paddling a surfboard, only his surfboard is shaped like a big, red, greasy engine block. Instead of paddling his hands in the sea, he wields a wrench in one and a voltage meter in the other. And his feet sort of kick and flail midair behind him. Graeme routinely wears threadbare boxers while doing all of the above because, well, it's hot. Plus he pretty much starts surfing upon rolling out of bed.

Not that this is anything new. Graeme's always working on something on the boat because something on the boat always needs work. If you're a homeowner perhaps you can relate—as long as you multiply it by like a thousand. The marine environment is particularly harsh: water seeps, salt corrodes, and the whole "house" is rocked and rolled, beaten and bashed regularly. Stuff just breaks. So, apart from the dangers posed by crossing really big oceans, most sailors would say the toughest part of cruising is the incessant boat work. Hence the joke:

cruis·ing (krooz-ing) *n.* doing boat repairs in exotic places.

Since Graeme is stuck doing boat repairs, and since the Galápagos Islands are indeed exotic, I'm thinking maybe I should go visit them. With or without Graeme. So, one day, I abandon my task of handing him tools and serving him meals and positioning clip-on fans to blow hot air his way, and I head off to a giant tortoise sanctuary (the tortoises being giant, not the sanctuary). I go with a fellow cruising family that is giant, too: three kids, two parents, and one uncle all on one boat. Their family motto appears to be the more the merrier.

I'm below when there's a knock on the hull accompanied by a kid's shout of "Ahoy, *Dragonfly!*"

I grab my camera and climb apologetically over Graeme's surfing back. "I'll say hi to the turtles for you," I tell him.

Graeme grunts and throws me a hang-loose sign. The youngest girl claps gleefully as I step aboard the water taxi to head to shore.

The bay at Puerto Ayora is large, which is a lucky thing, because half of it is taken up with cruising sailboats, the other half with local tour boats. The way tourism works among the Galápagos's almost two dozen islands is that guests stay aboard tour boats like traveling hotels; meals are provided. Most of the islands don't have large population centers to cater to tourists, plus tourism here tries to be eco-friendly. The use of live-aboard tour boats is a unique, if expensive (and for some visitors, queasy) solution. The other thing that's expensive is the permit process. Every single island requires a tourism pass, and the more islands you want to see, the more permits you must buy. It adds up. On the other hand, there's none of the crass, concrete, carnival sprawl in the Galápagos that you see in regular tourist spots. So even for tightwads like Graeme and me, the cost seems worth it.

When the giant family and I get ashore, we cram into a tour van like reverse circus clowns and trundle loudly down the road. Being away from my teacher life for so many months, I've forgotten the sheer noise that the shorter of the human species emits. Though their voices go magically still when the guide at the lava tubes extinguishes his flashlight mid-pitch-black-cave. *Spooky.* And by the time we reach the viney but not exactly verdant grounds of the giant tortoise reserve, the midday sun seems to have shrunk their vocal chords slightly. They hoop without hollering through the jungle, which is not lush and green, as I expected, but the color palette of a hospital waiting room—tan, gray, muted greens. I guess I imagined that a place so famous for its wildlife would be waxy, wet, fertile green like Isla del Coco, but the Galápagos aren't. They're arid and hot, with some parts of the islands being downright moonscape-ish.

The most stunning thing, though, are the giant tortoises whom we've come to visit. They are HUGE. Smaller than a Volkswagen bug, sure, but definitely bigger than a beanbag chair; perhaps the size of a large leather ottoman or a big, greasy diesel engine (poor Graeme). The kids say over and over again "Watch this!" and then pretend to climb on the turtles' backs. This cowboy mime becomes more elaborate each time, with imaginary ten-gallon hats placed atop heads and outstretched legs reaching perilously close to tortoise humps. The parents act appropriately horrified; the kids high-five with laughter.

Of course, turtle cowboys wouldn't get very far. These creatures are slow, spending hours, even days, our guide says, trying to get over a fallen tree branch or through thick brush. A tortoise can go eighteen months (yes, a year and a half!) without food and water—which, to the old sailing ships, meant free, nonperishable food, requiring no feeding or care. The resultant overharvesting is one of the reasons some turtle species have gone extinct.

Which brings us to the Charles Darwin Research Station, back in Puerto Ayora, to the home of poor, old Lonesome George. Unlike those we've just seen, Lonesome George is not the largest type of turtle in the Galápagos. But he's definitely the most famous. In fact, the *Guinness Book of World Records* calls him the rarest living creature on earth. Hailing from Pinta Island, one of the northernmost islands in the Galápagos, Lonesome

George is the last tortoise of his kind. When he dies, so will his species. Which makes him a powerful icon for conservation in the Galápagos and worldwide.

Upward of 50,000 people each year visit George in hopes of getting a glimpse of the old guy before he croaks or, better yet, while he's in the throes of passion. See, George is housed with two fetching tortoise lasses from a neighboring island; they nod their long necks and wink their droopy eyes at him all day long. They're not of his species, of course, but the thought is better to have a half-Pinta George Junior than no more Pinta Tortoises at all. But apparently these turtle ladies aren't George's type. Because, after thirty-some years of cajoling and close quarters, George has yet to make his move. It seems Lonesome George isn't just lonely; he's also lost the spark.

When I return to *Dragonfly* late in the afternoon, I give Graeme a full report about the day's adventures. The hugeness of the tortoises. The expensiveness of the sightseeing. The loudness of a van crammed with three kids, two parents, one uncle, and one woman who's spent far too much time cooped up on a small boat. Graeme nods and laughs and acts surprised in all the right spots. But when I tell him about Lonesome George and his missing spark, Graeme looks downright distressed. Probably because the loss of a species *is* distressing. Maybe because it hits a little too close to home.

Graeme and I are having trouble with our own sparks lately—and not just in the engine room. Now, I am neither bold nor crass nor creepy enough to lay out my own personal sex life for you, my Uncle Bob, and my former students to read about. And yet it seems nigh on impossible, or at least disingenuous, to write a book about one's honeymoon without talking at some point about sex. So let's approach this like one would a rare, old, impotent tortoise . . . very carefully.

As has been mentioned before, Graeme and I are Average Joe cruisers. And, despite our exotic surroundings, we're Average Joe people, too; we're your neighbor down the street, your friendly face at the watercooler, your fellow nose picker on the highway. *Average folks*. So it stands to reason that we're Average Lovers, too. Back when we were in the rat race, treadmilling sixty hours a week and sleeping forty, our sex life was like that of most busy cohabiters I suppose: fun, frolicky, and squeezed in haphazardly when we had a minute—or thirty. It was a (yummy yummy) piece of cake . . . not an upside-down baked Alaska bananas Foster flambé.

But now, being exotic honeymooners on a long boat ride without a single care in the world—except maybe survival—the ante has upped. It seems like, since we have all this time now, our love life should have a little more, I don't know, va-va-va-VOOM. Like we should invest in aromatherapy candles and incense and sex toys and Andean pan-flute music. And we should spend hours with massage oils and icy-hot solutions and blindfolds and whipped cream canisters. And we should study *The Joy of Sex* or the *Kama Sutra* or *Twelve Steps to Tantric Love*. OK, or maybe just have sex more often.

But, you know, we don't do that stuff. Well, not *all* of it. Because that would be kind of . . . scary. I mean, we were happy with our sex life before we stumbled upon all this free time together, so what if we try to become titillatathoning, pretzelizing, supremo-orgasmo-sexual gurus and realize that we're not just Average Lovers, but crappy ones.

This is not a totally irrational fear. Because when you really get down to it, men and women have lots of barriers standing in their rockin' good sex life's way. Namely: 12 percent of women never reach orgasm. Seventy-five percent don't climax during intercourse. And those that do orgasm take ten to twenty minutes to get there. Men, on the other hand, are washing their hands of the whole shebang (or falling asleep) just two minutes after penetration.

All this comes to a head, so to speak, in a culture like ours, which really values penetration. It's like, you say "sex" and you're assumed to mean (not to get too textbooky here but) vaginal intercourse. But, and here's the rub, most women require clitoral stimulation for orgasm . . . and yet most women's anatomy precludes it during intercourse.

And that's when Charles Darwin enters the bedroom.

Stephen Jay Gould, a famous evolutionary biologist, believes that the female orgasm is a paradox of Darwinism. Why? Because a woman's climax is a quirk. An afterthought. It is in no way required for reproduction.

"How can our world be functional and Darwinian if the site of our orgasm is divorced from the place of intercourse?" Gould writes. "How can sexual pleasure be so separated from its functional significance in the Darwinian game of life?"

Well, there are lots of complex, scientific, highfalutin theories out there to address Gould's question, but the nutshell answer that makes most sense to me goes something like this: Men's reproductive mandate is to spread their seed far and wide. Hence:

Intercourse ——▶ Ecstasy ——▶ Reproduction

But a woman's evolutionary mandate is to find the best mate, not just to impregnate her, but to stick by her and help raise her brood. And a guy who might be good at *that* might also be willing to invest the extra time and energy it takes to figure out his partner's body. Hence, the evolutionary justification for women's anatomy.

And so Darwin is not dead. Neither is Graeme's and my love life. But with all this extra time and scrutiny, and these new gourmet expectations, it just might require a tad more bananas-Foster-flambé work.

Work is something we'd thought we'd set out on this trip to avoid.

Yet boat work certainly can't be avoided. Thankfully, though, Graeme's engine surfing is finally over. Which brings to mind what Dad used to say every day when he came home from work. He'd walk in the door and yell: "The moment you've all been waiting for has finally arrived!" Meaning: Dad was home. My brother and I just rolled our eyes: *As if.*

But on the eve of Graeme's and my crossing, it really does feel like the moment we've been waiting for has finally arrived. As if our entire trip up until now has been practice and preparation for tomorrow. Because what really sets the cruising life apart isn't just skirting big oceans, but crossing them.

So often when we think about crossing, we imagine it being from one point to another. As if it's those two points—the north side of the street and the south side of the street, single gal and married wife, personhood and parenthood—that matter. When really, it's the space in between, the getting from point A to point B, that terrifies and teaches us most.

I remember, back when I was in my post-TFA funk, one of my girl-friends told me I had to "embrace the bridge." She said I was in limbo, on a bridge between my old self and my new self. And instead of staring down at the heights in fear, instead of racing across the bridge in excitement or terror, she said I had to embrace that bridge and really *be* in that space of displacement and discomfort. It's on life's bridges, she said, that we catch a glimpse of who we really are.

I imagine crossing an ocean is much the same. There's the security of the land we're leaving. And the enticement of the land we're heading for— in this case, the quintessential South Pacific: white sand beaches, waving palm trees, turquoise lagoons; one can certainly understand wanting to race *there*. But in between these two terra firmas, there's that potentially danger-ous, totally unknown, perhaps boring, perhaps thrilling place called cross-ing. I'm crossing my fingers I can somehow embrace it.

In preparation for this passage, I've loaded up on provisions like some-one who won't see a grocery store for a month. I probably won't. I've got three cabbages, a bin full of green tomatoes, scores of canned everything, and a dozen boxes of thirty-year-shelf-life milk. In the bilge (the coolest part of the boat—we've totally given up on the refrigerator now) I've got baskets of other veggies, condiments, and eggs, the latter of which I'll turn every couple days in an attempt to prolong their lives. I have potatoes, pasta, Top Ramen (of course), and a couple Betty Crocker cake mixes. We've also stocked up on fishing gear in hopes of catching fresh meals on the way.

For his part, Graeme has finally gotten our new alternator working. For once in his life, something took three times longer than he thought. It also took twice as much money, and it was one giant, lonesome headache. The upside is that all that incessant waiting performed some bizarre psychologi-cal trick on me; instead of being scared and hesitant about our crossing, I'm now chomping at the bit.

We saddle up *Dragonfly* and ride . . . tomorrow.

Part 4

Crossing

13

The Green Box of Love

Day Zero

We should have left today. We could have left today. We were ready to leave today.

But today is Friday. *No* one starts a voyage on Friday. It's seafaring superstition. *No* one messes with seafaring superstition.

Day One

Ba-bye, Galápagos! Hellooo, Pacific!

Day Two

Put your hands in fists. Cock your thumbs out just slightly. Now hold out your arms like you're riding a motorcycle. This is your map of the Pacific. Washington State is your right fist and your left cocked-out thumb is Japan (a bit out of scale). There's more land out beyond your fists, too—Russia beyond your left, Canada and Alaska beyond your right—but the part that matters most is everything in between: the Pacific Ocean. The crook of your right elbow? The Galápagos Islands are near there. And the crease of your left elbow? That's our westernmost goal: Hong Kong. And then just in front of your right nipple, maybe even closer to your cleavage (if you happen to have cleavage), are the Marquesas Islands. That's the next time we'll see land.

Sailing from the Galápagos to the Marquesas is like driving from the West Coast of the United States to the East Coast of the United States at its widest point (3,400 miles). Except, the whole way, you're only going 5.75 miles per hour. So. If you trundled your family into Chevy Chase's pea green fake-wood-paneled station wagon and took no gas/eat/pee stops on the way, you would reach Wally World in about twenty-four days. Which is what Graeme and I expect this trip to take. Except our Shakedown Crossing went, um, not exactly as planned. So, in addition to overprovisioning, finger crossing, and agnostic praying, we've mentally prepared for a month.

Or two.

Day Three

What I haven't prepared adequately for is what to wear while crossing an ocean in the tropics on a boat with limited shade. Pants are too hot. Shorts leave dorky tan lines. And besides, I wouldn't mind getting a *little* tan. So the first two days I wore my bikini. But today, when I go to don my bikini again, I realize that wearing the same piece of nonbreathable fabric for who-knows-how-many weeks might not be the most hygienic arrangement. So I decide to wear underwear. Just—as in, no bra. I'm going Euro. Sounds dangerous but don't worry—*Moby-Dick*, my current book of choice, sort of shades my girls anyway, and I've used a quarter tube of Banana Boat SPF 50 already. I've got to be vigilant because the temperature is deceptive; the wind (we've got wind!) keeps things cool despite the sun.

Day Four

Dragonfly's best time ever! She made 170 nautical miles in the past twenty-four hours. That's 195.6 miles to you landlubbers. Which may sound dreadfully slow, but really is quite speedy, especially when you consider that we're traveling through the Intertropical Convergence Zone (ITCZ) near the equator, aka the doldrums. Usually there's like No Wind. But we've got plenty, which makes me nervous, because what's it going to be like when we reach the Trades where there's *supposed* to be wind?

Anyway, I'm on watch, so I'm watching: the sea and the sky and that sometimes pencil-lead-thin, but right now blurry line where they merge.

The seas are bumpy, meaning we've got moguls on an already undulating ski hill. Melville's words roll, bounce, and dip across the pages of my book. Winnie, our trusty wind vane (a nifty paddle gizmo that steers the rudder without electricity), is keeping us on course. Willie, our trusty autopilot, requires power. But the alternator's busted again. Graeme is back to engine surfing.

For me, though, it's an easy watch because there's not much in the way of dangers stalking us. No ominous clouds. No squalls. And no whales, like Moby, trying to ram us. (Melville wasn't making that up. It really can happen, though it's rare—usually it's a case of the boat ramming the whale, interrupting its afternoon nap.) Collisions between ships are also rare, since the odds of touching toes on such a huge dance floor are unlikely—we've only seen one other ship so far. I check regularly anyway. They say the dot of a ship on the horizon—the size an *o* makes on a book's page—takes at least twelve minutes to reach you. I check every ten.

Day Five

There goes Graeme, pissing over the side again. He's standing at the rail, his bare back to me, a scattering of those crazy, pubic-looking hairs on his shoulders waving in the wind. His hips are wedged between two vertical wires called shrouds that run from the deck of the boat up to our two masts—as if this wedged-in position of his is supposed to make me feel better. It doesn't. In fact, it's this banal moment, watching Graeme relieve himself over the side, that terrifies me most about this crossing. Because if Graeme falls over, I'm dead. Metaphorically at least. He'll be dead literally.

Yes, of course, we've done the overboard drills, and I know what I'm *supposed* to do if Graeme takes a header. But half of those drills resulted in the fatal drowning or at least loss of the sticks we tossed overboard to save. Even Scout, who couldn't understand why we would squander such perfectly good fetching material, eventually lost scent of them in *Dragonfly*'s dizzying circling. And now. Under ocean conditions—small ripples on larger waves on hefty swells in endless sea with absolutely no he's-just-off-that-gravel-beach visual aid—the odds seem even grimmer. I'd have to keep my eyes and finger pointed at Graeme's quickly receding body, all while executing the about-face of a boat with full sails set, moving steadily in the opposite direction. Obese chance.

And let's just not even mention the fact that Graeme could fall overboard in the middle of the night, without my knowledge, while I'm sound asleep in my bunk. This is by far my biggest fear. I mean, imagine waking to another bluebird day at sea to find the love of your life missing. Imagine him floating somewhere, out there, nowhere, just waiting for the dawn. For the sharks. For you. And imagine yourself single-handedly circling the boat in a desperate search for him, sending out frantic radio transmissions to anyone nearby, trying to calculate current and timing and position and where in the middle of the goddamn Pacific your husband might be floating. Or drowning.

And then imagine that dreadful moment. After circling for days. When you finally have to give up. And stop searching. And continue to the other side. Alone.

Cannot.
Discuss.
Further.

So, yeah. It freaks me out, just a little bit, when Graeme pisses over the side.

Day Six

Blue jay blue, blueberry blue, velour seats in a sedan blue, pansy blue, iris blue, is that suit black or blue? blue, violet blue, violent blue, fingernail polish on toes blue, sky blue, midnight blue, Blue Morpho butterfly blue, Bluebeard blue, blue balls blue, crisp navy uniform blue, royal blue, blue suede shoes blue, Kmart blue light special blue, computer screen blue, Smurfy blue, swear a blue streak when you're mad blue, smoky blue, guitar blue, almost heaven Blue Ridge Mountains blue, sapphire blue, lapis blue, blue ribbon at the county fair blue, blue jeans blue, recycle bin blue, my mom's old apron with stains blue, iceberg blue, damselfly blue, Galápagos Blue-footed Boobie blue, "Go Blue!" blue, Blue Angels blue, Babe the Big Blue Ox blue, bayou blue, Great Blue Heron blue, Polish pottery at a yard sale blue.

The only things out here that aren't blue today are *Dragonfly*, Graeme, and (thank goodness) me. Not even a bit. Oh, and also our friends on *Journey*. They're a nice retired couple on a catamaran, and we've been checking in with them regularly on the radio: we write down their position; they write down ours. Anyway, catamarans are generally faster than monohulls, so *Journey* left a couple days after we did, eventually saw our sail on the horizon, and steered right for us. (Graeme and I put on clothes for the occasion.) As they passed, we all waved and shouted and took photos of each other. And now we're watching their boat get smaller and smaller till, pretty soon, they'll be just an *o* on the horizon. Then gone.

Day Seven

Sailing 3,400 miles across an ocean gives you lots of time to think. About where you've been. About where you're going. About what's in that green box sitting by your pillow. *Shake. Shake. Shake.* Like a kid at Christmas, I'm holding it to my ear. *Shake. Shake.* Only it's April. *Shake.* It's a bon voyage gift, given to me nine months ago by my matron of honor, the pregnant one I inflicted with varicose veins by making her stand at the altar with me on her due date. Well, somehow, she forgave me and bequeathed to us this box in sage green wrapping paper with detailed instructions on the side. It says:

Open for any of the following circumstances:

1. You are seven days into a major passage/crossing.
2. You've crossed the equator.
3. You're sinking.
4. You are restless, bored, or need a pick-me-up.
5. You've finished all of your books.
6. You don't have room for an 8-by-8 box on board.

Let me address her list bottoms up:

6. We do have room for an 8-by-8 box on board, though it was ousted from deep storage when I superloaded provisions last week; that's why it's by my pillow now.
5. There's no way we could finish all our books on board; we've got enough to keep the International Bibliophiles Conference busy.
4. We're neither restless nor bored, though I did entertain myself last night plucking leg hairs with tweezers and a headlamp while listening to Salman Rushdie's The Ground Beneath Her Feet on audiotape. (Normally, I write on night watch, but our solar panels didn't fill the batteries enough to run my laptop.)
3. Nope. Not sinking. Yet.
2. Crossed the equator way back at the Galápagos where we made a toast

and tossed over some fine tequila for Neptune, Mother Ocean, and other VIP deity types.

1. We are indeed seven days into a major crossing/passage, which means we get to open the mysterious green box. . . .

Tonight! At our daily 5:30 P.M. nonalcoholic happy hour where everybody (that would be Graeme and Me) gathers in the cockpit to eat Graeme's surprisingly tasty sardine dip, drink warm Coke, and talk.

Day Eight

We instituted our daily 5:30 P.M. non-alcoholic happy hour purposely so Graeme and I could have quality time together. Because one of the most surprising things we've learned about crossing an ocean on a ten-foot-wide, thirty-five-foot-long sailboat is that it would actually be quite easy to go days without really talking. Or, as we discovered on the Shakedown Crossing, doing other things newlywed couples like to do. Because someone's always on watch and the other person is usually busy—sleeping, doing the Pink or Blue, reading. . . .

JANNA	TIME	GRAEME
Wake Graeme with steaming pot of coffee and go to sleep	4 A.M.	On 5-hour watch
On 3-hour watch	9 A.M.	Wake Janna with steaming pot of coffee and begin boat projects
Make lunch and do dishes, then read, write, or do boat projects; take nap at 2:30 P.M. and wake luxuriously to . . .	12 P.M.	On 3-hour watch
Sex	3 P.M.	Sex
On 4(ish)-hour watch	Sometime after 3 P.M.	Fall asleep (immediately) for afternoon nap; get up to read or putter; serve nonalcoholic happy hour at 5:30 P.M.
Make dinner and do dishes; go to sleep around 9:00 P.M.	7 P.M.	On 4-hour watch
On 5-hour watch	11 P.M.	Wake Janna and go to sleep, so we can do it all over again

Oh, and in case you're wondering, our 5:30 P.M. happy hour proceeds sans alcohol because our entire crossing is sans alcohol; we want to be ready for anything. Anytime. (Plus, after all those happy hours cruising south, we could use a little time to dry out.)

Day Nine

Besides happy hour and sex on a schedule, the other thing we instituted at the beginning of this trip are rules. Rules to prevent the unspeakable (which I spoke about on Day Five) from happening. For instance, while we may be mostly naked during the days, we've got a Must Wear Life Jacket And Be Clipped In rule on night watches. We each wear an automatic life jacket that'll inflate if we ever hit the water. And we each wear a harness with a tether and carabineer, to avoid being sloshed over the side. We "clip in" either to the cockpit or, if going forward on deck, to lines we've rigged that run the length of the boat. Which brings us to a corollary rule: If you go on deck at night, you Must Wake Sleeping Mate First. And s/he must not fall back asleep until you return safe and sound. (If you don't return safe and sound, see Day Five.)

I must say that (most of) the fears I had leading up to this crossing have been alleviated. By our rules. By our routine. And by *Dragonfly* herself. It may sound a bit woo-woo, but ever since I got mad at her for losing her steering back in California, she shaped up—and shipped out. I feel like she's taking care of us now. For instance, Graeme and I don't actually have to go on deck very often because we each can sail *Dragonfly* from right here in the cockpit. Lots of boats can't do this. But *Dragonfly*'s got this clever thing called roller furling, which means both her forward sail (called a genoa) and her center sail (called a mainsail) roll up on tubes like yards of fabric at the fabric store. This is important because, when the wind kicks up, you can roll the sails in however much you want. (Less sail area = less scary.)

This roller-furling thing may seem like a no-brainer, but lots of sailors opt for old-fashioned "hank-on" sails because they're higher performance (aka faster). And yet, if the wind picks up, hankers-on actually have to go out on deck, to the pointy end of the boat, to hank down the big sail and replace it with a smaller one—so the ship doesn't get knocked over. Plus, hankers-on often have to turn the entire boat into the wind, going broad-side to big nasty waves, in order to reef or reduce their mainsail. Scary. So *Dragonfly*'s nifty rig really does make me worry less.

Though I do still worry about Graeme falling overboard midpiss.

Day Ten

Squally and rolly. During my 4 A.M. sleep, the *vrrrooosh* of speeding trains keeps startling me awake; *Dragonfly* careens, leaning hard on her ribs. I remind myself this is just like driving: how you feel safe when you're behind the wheel (my midnight watch had been windy but fine), but you slam imaginary brakes when you're a passenger (I call to Graeme, "Is everything OK?").

Once morning comes, I can actually see the elements we're up against—big brash waves, petulant surface, gray brushstrokes leaping off wet canvas. And I realize it's actually a lot less nerve-wracking at night when I can't see these huge surges rising behind us. Though, in the dark, you also can't see or prepare for the squalls. Each squall brings rain and its own schizophrenic wind, always more fierce, usually more chaotic than the air around it. If we had enough power to flip on the radar (no such luck), these systems would show up as bold black blips stalking us. While it's sort of Space Invaderish to watch, it would be nice to know they're coming, because then it's possible to reef before they strike.

In the light of day, though, it's easy to see each squall approaching, a little (or big) black rain cloud on a gun metal sky. The squalls are so dark, so delineated, so compact, they're almost fake-looking. They remind me of a muddy Winnie-the-Pooh masquerading as a cloud, trying to steal honey from bees. We can sometimes even steer our way around them. But when they do hit, it's a wet swarm. Rain, wind, butter knives on the sea. Warm though, and we try to funnel as much freshwater as we can into buckets for laundry. As our mostly naked bodies get drenched, we rub our hands under armpits and down legs; we pull the elastic of our skivvies from our bellies and scrub scrub scrub. And then it just stops. The little black rain cloud with its swarming bees floats on. Past *Dragonfly*'s bow, toward the horizon, and out of sight.

Day Eleven

There's this guy named John Vigor whom Graeme considers his personal boating guru. (Graeme has many personal boating gurus.) Though the way Graeme talks about this guy is starting to sound a bit voodooish to me. Mainly because Graeme has become obsessed with Vigor's Black Box Theory of Luck at Sea, the premise of which is: There is none. Well, not exactly. According to Vigor, there is only *earned* luck, which is created by "diligent and constant acts of seamanship." The idea is that you do as much upkeep and repair and safety-conscious nitpicking as you possibly can, and then in bad weather or emergency situations where, as Vigor says, "human effort can do no more," your points are cashed in. If you've earned enough luck in your box, your account stays in the black: Your boat weathers the storm, or you're able to fix the problem, or you simply have fewer problems. But, of course, you immediately have to start earning more luck for the Black Box.

So, over the past eleven days, Graeme has pumped the bilge, greased the propeller shaft, added coolant, rewound the furling system, rigged Winnie, fiddled with Willie, replaced the regulator, and fixed the alternator—twice. Me, I've cooked a lot.

And did I mention I found weevils in the flour today? It's only Day Eleven. So I consulted my own personal boating gurus—the ladies who write cookbooks for cruisers—and followed their instructions. I sifted the flour through a fine mesh colander (the weevils writhed like miniature Mexican jumping beans). Did it again (fewer writhers this time). Then I baked with it.

Ew.

Day Twelve

Halfway! Or at least that's what the mileage suggests. To celebrate, Graeme shaves his facial hair all wackylike: soul patch and mustache with weird hooky wings around his mouth. He looks like a '70s drug dealer, or our UPS delivery guy. I add deodorant and a dress to my usual ensemble of underwear. And at five-thirty we drink warm Coke with colorful mini-umbrellas stuck in the cans. We're literally, and happily, in the middle of nowhere.

Day Thirteen

I should amend that. We're actually about one-quarter of the way across the entire Pacific Ocean as its widest point. You, of course, already know that this is the largest ocean on earth, but to put things in perspective, the square mileage of the Pacific is larger than all the world's land masses combined. It's kind of huge. But once we reach the Marquesas, we'll be able to stop at different islands every two to ten days as we move west. It's like learning to walk in reverse; you make a huge giant leap and then revert to baby steps.

The weirdest thing about being out here is the push-pull of emotions. On the one hand, I'll admit it, there is a fervent desire to get to the other side. I can't help it. Neither can Graeme. We count off miles like kids in the backseat—"Are we there yet?" But who can blame us? There is something mildly enticing about what we're heading for: tropical beaches, physical safety, living creatures besides weevils. On the other hand, though, there's this electric feeling of freedom out here. It jolts me at the oddest moments—while popping popcorn on night watch, while looking out the bathroom porthole at rushing water, while slathering on sunblock for the umpteenth time. This is it! We're living our dream! This is what sailing to the South Pacific sounds and smells and looks and feels like! Who knew?

It reminds me, actually, of that time in my life when I was young and single and living on my own. This was post-grad-school, post-TFA, post-depression. I was still crossing that bridge between identities, I suppose, but I was nearing the other side, growing more and more comfortable with the new me. Plus, I had a challenging job, a fixer house, a small group of close girlfriends, and, of course, Scout. It was me (and all those accoutrements) against the world—I was happy!

And yet, I must admit that I spent crazy amounts of time during those years daydreaming about my future mate. Who would he be? What would he be like? How would our life together smell and taste and feel? It was like a sprawling Mad Libs of a love story with endless blanks to fill in with whatever adjectives (cute, outdoorsy), adverbs (precipitously, patiently), and verbs (talk, screw) I chose. (Sorry, but no Mad Libs in the history of the world has ever been completed without a dirty word.) My point is it's a yin-yang of emotions out here. One moment I'm wishing this crossing would never end. The next I'm wishing it already had.

Day Fourteen

I never realized the sheer diversity of my husband's boxer collection. He's got some of those cheapo almost-see-through white boxers, and a couple fancy Patagonia pairs. He's got maroon boxers made of thick cotton. And green boxers with hula girls. And one pair that's cut almost tighty-whitey but not. There are gray, holey plaid boxers. And blue striped ones, also with holes. And a pair of flannel, red-and-green Christmas boxers with wrapped presents on them. And, as his last resort (there's always a last resort), he's got this quirky pair of yellow-and-red boxers with Chinese characters scrawled across the place the fly should be. He's wearing those today. Which tells me it's time to do laundry.

So I haul out our collapsible green bucket, lower it to sea on a rope, and haul it aboard. Water sloshes on deck and over my feet. It's hot out (of course), so it feels good. I scrub the skivvies against each other with a cup of detergent, a handful of my undies in there, too. Then I rinse in saltwater. Rinse salty again. Rinse in semifresh rainwater. And finally commit a bit of our precious potable water to the cause (we loaded up extra jerry jugs of the stuff before leaving the Galápagos). I wring everything out and clothespin our collective unmentionables to the life lines, which now resemble those colorful strings of flags at a street fair, flapping and yapping in the wind.

Meanwhile, Graeme's been warming fresh water in the sun shower gizmo we normally use camping. We've been relying on solar for two weeks now, and despite occasionally wishing we had more juice, it's a cool feeling being totally off the grid. We hang our hot shower bag from the mast, stand on the overturned dinghy stored on deck, and suds up in front of the Father, the sun, and the holey boxers. Hard to imagine a shower stall with a better view.

Day Fifteen

Morning and night we listen to the weather, and every six hours we talk on the radio. We're no longer checking into an official Net, just a small group of friends who're crossing with us. We've already said good-bye to so many people we've met: our young cruising friends; the king and queen; other boats we lost track of but hope to meet again in the South Pacific. But the thing about cruising is that every time you have to say good-bye to one boat, another friendly boat comes along. And pretty soon you've got a new fleet of friends, all traveling, for a time, to the same places, at the same paces. Until you part ways again.

Truth be told, though, none of our current friends are as slow as we are. *Journey*, as I said, passed us on Day Six. *Freebird*, another catamaran, passed us on Day Nine, even with their headsail busted. And *Sea Hawk*, a fifty-some-foot monohull, is bound to catch us any day now. We're the slowest, the cheapest, and the youngest in the bunch. But they seem to enjoy the dirty jokes we tell on the radio.

Day Sixteen

Me [in a high-pitched Mickey Mouse voice, squeaking into the mic]: "Mickey and Minnie were experiencing marital strife, so they went to see a marital counselor. After much discussion, the counselor said, 'Mickey, I don't think you should divorce Minnie just because she's a little bit crazy.' Mickey replied, 'I didn't say she was a little bit crazy, Doc, I said she was fucking Goofy!'"

Day Seventeen

"Fish on!" Graeme yells.

I look back, and sure enough, the green hand line stretching behind *Dragonfly* is taught and slicing the smooth sea like a scalpel. Graeme grabs the plastic spool from the starboard cleat and takes patient wraps, a few at a time. Soon Graeme's standing on the back deck, playing the fish, leaning and bending and crouching—oblivious to the fact that he's forgotten to don even his threadbare boxers today. A fact to which I cannot, however much I try, be oblivious. And so I offer for the record: Naked man lounging in tropical sun on sailboat? Sexy. But(t) naked man fishing? Repellant.

Soon there's a long, fat tuna on deck, slapping and bleeding all over the place. Naked Man bonks it with his fish bonker. Naked Man bonks it again. The fish gives one last quiver and then Naked Man is crouching with knife, slitting the belly and slicing out guts. Let's hope he doesn't slip with that knife. I avert my eyes for about the fiftieth time and busy myself gathering chopsticks and soy sauce and wasabi. I also grab a pair of boxers from Graeme's clean pile of laundry. I'm eager to enjoy my fish naked and raw. The company might be better dressed.

Day Eighteen

I never knew monotony could be so fascinating. The scenery out here is like Heraclitus's observation: *You never step in the same river twice.* Because even though it's always the same (sea and sky, sky and sea), it's always changing, too. Today we've got a silver blanket above and a shimmering gray sheet below. Not much wind, though there's a squall line on the horizon. I'm sitting on the elaborate throne I've created: beach towel over cockpit cushions atop Igloo cooler. Homer drapes across my chest (I finished

Moby-Dick, read *Ahab's Wife*, and am now into *The Odyssey*). This seems the perfect place from which to watch everything. And nothing at all.

Seeing this sort of scenery day in, day out is, I imagine, kind of like owning a really masterly piece of art. I mean, if there was a Dale Chihuly glass vase, say, and you went to the museum to see it, you'd just get that one glimpse of it, at that one moment, in that certain strand of light. But if you (were a millionaire and) had it sitting on your dining table, you'd be able to look up from making coffee in the morning or chopping bok choy in the evening or turning off the stereo at night and be surprised again, and again, and again, at its changeable color, its deceptive shape, its ephemeral yet eternal beauty. The piece as a whole would always be the same, you know, in its essence, but the way it looks, the *effect* of it, would be different.

That's how the sea is. Moody and fleeting and beautiful and monotonous. I'm just watching it go by.

Day Nineteen

I think there's also a monotony in marriage that's equally delightful and dangerous. I mean, there's something very reassuring about believing, and trusting, and *knowing* that your marriage is going to last forever. That it will keep its same essence or form, that, like sky and sea, it's always there. But if you don't really *look* at your relationship, pay attention to it, *stand your watch*, then you might have it, but not really *get* it. Because, you know, it changes. The blue goes gray, or the white puffy clouds turn dark, or the wispy horsetails signal a change in the weather. You've got to be attentive.

But maybe even worse than missing warning signs, at sea or in marriage, would be missing those simple but intense moments of beauty. The scent of fresh rain peppering the sea. The smell of wet skin, freshly scrubbed. The *shhhh* of white horses tumbling down waves. His coughing laugh when you really crack him up. The buck and roll of the motion of the ocean. The press of a cool hand on the small of a hot back. You know. The little stuff. The stuff that's hard to pinpoint. Even harder to remember. But the stuff that, when those moments are gone, you miss without even knowing.

Day Twenty

Graeme's working on the alternator again. He's been working on it almost this entire trip because as soon as he fixes it, a few days later it breaks. And then he goes back to engine surfing. I suppose we could just sail the whole three-thousand-some-odd miles without it, but in the back of your mind there's always this thought: What if we really *did* need more power? Say, in a nasty storm where radar could really help? Or if the unspeakable (which I spoke about on Day Five) happened and I had to cry and snot and holler into that radio for days on end, calling for any sign of my husband? You never know. And so Graeme keeps at it. Fixing what appears to be unfixable. Getting closer to solving the mystery, he says, each time it breaks.

Plus, there's no wind. (That's right, in the doldrums we had great wind; in the Trades, which are supposed to be steady, we have none.) So we'd like to run the engine a bit, you know, just to make way, but it's hard to justify the engine when it gives no juice. On the bright side, for the past five days we've been flying our bright orange-and-yellow spinnaker; that's the big parachute of a sail you see on '80s calendar covers. Up until now we'd only used it a dozen or so times, but now we're getting pretty good at it. We've only dropped it in the ocean and run over it twice.

Good thing I have a sewing machine on board to fix those rips.

Oh wait. That requires more juice.

Day Twenty-one

If I eat one more goddamned canned bean salad or another meal that involves cabbage, I think I will hurl. Those are pretty much the only veggies we have left. The green tomatoes ripened and (the ones we didn't eat) rotted by Day Fifteen. The carrots went from rubbery (Day Eight) to fuzzy (Day Eighteen). And we ate the last of our eggs this morning (I figured they were OK, since the rotten eggs I discovered along the way smelled like, well, rotten eggs). To make up for our dearth of fresh food, Graeme's hoping to catch more fish, but after eating that tuna four different ways (raw, sautéed, fried with rice, in a stew), I'm not even sure I can stomach that. What I *really* want? A double-bacon cheeseburger, corkscrew fries, and side salad with bleu cheese dressing, please.

Oh, and a beer. An ice-cold beer.

Day Twenty-two

Like I said, sailing 3,400 miles across an ocean gives you lots of time to think. So if John Vigor has that Black Box Theory of Luck that Graeme likes so much, then I offer another box-based theory about the stuff I really care about: Frits' Green Box Theory of Love. It's named after my matron of honor, who gave us that green box to open back on Day Seven. Incidentally, she also gave us most of the advice. Here's how the theory works:

1. Love in a lasting relationship is not random. Just like luck at sea, it has to be earned.
2. You earn love points to put into your Green Box through constant maintenance, upkeep, and repairs.
3. E.g., the Little Stuff: Offering thanks for folded laundry. Walking the dog on a rainy day when it's not your turn. Fixing a mistake without an I-told-you-so. Appreciating a repaired alternator (even when it's bound to break two days later).
4. And then there's the Big Stuff: When part of your relationship (like that alternator) is busted, you've actually got to try to fix it. Not just pretend like everything's hunky-dory and carry on without it.
5. Because down the road, when your relationship encounters serious storms, when tragedy strikes or emergency calls, or when as Vigor says, "human effort can do no more," you'll cash in the points in your Green Box. And if your love box is full enough, you and your mate will weather the storm. Together.
6. And then, of course, you'll have to start depositing more love points into the Green Box.

Of course you may wonder, how many points do I have to put in? How many loving gestures or relationship repairs will make the box full? How much work is this going to take? Well, my matron of honor's advice at my wedding was this: *Give sixty; expect forty.* Why? Because if you give 50 percent and expect the same in return, something always gets screwed up with the math; you're always more aware of your own deposit slips than your mate's. The other thing she said, irony notwithstanding, is *Don't keep score.* This one's tough for me. Graeme says that for someone who is abysmal at math, I'm astonishingly good at keeping score.

The thing about the Green Box of Love is that no one knows the exact value of a graceful apology or a back rub or a squeezed hand; no one knows what a broken promise or an unkind word extracts from the account. A bank statement cannot be waved about and used as evidence of deposits and withdrawals. All one can do is make conscientious and continual contributions to the Green Box of Love. And hope that, in the end, it's enough.

Day Twenty-three

I guess what I'm trying to say is most things in life worth doing—even the really magical things like love and sailing—take a lot of hard work. Neglecting that work, or leaving those things to chance, is a little like abandoning the good things in life. This Green Box idea is just one way to hold tight to the good stuff.

Speaking of good stuff, I should mention what my girlfriend packed in that eight-by-eight sage green box we opened on Day Seven. In addition to the sweet card, the homemade jams, and the travel Yahtzee game, my friend followed the Green Box Theory to a tee: She was "diligent and constant" in her acts of friendship; she filled the box chock full of love.

Day Twenty-four

At 10:41 A.M., Graeme, on the bow with his binoculars, shouts, "Land ho!"

I stand up at the wheel and squint into the distance. I don't see a thing. "Where?" I holler back.

Graeme walks back to the cockpit and points. "There. Under those clouds. There's a long, low, dark mass." He puts the glasses in my hands. "Look."

I hold the binoculars to my eyes and I see it. Land. And it's the exact jolt I used to get in Graeme's and my dating days when I'd see an e-mail waiting from him in my in-box. I'm giddy. I'm sprung. I hop up and down from one foot to the other.

Graeme's giddy, too, but he shows his excitement by stepping to the GPS. "OK," he says, after pressing a few buttons, "if we can keep up our speed, we'll get there by dusk. And, let's see"—he does a few more calculations—"if you divide our trip out by twenty-four-hour segments, that makes for a twenty-three-day crossing. Give or take a few hours." He looks back at me. "Not bad."

"Not bad at all," I say, patting *Dragonfly*'s salty dodger. "She made it."

Graeme steps up to where I am behind the wheel. He slips an arm around my bare shoulder and squeezes. "*We* made it," he says.

And that afternoon, instead of enjoying the usual activity penciled in at three o'clock, we do something just about as exciting. We watch the small greenish gray island off our port bow get bigger and bigger and bigger. As we inch closer, the grays ashore articulate into cliffs, boulders, and stones; the greens divide and multiply into palms, bushes, and vines. And in that last hour, sailing into the shadow of that tall island, we retire both trusty autopilots, Winnie and Willie. We take the shiny, albeit rust-bitten wheel in our own hands. And we take turns guiding *Dragonfly* to the other side.

The Night Watch

*t*wenty-four hours after making our first South Pacific landfall, we're tossed back to sea. It turns out Fatu Hiva, the southern- and eastern-most island in the Marquesas, is not an official check-in port for French Polynesia, so you have to get permission to visit from a larger island first.

OK, so our guidebook told us this. But we thought we'd risk it anyway, since it was the closest island in reach. And we hadn't seen land in twenty-three days. And we, of course, wanted to visit the place famous for penises and virgins.

Sailing into Hana Vave Bay, even in fading light, it's easy to see where the talk of penises comes from. The bay is flanked on both sides by towering basalt spires that put my mom's collection of phallic rocks (yes, Mom collects penis rocks) to shame. Dropping anchor beneath these behemoth pricks, you really can't help but get the giggles. But maybe that's just the effect of seeing land, *any* shaped land, after so many days at sea.

Legend has it that the original French name for this place was, fittingly, Baie des Verges, or Bay of Penises. But then, when the missionaries came along, they fudged a little on the spelling, renaming it Baie des Vièrges. That's Bay of, ahem, Virgins to you. Oh the difference a wee *i* can make.

And what a difference a shower can make, too. As soon as Graeme and I drop the hook, our friends on *Journey* insist we board their palace of a catamaran for hot showers in an indoor, full-size stall with water-impervious walls, stainless steel fixtures, and a massage-setting showerhead. We don't make them ask twice. When I emerge fifteen (OK, thirty) minutes later onto the back deck, the Usual Suspects (*Freebird*, *Sea Hawk*, and, of course, *Journey*) have gathered to celebrate. Only this isn't our official celebration, they explain, because we're not officially accepted into French Polynesia yet. As soon as we step foot ashore tomorrow, they predict, we'll get booted back to sea.

And that's precisely what happens. The next morning the local gendarme, a serious gentleman with hands folded high on his puffed-out chest, announces that all un-permit-ed boats must leave by day's end. He is placid and soft-spoken, but firm. So Graeme and I apologize profusely, calculate the distance to the official port of entry at Hiva Oa—an easy overnight run—and realize we don't have to leave until evening to get there. We decide to spend as much daylight as possible frolicking illegally in the land of penises and virgins.

We walk with our friends Jane and Doug from *Sea Hawk* through the village of Hana Vave. It's a smattering of small, tidy houses strung along a main cement road, the cement a debatable perk of French rule. At the quay there are locals looking to trade their carvings and *tapas* (no, not tasty, overpriced Spanish vittles but black geometric paintings on bark cloth) for baseball caps, booze, and, one particularly brazen woman asks, a brassiere. They'd rather trade than sell their wares because the local store's selection is slim pickings compared to what the yachties, as we're called throughout the islands, might have stowed away. But, alas, Graeme and I have brought nothing ashore to trade. Graeme eyes the brazen woman's intricately patterned *tapas* and considers offering the shirt off his back. I contemplate trading the bra off my rack. But too small, I think, looking down at my chest and seeing, instead, my toes. We thank the busty woman with the pretty *tapas* and continue with Doug and Jane up the road.

As we amble through the settlement we pass a gray horse tethered in a yard, and a painted wooden house with divided window panes, and a picket-fenced garden so meticulous it belongs in a Cotswold village. There's a man straddling the branch of a *pamplemousse* tree, picking yellowy green grapefruit the size of Frankenstein's head. And an older sister on a front stoop, brushing her younger sister's dark hair. Then we reach the end of the houses and the beginning of the dirt road. The goal is a waterfall high up on Fatu Hiva's mossy flank. As we hike we chat.

"So, were you guys ever really scared?" Jane asks, her voice like two hands rubbing together. This is a common topic among sailors, and by far the most common question we get from landlubbers. I suppose most people consider it small talk. Though Graeme is about to reveal a secret he's been keeping from me for nine months now, and when that bomb drops, it doesn't feel so small at all.

I respond to Jane's question with my old standby—"Scared, sure, but I never feared for my life"—though this, I realize, is not a very satisfying answer. Really the asker wants to hear about fifty-knot winds and fifty-foot waves and, if possible, a helicopter evacuation, please. But fear isn't always as obvious as playing Frogger with freighters or losing steering on a lee shore or being caught in a lightning storm near a pirate attack. There are other things, not actual crises, that have scared me just as much. Like my incessant worry that Graeme will fall overboard pissing. Or the fear that our toilet will overflow with sewage (it did once, and it was *scary*). Or—and this is really weird—that inexplicable terror I feel every time I detect a leak. I swear I practically have heart palpitations. Which is ridiculous, because these leaks are not in the hull or anywhere vital. They're just drips down the walls or slow seeps that dampen the cushions. They couldn't sink us. So why do they freak me out so much?

We're making our way through hip-high meadow, walking a dirt path two people wide. I grab a strand of tall grass, strip it of its seeds, blow them off my palm, and pluck another. Some seeds stick to my palm because it's so humid out.

While I'm not ready to open the psychological can of worms that my oddball fears are, I figure Jane deserves a better answer than "I never feared for my life." So, after some thought, I offer her this: There was that scary night we had on passage between Mexico and El Salvador in a stretch of water called the Gulf of Tehuantepec. It's so notoriously nasty there that the winds have a signature name, Tehuantepeckers, which seems to both personify the winds (damn peckers) and make them seem way too cartoonish for how bad they really are. Anyway, we were bashing into waves constructed of cinder block, bashing so hard that our cap rail ripped off (though we didn't discover that till morning), just bashing and bashing into angry black sea. I stood under the dodger, wrapped in yellow foulies, staring blind into the blind night, sailing by braille I suppose. I was so intent upon not freaking out about the waves crashing against *Dragonfly*'s hull that I started singing camp songs as loud as I could. Just Hail Marying them out to sea. I suppose I sang because it's something I've always done with my mom, a sort of happy place, and I figured a few rounds of "I've Been Working on the Railroad" would keep my mind off the storm. Especially once I switched to the dirty version my friends and I used to sing in college.

Jane, walking just right of me, offers her own off-key variation on "Dinah won't you blow" complete with hand gestures.

We laugh.

But Graeme interrupts our laughter with his own memory of the night of the Tehuantepeckers.

"The weirdest thing," Graeme says, "is how Janna was totally solid during that storm. I mean, she was fearless. But then, a few days later, we were on a nice, pleasant sail, in daylight, low seas, only half as much wind, and she freaks out about the boat heeling—"

"Hey, lots of people freak out about heeling," I say. Almost every friend who's ever sailed with us tenses up when the boat starts to lean way over.

"Yeah, but you're not a novice. You know sailboats are meant to heel. And you know *Dragonfly*'s not going over in just twenty knots with a reef in the sail—yet that seemed to scare you more than the storm did. It didn't make any sense."

"Yeah, well." I shrug. "Fear isn't exactly rational."

He's right though. My reaction to storms is totally different from my reaction to regular discomforts aboard. During bad weather I gear myself up for sheer survival, my mental mantra being: "If she goes over, she'll come back up. If she goes over, she'll come back up"—which is because, the way sailboats are made, the heavy keel will always, no matter what, bring the boat back up. My parents' double capsize in that Japanese typhoon convinced me of that.

And yet, little things like heeling and leaks and overflowing toilets unnerve me. I'm much more addled by the small, daily discomforts of cruising than by the big, hairy, scary stuff. Like I'm more scared of not liking our honeymoon—than of dying.

Our wide path has dwindled to a narrow track now and is slowly becoming more jungly. We pass a bush of fluttery pink hibiscus flowers, their yellow stamens swaying like Zippos at a rock concert. I point and say, "Pretty."

Then I ask Jane and Doug, "What about you guys? Were you ever really scared?"

Before Doug or Jane can answer, though, Graeme says, "Actually, Janna, I think I've been more scared than you have on this trip."

I stumble slightly on a dip in the path and almost choke on my own saliva. We've moved into the shade of the jungle now and Graeme's leading the way. The back of his T-shirt is wet with sweat; his voice sounds serious.

"What's that?" Doug calls from the back. "You say you been scared, Graeme?"

"Yeah. Definitely," Graeme says, turning his head so we all can hear. "Watching that barometer drop. Seeing those big *L*s on the weather fax. Knowing the ocean doesn't get big and lumpy unless there's a big, lumpy system causing it. . . ."

On *Dragonfly*'s wall, a brass-encircled barometer measuring atmospheric pressure hangs like a clock. Graeme taps its glass face throughout the day to make the needle inside jump and settle on its latest reading; even the slightest drop can mean gnarly weather. He also downloads weather maps onto our laptop from the SSB radio to track every storm. The *L*s show the location of low pressure systems, along with lots of squiggles and arrows to indicate projected wind, waves, and current. For Graeme, I'm now realizing, reading these indicators is like getting a doctor's dreaded diagnosis, the only advice ever being to wait and see.

Graeme climbs up over a gray boulder in our path. He turns and holds out his hand; I grasp it fireman-style, and he hauls me up. Then he helps Jane.

"For me, it's not so scary *dealing* with a storm, the elements right in front of you," Graeme says, "but I'm constantly worrying about how much worse it's going to get before it gets better. Or, before a storm hits, I'm always trying to read the signs and figure out what to do. It's that anticipation, the waiting, the worrying part that's scary. I've worried more on this trip than I ever have in my life."

I stare at Graeme like I'm a fish gaping for water. In the thirteen years I've known him, Graeme has never been a worrier. And all this trip, I had no idea he was so freaked out by those *L*s and squiggles and arrows. What a shock to learn there's been fear—serious fear—streaking through my husband's veins while I thought he was rock solid, confident, even cocky. It's disturbing to be wrong about someone I thought I knew so well.

"So you've really been scared on this trip?" I ask, pushing a Tarzan-like vine out of my face and holding it aside for Jane.

"Of course," Graeme says, the implication of his tone being that he'd be an idiot not to be.

"More scared than I've been?" I ask.

"Yyyup," he says. "Or at least scared of different things."

And that's when I realize that my ability to sing into the face of a storm probably has more to do with dumb ignorance than any so-called courage. Instead of worrying about what's coming next, I pat myself on the back for being able to ignore what's right in my face. Apparently ignorance, as the saying goes, has been my bliss.

The four of us walk on a bit farther in silence. It's fully shaded now among the trees and vines, and the jungle smells cold compared to the open meadow, though it's still probably seventy-five here. Jane stops to adjust her fanny pack, so Graeme slows his pace so they can easily catch up. When they do, I cast about for a new bit of small talk. I ask the old standard: "So, Jane, how did you guys meet?"

Turns out this isn't small talk either. Doug and Jane's love story is a painful one, one they almost cringe to tell. Not because of some you-broke-my-heart, I-broke-yours history, like Graeme's and mine, but because they were both married to other people when they fell in love. Neither of them says much about the details, and I don't press, but their relationship story gets me thinking about how complex and meandering and unpredictable love can be. However imperfect their path may have been getting here, though, Jane and Doug seem perfect for each other now. And Graeme and me, our path hasn't always been perfect either. In fact, long ago, back when we were both young and one of us was stupid, some-one in Graeme's and my relationship strayed. . . .

That someone (at least according to Graeme) was me.

Remember how I said that back in college Graeme balled up my heart and threw it away like a crumpled-up term paper (the jerk)? Well, I sort of put a few wrinkles in his heart, too. Though I *didn't* cheat on him. Not technically at least. I just said at the end of my freshman year, after we'd been seriously head-over-heels for about four months, that I wanted an "open" relationship. Just for the summer. So I could get it on with some hot counselor guy I had yet to meet at the summer camp I'd be working at come June. (I didn't tell Graeme that last part.)

Anyway, I was the only one who took the "open" part of our relation-ship seriously. Graeme stayed faithful all summer. And when I told him I hadn't, he was, like that balled-up wad of paper, crushed.

In my defense, though, before I met Graeme I'd been dating my high school sweetheart for three, count 'em one-two-three, years. I started dat-ing Graeme pretty soon after that. Which is a lot of commitment for a young woman who's just figured out that, despite her horse teeth, limp hair, and mannish walk, she might be considered attractive. By some. And the other thing is—and this is probably more to blame—I'd been attending that coed summer camp, Camp Sealth, for ten years. And all those ten years I'd been meticulously constructing a dream—a very *vivid* dream—of someday becoming a counselor, and falling in love with a hot counselor guy, and singing Kum Ba Yah, and kissing around the campfire.

The counselor guy I ended up with was called Flurby. (My camp name, inexplicably, was Kiwi-Lips.) But Flurby was *not* hot. And we did *not* fall in love. Though we did sing Kum Ba Yah around the campfire. We also kissed for about 4.5 seconds on Flurby's thin, mouse-bitten, vinyl-covered mattress whose sheet, sadly, was in the laundry pile growing mold on the cabin floor. *Blech*. Flurby was one of those virginal Christian guys who tells everyone he's against premarital sex yet proposes it (sex, not marriage) 3.5 seconds in to the slobberiest, thrustiest, most gag-inducing kiss I've ever had the misfortune to experience. *Double blech.*

Needless to say, I smoothed things over with Graeme the first chance I got. But the damage was done. And our ensuing relationship just wasn't the same. (He became a jerk, remember? And I a needy nag. And he balled up my heart and threw it away with the finality of a slam dunk.)

Looking back, I'm floored that I asked for this "open" relationship from Graeme in the first place. I, who was so smitten. How could I have done that to him? But that's the thing about love: No matter how you slice and dice it, love, like fear, is neither straightforward nor rational nor easy to pin down. It's downright squirrelly. And just as I don't want Jane and Doug judge-and-jurying my screwy, neurotic fears, I doubt they want me second-guessing the decisions they've made in love.

When it comes down to it, why we fall in love, why we fall out of love, and why we (cross your fingers) *stay* in love is about as easy to understand as camp songs hurled at a storm, as *L*s and arrows marking the mad-capped sea, as the hidden fears pulsing in my husband's not invincible heart.

In response to the gendarme's booting, we're back to boating, and I've got one more night to survive till we can officially call off this crossing. Only the weather is a bit squirrelly, not bad really, just inconsistent. Which is what I hate most on a night watch, because then I can't just set the sails and let them do their thing, set Willie and let him do his thing, and settle myself into the cockpit to do my thing (read, write, pluck armpit hairs with tweezers).

Instead I'm watching the anemometer (wind-o-meter in Janna speak) rise and fall like that carnival game with the massive mallet and the red dinger. Uuup. Down. Uuup. Down. *DING!* The ding comes when Willie gets overpowered by the wind and lets *Dragonfly* swing off course, and then the sails start flapping and the lines start zinging and I have to take the helm to get us back in the direction we want to go. Which wouldn't be such a big deal, except that then I have to open the hatch directly above Graeme's bunk—*THUNK-THU-THUNK-THUNK*—to fiddle with Willie's control panel. (And stop reading, writing, and plucking hairs.) There's *got* to be a better way. And I know it's got something to do with this thing called sail trim.

In the year leading up to our cruise, Graeme read about sail trim like a preacher on his deathbed reads his Bible. He devoured everything— magazines, blogs, guides, handbooks—anything he could find on the topic. He was obsessed. Partly because he was truly passionate about sail trim, and partly because, like Socrates, he knew how very much there was to know . . . and how very little he actually knew.

I remember one book in particular that lived between the toilet and the orange tile wall in our old house's bathroom. It was called *Racing Sail Trim*, a white, floppy, oversize paperback with drawings of white and red sailboats on the front. I never once cracked open that book, preferring, instead, to judge it by its cover. And now I must admit the truth. During an entire year of toilet sits, I somehow thought those crisp white boats with their bold red accent stripes meant the book was about paint colors. Like sail trim, as in house trim, as in: What pretty color shall I paint my boat?

For the record, I was a tad off. Sail trim is actually how you position the sails in relation to the wind in order to maximize forward motion. So, for example, if the wind is directly behind the boat, you push the sail waaay out, perpendicular to the boat, to best capture the wind. Sort of like how, if you put your open palm out the car window, perpendicular to the wind, your arm gets thrown back? That's the same force that propels a boat forward on a downwind run. The other obvious sail position, called luffing, is when you're not catching the wind at all, e.g., your hand or your sail acts like a blade with the wind rushing parallel to it, right past it. Your sails billow and rattle and snap like flags, but the boat doesn't get pushed forward at all.

All the other points of sail, at least in my estimation, are a lot more confusing. The angles get fancier and the effects of the wind more nuanced.

(Like did you know a boat can actually make its own wind and, so, go faster than the wind itself?) You have to pay really close attention and know lots of things—you know, *little* things—if you want to get your sail trim set exactly right.

It's sort of like balancing a relationship. Because, even though you can nail all the big stuff with your partner—shared values, common goals, mutual interests and passions—something little, something seemingly insignificant can come along and screw everything up. Say he forgets to pick up the dry cleaning. Or doesn't say you look nice on a Saturday night. Or tells his annoying version of your engagement story at your birthday party. Too many of these little things—or one little thing at a really big moment—and the relationship can get thrown completely off course.

That's what balancing *Dragonfly*'s sails is like. And while I've got the Big Things taken care of, I'm pretty sure it's just something little right now screwing things up. Thus, a little fix would likely solve the problem. Of course, wielding hatchet instead of scalpel I could: (A) hand-steer *Dragonfly* all night long (way too much work); (B) wake Graeme and ask for help (God forbid); or (C) reef (but that would slow us way down—and did I mention there's a burger joint in Hiva Oa I'm jonesing to get to?). So, if I can just figure out that one little thing . . .

And that's when it hits me. Graeme's voice yelling "Release! Release! Release!" back when I thought he was an asshole fifty miles off the coast of Oregon. Granted, that was different; it was an emergency, and I knew exactly what to do. But this isn't an emergency; it's just an everyday thing . . . and yet, what would happen if I released the sail just a bit to dump a stitch of wind the next time it gusts? Would a little move like that do the job? And as I'm thinking this, the wind vibrating *Dragonfly*'s rigging goes from a low moan to a higher-pitched hum. I look at the wind-o-meter. Definitely a spike. And, sure enough, Willie starts letting us drift too far to port.

I take the mainsheet in my hands and ease it. Just a little bit. A little bit more. There.

I watch.

And the old girl brings her nose right back on course. No sweat!

When the gust subsides, and *Dragonfly* returns to her moaning, I tighten the mainsail back up. Our speed resumes. And I'm free to read and write and pluck, or just sit back and bask in that splayed-toes, dumb-grinned feeling you get when you figure something out. Finally. On your own.

• • •

OK. If you're a sailor reading this, I am *really* embarrassed right now. Truly, that little mainsheet trick is something I should have figured out a long time ago. Long before sailing ten thousand miles and crossing half the Pacific Ocean for crying out loud.

But (and there's always a but) I was not an experienced sailor when we left. A few trips with my folks growing up, a year's coastal cruising with Graeme, and a refresher sailing course before we left—that was about it. I knew the basics, sure. Enough to be safe. But the technical stuff was (and is) a struggle. I have to see things, feel things, and furrow my brow a lot before a concept registers. In teacher's lingo, when it comes to sailing at least, I'm an experiential learner; whereas Graeme grasps sailing mechanics in a more theoretical, academic, finger-snapping way. Which is not to say that I can never conceptualize the physics of sailing, or that Graeme doesn't benefit from lessons of experience. I just require a time-intensive, hands-on, trial-and-error style of classroom. A classroom that exists for me, I now realize, on night watch. Alone.

At the beginning of our trip Graeme used to try to teach me things about sailing. I would even get mad at him when he didn't explain stuff. But now I get it: Smart lovers play doctor, not school. Because, despite Graeme's best intentions, I never really enjoyed or appreciated sailing instruction from him, just as he never relished downhill skiing pointers from me. It's too easy to take things personally, get defensive, let a little comment throw everything off course.

I think that's why the best sailing lessons occur for me at night, when no one's pushing my buttons, or being misconstrued, or looking over my shoulder, or there to fall back on. For better or worse, it's just me and the wind and *Dragonfly*, who, I now realize, has been coaching me all along. She leans in, she hums, she taps, and she hollers to let me know what's working for her. And what's not. All she needed was for me to listen.

Finally, I'm all ears, and *Dragonfly* and I sail the last moonlit night of this crossing like two old friends.

The next day Graeme and I are on our way back from officially checking into Hiva Oa, on our way back from the overpriced, overcooked, but still-worth-it burger joint, when we hear some dreadful news.

"That boat arrived a couple hours ago," a cruising friend at the dinghy dock says, stretching his finger toward a new sailboat lolling at anchor in the bay. He shakes his head. "Guy came in single-handed."

Turns out the fellow didn't *start* the crossing single-handed, though. Over a month ago, when he set sail, it was he and his friend aboard. Sailing together. A team. His friend took the dog watch, the middle of the night.

Then one bluebird morning, the fellow woke. Looked around. And his friend was gone. He was all alone.

My belly goes from full to hollow. I look down at my clasped hands. I can't look at the lone sailor's boat. Or our friend sharing the news. Or at Graeme: my first and last and only and utterly indispensable mate.

The rest of the day is a fog. I go through the motions of cooking and cleaning and scrubbing scum from the hull. Graeme lugs jerry jugs of diesel and water, and begins work on the alternator again. But the image of that too-tanned, half-bearded, middle-aged guy sailing his boat in frantic circles—apparently he spent a week searching for his lost mate before giving up—keeps rising to the surface of my brain.

I'm not sure what to do or say or think or feel. Except horror.

And then, around dusk, while I'm chopping newly bought carrots and onions and potatoes for a curry, Graeme lifts his body from engine surfing, sets his rusty wrench down, and says, "I think I did it. She's finally, really, truly fixed."

An inadvertent jolt of happiness rushes through me. When Graeme turns the key and the voltmeter jumps, my spirits jump, too. And I realize it's not just at Graeme's having fixed the alternator (for real this time). But at the fact that he's here, on this small boat, in this beautiful place, living this B-HAG with me.

Standing watch over a heavy gray skillet, inhaling olive oil and caramelized onions and curry, this is what I come to: There are 42,000 fatalities from car accidents each year, and yet we still drive cars. There are 40,000 deaths from breast cancer each year, and yet Graeme's mom fought it and won. Roughly half of all marriages end in divorce, and yet we still said I do. I wear a seat belt. I do breast self-exams. I try to create something wonderful in my marriage every single day.

The point? While it's hard for me to imagine a more terrifying way to lose one's mate than waking up at sea alone, life is inherently risky. None of us is getting out of it alive. And yet some of us will go having lived—or even *while* living—our wildest dreams. I hope that's me.

I'm no daredevil and I have no death wish, but I certainly do have a life wish—a long list of them. And *that's* why I've been able to sing into the face of storms. That's why I've been able to miss friends and family, yet venture farther. That's why I've been able to endure leaks, and piss on the tilt, and sift weevils, and not strangle my husband. Because my dream of sailing into the sunset with him is, in the end, more powerful than my fear of it.

Or, put another way, my fear of not having lived life is more powerful than my fear of living it.

Marking the Passage

S niff sniff sniff. "What's that funky smell?" I ask, bunching my nose.

Sniff. "I don't smell anything," says Graeme.

Sniff sniff sniff. "Are you sure?" I say.

Sniff. "No," he says. "I mean, no I don't smell anything."

Seeing as how my sniffer is at the same altitude as Graeme's seated rear end, I'm wary of all unidentified flying odors. But no, *sniff sniff sniff*, this smell is acrid, maybe a little sweet. Decidedly not flatulatory.

I'm lying facedown in a dusty cabin on a large cardboard box marked YAMAHA. Graeme—like a birth coach, or a boyfriend who holds your hair while you puke—is stationed near my head, which is bobbling precariously over the box's edge like a turtle. My blue tank top is hitched above my belly, the band of my shorts is pushed low, and the precise horsepower of the box's contents is pancaked beneath my boobs. More to the point, a very large man with a very scary tattoo gun has been doing strange things to the small of my back. Right now he's turned toward his wooden desk, taking a break.

Sniff sniff sniff. "Maybe it's the smell of my suppurating flesh," I say, only half-joking. "Or, maybe it's the lingering scent of his. . . ." I raise my fingers to my lips, as if holding a joint.

"Janna," Graeme hisses, "he doesn't speak English. He *does* speak body language."

Criminy. I exagga-scratch my cheek to cover up my mime, and that's when I get a whiff of precisely where this scent is coming from: my sweaty (and slightly hairy) armpit. *Pee-ew.*

"Brace yourself," Graeme says. "Here he comes again."

PEE-EWW, I think more loudly as I inhale more deeply, in hopes that tantric breathing is to tattooing what Lamaze is to childbirth.

Works, I suspect, about as well: *Shitfuck shitfuck shitfuck.*

The tattooist pulls back briefly. Leans in again. *Shitfuck shitfuck shitfuck.*

Again. *Shitfuck shitfuck shitfuck.*

Again . . .

From this vantage point, I see Graeme's craggy toenails attached to his grime-creased toes attached to his dust-caked feet. The wooden cabin, with its wooden floor, wooden shelves, and wooden benches, reminds me of the dusky wooden cabins of that summer camp I loved. All that this one needs are some wooden bunk beds and a few more screaming girls; I'm currently alone in that department. My eyes water. My armpits sweat. My lips curse. When the tattooist takes another break, Graeme thrusts a red Hinano beer can in my face and I take an awkward sip. It's the closest I've come to doing a keg stand since college.

Withdrawing the warm beer from my lips, Graeme says, "OK, he's ready again."

Shitfuck shitfuck shitfuck.

Between hernias I say, "Talk to me."

Graeme swivels his attention from the fresh black markings on his upper arm, still welling with blood. Though his new tattoo is beautiful, I can't help but think in my current mood that Graeme's been examining it with the intensity of a dog licking its nether parts. "Talk to you about what?" he says.

"Anything," I say.

Shitfuck shitfuck shitfuck.

Graeme says, "Did you know traditional tattoos were made by hammering needle-sharp combs, often made from shell or bone or shark's teeth, into the skin?"

Holy shitfuck. "Not *anything*, Graeme," I say through gritted teeth.

I throttle my husband's wrist and try to recall, precisely, how I ended up in this *shitfuck shitfuck shitfuck* position in the first place.

Two Days Earlier . . .

Though it's been a few days since we made (unofficial) landfall, tonight is our (official) celebration. The Usual Suspects have agreed to meet in Tahuata, the Marquesas' smallest inhabited island, to celebrate, and we've of course invited every other boat in the anchorage to join us. Sailors crowd *Sea Hawk*'s cockpit like circus animals in a hot tub. We revel in the scenery (green palms, white sand), tell tales of the crossing (hash, hash, and rehash), and drink copious amounts of beer until all we see are stars and black and a dozen swaying mast lights. I'm not sure how this makes tonight any different from any other night this week. But I'm not complaining.

Oh wait. I am complaining. Because this morning when I opened my new box of cereal, bought fresh from Hiva Oa's general store, a cockroach scuttled out and dropped onto the floor. I shrieked. And even though Graeme stomped it with his flip-flop till it crunched, it gave me a serious case of the Yucks. So now Jane is explaining how they remove all the cardboard packaging from their food before bringing it on board. Apparently, cardboard is where cockroaches lay eggs. I'd heard this before, but then I'd read somewhere that it was bunk. I'm hedging my bets; cardboard will not be gracing *Dragonfly*'s decks ever again.

Jane gets up to give someone a tour of the boat (their boat is big enough to merit a tour), so I lean back to enjoy the still, starry evening. The lip of my beer can drips with lime, sufficiently limed beer being the only way I drink it anymore. I roll the tiny specks of green pulp on my tongue and pop them between my teeth. Yum. Meanwhile, I eavesdrop on the conversation wafting in, along with barbecue smells, from the back deck.

"I've dreamed of sailing since I was a kid," Doug's familiar voice says. "I feel so lucky to be here." Sound of metal spatula on metal grill. "After the crossing, things are different somehow. The world seems different. *I'm* different." I imagine his listeners nodding their heads, and I'm starting to contemplate how crossing has changed my life, too, when Doug adds, "So I want to get a tattoo."

A tattoo?

Doug looks more like a clean-cut yuppie than a salty sailorman, the kind of guy you take home to Mom, not to Sturgis. And yet, after a moment's thought, I'm not surprised by his declaration. Tattoos are an ancient Polynesian art form and a sailing tradition, too. For centuries seamen have marked ocean passages with celebratory tattoos.

Even so, I am definitely startled by the voice I overhear next, saying, "I think I'll get a tattoo, too."

Naw . . . that couldn't possibly be Graeme. The man who considers tattoos faddish. Permanency a threat to freedom. Needles instruments of torture.

Graeme has nursed a needle phobia all his life. In addition to tattoos—which he's always said were silly—this phobia has precluded flu shots, dental visits, blood donations, and physicals. But now, in a voice simultaneously sonorous with machismo and nostalgia, phrases like "sailor's rite of passage" and "seafaring tradition" and "since the voyages of James Cook" spill across the water like fog. Rolling my neck in lieu of my eyes, I turn to see my husband orating on the aft deck. He looks sincere, confident, and— empty glass in hand—a bit tattooed already.

Marquesan tattoo art, with its intricate design, painstaking precision, and languagelike symbolism, is famed to have been the best in the world. Tattoos marked initiations and provided protection; they augmented social status and sex appeal; they could be as frivolous as jewelry or as solemn as sacred rites.

On all the Pacific Islands except Samoa, this native cultural institution was zealously decimated by nineteenth-century missionaries. The jerks. But after a hiatus of about a hundred years, tattooing in the Islands has been revived—and not with airbrushed dragons, cartoon Popeyes, and red arrow-pierced hearts. Polynesian tattoos use black ink and ancient symbolism to create what Robert Louis Stevenson in 1888 called "awful" patterns. With the resurgence of the art in the 1980s, though, "awesome" seems more apt. These days practically every island in French Polynesia has a tattoo artist.

Our task simply is to find one.

The morning after our official celebration, four dinghies of sailors optimistically set off for Tahuata's main settlement, Vaitahu, a few coves south of our anchorage. It's a picturesque village, rioting green, crisscrossed by paths and footbridges. Small wooden and concrete houses, which long ago replaced the naturally air-conditioned homes of thatch, march up the valley. And in the town's center bursts the red roof of the Catholic Church, a flashy stamen on an otherwise unfussy flower. Tonight we'll watch men playing *pétanque* on the laned lawn, women gossiping in floral dresses, and children running and climbing and tumbling, like the race of children everywhere. But for now we sailors bob in our dinghies in the bay, having discovered the first hurdle in our tattoo quest: how to get ashore.

The surf is running high. The beach is mined with boulders. And the public quay is old and craggy, not amenable to mooring inflatable skiffs. What we need is a ferryman. Thankfully, the captain of *Freebird*, Dave, a firefighter with the matching physique, volunteers to drop everyone at the wharf, anchor the dinghies in the bay, and swim ashore.

Everything is going as planned. Dave has deposited all his passengers onshore. Marsha is berating Frank for forgetting the camera. (Oh, wait, Frank remembered the camera?) Marsha is berating Frank for forgetting the sunblock. And I'm asking a local on the quay about the resident tattoo artist. *"A gauche au deuxième pont,"* I say in rusty French, reviewing the man's directions to the tattooist's house.

Just then a loud group of guys pushes past us to the edge of the wharf. Conferring in Marquesan, they shake their massive heads, wave their tattooed arms, and glare at Dave, who is now approaching in an easy crawl. As Dave reaches the wharf, the locals, big as linebackers, switch to a flurry of French words—*"Attention! Attention! Uhr-SHAN! Uhr-SHAN!"*—and point menacingly down at him. Whether they're angry or drunk or crazy no one can tell, until Dave, tiring of treading water, clambers up the side of the quay. Immediately, he gets the point.

Hidden below the water's surface, clinging to the cement steps, are dozens of sea urchins ("Uhr-SHAN! Uhr-SHAN!") whose toxic quills are now embedded in Dave's bare feet.

Dave howls in pain, "Fuckfuckfuckfuckfuck!"

The locals shout their new directive. "PEE-say! PEE-say!"

And I, the failed French interpreter, translate, "Pee on it! Pee on it!"

So now imagine four white guys on the public quay of a heretofore peaceful Polynesian village trying to urinate on command over their buddy's writhing feet. Doug, looking down dejectedly, complains he went an hour ago. Jim, his penis poised perilously close to Dave's quills (not that I'm looking), has produced nary a drop. And Frank, our senior member, is still fumbling with his shorts. Meanwhile, the locals have taken an extreme interest in their toenails.

I turn to look for Graeme. He's standing, his back to the crowd, a few good steps from Dave. A gray cliff wall looms to his right, Polynesia lazes behind him, and Graeme is examining the turquoise water below him.

Taking a step forward I say, "Graeme, what are you—"

But then I stop. I note his studied stance. Feet shoulder-width apart, heels lifting and settling like an NBA player at the line. I watch the subtle movements of his shoulders, hunching then easing as his hands find their position. The man is focused. His head is lowered. But then, with a hint of cockiness, he lifts it and looks to the horizon to wait.

Behind me stand the Polynesian locals sporting well-worn shorts and flip-flops, no doubt amused by the antics of their Western guests. I, too, stand transfixed on the scorching cement quay, breathing the mixed scent of sea and hibiscus. I trust a more acrid odor will be rising from the quay. Soon. I stare at Graeme's back; he looks down again. I wait for the golden arc to appear between his legs and imagine him rushing the few steps to Dave as soon as it begins. But no. No arc. His butt cheeks clench briefly; his knees crease forward. Looks like somebody's got stage fright.

But Graeme has prepared himself with precision. Unbeknownst to us spectators, who are watching for a golden stream, Graeme has picked up a Costco-size blue mayonnaise lid from the litter on the quay and is, after an initial case of nerves, successfully filling it to the brim. One hand zipping his zip, the other trembling with his petri dish, Graeme approaches Dave and presents him with his precious piss. Immediately the other guys take the hint. Doug offers a half-crushed Hinano beer can of antidote. Jim fills an old water bottle (BOTTLED AT THE SOURCE the tattered label claims). And Frank's wizened fingers, now clutching a rusty tin can, continue to fumble with his zipper. Splayed on the quay, his feet awash in piss, Dave sighs with relief.

More quickly than it began, the show is over. Our island spectators pound the shoulders of our proud sailors, who, in turn, readjust their trunks and double-check their zippers. Someone has flagged down a tired old van (the only vehicle we see in Vaitahu), and the Marquesan hulks lift Dave inside. We women coo and fuss.

Soon Dave sits at the local infirmary just a few hundreds yards down the bay, where the motherly clinician expresses surprise that Dave isn't in more pain. I, sheepish translator, explain that the guys peed on him. She nods knowingly—sea urchin stings are nothing new in the islands—and begins to wash, then nurse Dave's bruised feet.

Dave nurses his bruised pride.

Despite the day's setbacks, the quest for *le tatouage* continues. Back toward the quay, up the hill, left over the second bridge, up the path, our slightly diminished group of cruisers finally arrives at Félix Fii's tattoo studio. But peering into the dusty windows almost makes us run. The walls are mounted with vices, hammers, chisels, and picks. Graeme blanches, recalling the Discovery Channel's special on traditional tattooing methods. But when Félix soon arrives from the hills, where he's been harvesting noni fruit, he tells us these tools are for sculpting wood and stone, not flesh.

Félix's dark, tattooed arms are bulging from hours of fruit-picking, but when he finds his place teeming with potential patrons, he quickly gets down to business. Doug points to a photo of a turtle tattoo; that's the one he wants, he says. I translate. Félix, arms crossed over his imposing chest, shakes his head, *Non*. Turns out Félix never does the same tattoo twice. Doug can choose the location, size, and general image, but the tattoo will develop naturally, Félix explains, as he finds his muse. Doug frowns at my relayed message but then nods and rolls up his pink polo shirt to bare his white tabula rasa of a shoulder. Félix, meanwhile, goes out back to smoke a joint.

Soon Félix's meaty hands are creating delicate patterns with the tattoo gun. His movements are confident, his concentration intense, and the image emerging on Doug's shoulder, amid wellings of blood, is beautiful. To distract Doug from the pain, Graeme provides a constant stream of conversation and a measly trickle of beer. Félix has imposed a two-beer limit because, he says with no hint of irony, he has a policy against tattooing anyone under the influence.

"Pain is the power of the tattoo," Tihoti Tatau, a tattoist we'll meet a few islands later, will explain. "It acts as a test, a way to show one's valor."

Tihoti, a man literally divided in half with tattoos—the left part of his body snaking with symbols, the right half blank—certainly proved *his* valor. The tattooed side of his body connects him to his ancient culture, he says, while his unmarked half embraces the blank slate of his future. Tihoti admits that most tattoos these days are created for aesthetic reasons, not spiritual ones. Nonetheless, there is something transformative, he says, something powerful intrinsic to each tattoo. Doug's clenched jaw, Félix's trancelike focus, the image burgeoning in Doug's flesh . . . Tihoti's words make complete sense.

An hour later Doug's test is over. A magnificent turtle, the Marquesan symbol for safe passage at sea, rules his shoulder. Staring out from the shell is a traditional Marquesan tiki, its totemlike face both powerful and peaceful—the exact expression Doug hadn't known he wanted.

Now it's Graeme's turn to face the gun. Still undecided about the image he wants, Graeme begins to ask questions about various symbols. But Félix, hands clenching from fatigue, eyes red and glassy, shakes his head. This tattoo is not meant to be. Graeme can come back tomorrow, Félix says, and they can begin fresh, but he does not have the energy to do another tattoo right now.

And so, it seems, Graeme's off the hook, he won't be getting a tattoo after all, because tonight we're leaving for our next port. You'd think Graeme would feel relieved, overjoyed, like he'd ducked a screaming bullet. But having steeled himself all day to his terror of needles, Graeme returns to *Dragonfly* that evening not happy at all, but tired, tattooless, and utterly disappointed.

Now who'd've thought that a man so phobic of needles could become such a tattoo convert? And, really, how did this masochistic tradition of artistic torture—much more painful in its original form of hammers and bone—become popular among Polynesians in the first place?

Enter: the Allure of the Tattoo. Various forms of tattooing have been popular around the world for at least the past five thousand years; archaeologists have unearthed mummies to prove it. From punishing criminals to marking slave status, from treating arthritis to mourning the dead, from spiritual practice to decorative body art, tattoos have been a human tradition since, some say, the Stone Age. And the tradition continues. Even my brother and I—well-adjusted, respectable college grads—got matching tattoos when we were in our twenties, much to our mother's dismay.

But when it comes to Polynesians in general and my husband in particular, I have my own amateur theory about tattooing's allure. Beginning some three thousand years ago, a people of expert navigators braved storms, reefs, counterwinds, and countercurrents to settle the "many islands" of Polynesia. This is fact. And while their newfound lands were beautiful, island life was no paradise. The remoteness fostered both isolation and community. The climate brought disaster and abundance. The sea presented great risk and great bounty. So here's my theory: It's no wonder that tattoo, an art requiring intense pain to attain permanent beauty, became a vital expression of the culture.

Which brings us back to Graeme and his newfound interest in tattoos and his long-lived passion for sailing. Though crossing oceans with today's technology is no Polynesian migration, it still does require seagoers to confront fears, overcome obstacles, and endure a fair bit of discomfort. Ocean passages—like tattoos—are both extremely beautiful and extremely trying. And so I can understand why Graeme feels drawn to a tradition that, though it confronts his worst fear, also mirrors his passion. After all, the only phobia rivaling Graeme's fear of needles was his fear of getting married. And he (eventually) got over that.

So last night Graeme and I did not weigh anchor. We did not head to the next port. We did not turn sail and run. Instead, we decided to return to Félix Fii's tattoo studio today, together, to get tattoos incorporating the symbols we chose for our wedding: wind, water, fire, and mountain. Graeme now has a bold tattoo, a mixture of traditional Marquesan symbols and Félix's modern muse, gripping his bicep. And I'll have an airier version gracing the small of my back. Soon. *That's* how I got here, lying on this large Yamaha engine box, practicing Lamaze breathing, saying *shitfuck shitfuck shitfuck* over and over. All in the name of permanence and beauty, longevity and love.

Almost a year ago Graeme and I set sail to celebrate our passage into marriage. Little did we know that the couple at the barn door altar (giddy, idealistic, novice, nervous) would not be the same couple that reached the other side (storm-weathered, blues-hounded, worry-warted, competent). But then I suspect most couples experience this year to year, decade to decade, constantly reinventing themselves, rediscovering each other, recalibrating their relationship.

After all, the purpose of marriage, as Graeme said so long ago, is not simply to *last*. Rather, it is to mark the passage of life *together*—celebrating joy, mourning loss, embracing change, finding meaning—the pain and the beauty all rolled into one. Our tattoos, like wedding rings or anniversary toasts or eulogies, are one more special way to commemorate the passage of time.

And they remind us: You don't just mark the passage. The passage marks you.

Part 5

Polynesia

The Desert Isle Survival School for Sailors

Y es, your fantasies about the South Pacific are true. The water really is that turquoise. The sand really is that white. The palms really do sway as if dancing to an iPod shuffle of Jimmy Buffet's lifetime oeuvre. It's like landscape porn out here. And that Polynesian centerfold you saw in last month's *National Geographic*? Wasn't even airbrushed.

Ah, but one man's *Playboy* Bunny is another man's buzz kill. I remember describing my dream of sailing to the South Pacific to one of my girlfriends before we left. As I spoke, her face fell, pore by pore.

"Oh my God," she said when I'd finished. "The South Pacific is one thing. But sailing there, just you and your partner, imprisoned on a small boat that you have to somehow know how to operate all by yourselves? You've just described my very own personal version of hell."

Though hell is how some people describe summer camp, too, and we all know how caught up I got in *that* little world. So it's no surprise that I'm looking forward to our next stop, a deserted island called Suwarrow, where cruisers, I've read, get to learn things like coconut tree climbing and thatch weaving and lobster hunting from an elderly Polynesian man. I've heard it described as summer camp for cruisers. And, on top of that, Robert Louis Stevenson's wife, Fanny, called it "the most romantic island in the world." Romance and camp? Now that's a tough combination for me to resist.

Suwarrow, alternately known as Suvarov, Suvorov, Suvaroff, Souwaroff, Souworoff, Souvorow, and Suvarrow, depending on if you're consulting

Fanny Stevenson or *World Book Encyclopedia* or Lord Byron or an old chart or a Cook Islander himself, is a tiny atoll in the northern Cook Islands. Except for a few part-time caretakers, the place is uninhabited. Some might say uninhabitable. Because the truth about picture-perfect Suwarrow is it's comprised of narrow islands of crushed coral only as wide as, say, a freeway. And just about as fertile.

An atoll—the official name for a ring of coral islets like this—is an ancient and fragile ecosystem, the remnants of a high volcanic island long since vanished. The easiest way to understand how an atoll is formed is to imagine, if you will, Marge Simpson as a volcanic island blowing her top. When she finishes spewing invective at her husband Homer, she coifs her beehive of hair (tropical green instead of her typical blue) and begins sinking back into the ocean. Slowly. At first, with her lush green hair and stony face soaring upward from the sea, she looks like a tall jungly island like Isla del Coco. Billions of years pass. And around Marge's neckline (a shallow, warm environment where coral-forming microorganisms thrive) a necklace slowly emerges. So on an island like famous Bora Bora, you've got Marge's green beehive still standing, surrounded by a turquoise lagoon, ringed by a coral necklace. On an ancient atoll like Suwarrow, only the necklace remains.

The point is that this thin ring of coral islets—infertile, cramped, and washed over in a hurricane—would be a damned tough place to eke out a living. And yet it's been done right here on Suwarrow quite famously. Tom Neale, a gruff hermit originally from New Zealand, lived here on and off for about sixteen years between the 1950s and 1970s. Totally alone. He built a little cabin, and he planted a little garden, and he harvested fish and lobster and coconut crabs as food. The guy was a self-stranded Robinson Crusoe. He wrote a book about it called *An Island to Oneself* (1966). So now fifty or more cruising boats each year visit Suwarrow to see where Tom Neale hosted his own personal version of *Survivor*.

Graeme and I are sitting in *Dragonfly*'s cockpit at anchor, on the edge of this fifty-mile-circumference lagoon. It's hot. Damn hot. And the scrap of fabric I sewed into a sunshade before leaving Costa Rica isn't providing much shade at all. Most cruising boats have custom-tailored sunshades, called biminis, with stainless steel supports and full coverage so their cockpits stay relatively cool, even in midday. But my creation is a tattered, floppy blue fan, suspended from the shrouds with raggedy green granny knots. We strategically tie up bedsheets (very classy) to shade the places our bimini doesn't cover (very many). But even then, the sun always seems to find a hole to spy through.

I said that these Pacific isles are beautiful, like magazine centerfolds, and they are. Except for the parts that aren't. There are places in Suwarrow where the beach is dull brown and craggy, or lined with jagged bushes. Places in these islands where flotsam and jetsam gather, plastic jugs, plastic bags, ratty ravels of old line. Or just areas in the Pacific, not polluted or dour, but just not picturesque.

Sitting in the cockpit, I don't focus on these spots though. Instead I, like the magazine photographers, zoom in on crushed coral sand, baked dry and white by the sun, contrasting like Kodachrome with a tie-dye blue lagoon. We're anchored, along with a dozen other boats, off Anchorage Island, where Tom Neale's old house still stands among the palms. The atoll's tiny islets surround us, and in the lagoon, sharks are known to swim. I look at Graeme, leaning against the mizzen mast, his shoulder turning red in a bright patch of sunlight.

"Watcha doin'?" I ask.

A smile broadens under his scanning binoculars. "Bird watching," he says.

Suwarrow is a major stop for migratory birds in the Pacific, so his ruse could be believable, but really I know he's spying on other boats. Like eavesdropping on the radio, it's another unspoken but accepted practice among cruisers.

"There's a new boat in called *Nahanni*," he says. "They've got a Windsurfer aboard. Looks like a young couple like us." We've said good-bye to the old Usual Suspects and are now in search of new ones.

"Cool." I give a mellow head bob.

"I'm gonna go say hi, then maybe go on a dinghy cruise," Graeme says, lowering his glasses and stepping to the side of the boat where *Firefly* is bumping against *Dragonfly*'s hull. "Wanna come?" he asks, an extra lift in his voice.

I look down at my laptop, humming on my sweaty legs. A breezy dinghy ride would feel good. "Naw," I say. "I'm almost done with this article. You go ahead."

Graeme shakes his head but doesn't say anything. He disappears over the side. And I wonder if he's more disappointed that I've rejected his request for a playmate, or if he's jealous that I've found a passion that rivals paradise. I shrug my shoulders; either way, he'll survive. Besides, I'll see the island and meet the other cruisers soon enough, because Papa

John, the local caretaker on Suwarrow, is hosting a big shindig for every-one tonight.

Papa John, a fit and trim Cook Islander in his seventies, is the true survivor on Suwarrow. Unlike Tom Neale and his storybook experiment, this is Papa John's real life. He's stationed here by the government six months out of the year (forgoing hurricane season) for measly pay and with few provi-sions. His job is to take care of the island, the trees, and like a good camp counselor, *us*.

But why the Cooks administration would hire a caretaker for an un-inhabited, unfrequented desert isle hundreds of miles from civilization seems a bit crazy to me. Our guidebook's explanation is nuts. Coconuts. In the 1920s and 1930s, Suwarrow was a source of copra, dried coconut meat whose oil is used in foods and the health and cosmetics industry. Then ter-mites struck. According to our guidebook a "coconut watcher" is necessary to ensure that no infested nuts leave the island. Since Suwarrow is so iso-lated—and copra prices are so low right now that even convenient sources are being ignored—I wonder just who these feared coconut-nappers might be. I imagine coconut-toting swallows à la Monty Python winging away with infested nuts. This cracks me up. Until I realize the real suspect could be me. Many sailors gather coconuts for drinking and eating: I suppose cruisers carrying nuts from island to island could spread termites in their wake. So I half-expect a warning against coconut-thievery from Papa John at our first evening's potluck.

What I get, though, is an official government-issue sign greeting us: QUARANTINE: IT IS FORBIDDEN TO BRING FOREIGN ANIMALS, PLANTS, AND FOOD INTO THE COOK ISLANDS.

I look down at my plate of fresh-baked cookies. *Hmm* . . . Then we walk up to Papa John's open-air shelter and place our contribution of foreign food next to a dozen other foreign side dishes, salads, and desserts. Papa John provides the main entrées: dogtooth tuna, coconut crab, *poisson cru*, and breadfruit pudding.

Later that night Papa John, whose body language is better than his English, explains his flouting of the food law. He says the government has lots of rules; he holds out his gnarled hands, as if grasping the handlebars of an imaginary bicycle. But here on Suwarrow—he twists his wrists abruptly—we *bend* the rules. Papa John repeats this contortionist motion, mangling handlebar after handlebar, intoning, "We *bend* the rules. We *bend* the rules," just in case we didn't get it the first, or second, or third time. Okay. *Bend.* Got it. Needless to say, no coconut-toting warnings are issued.

That evening at the barbecue, "Pa Pa Kew" in Papa John–speak, we also meet our other hosts on Suwarrow: Papa John's nephew Baker and grandson Totoo (pronounced like Dorothy's dog, though I wouldn't mention the relation).

Totoo is a typical teenager, hooked into headphones most of the time with a bored look on his face. Over the next few days he'll fluctuate between sullenness, know-it-all-ness, giddy energy, and good humor. Happily, the latter two traits win out whenever he's demonstrating some gnarly survival skill (which is quite often) or finding pretty shells for the ladies.

Baker also has a penchant for the ladies, especially when he's shaking his bootie to Bob Marley after a few drinks. He's a quirky old fellow, jolly and helpful when he's around, but often reclusive for days. It's also never really clear what Baker's true relation to Papa John is. While tonight he's introduced to me as Papa John's nephew, I've read articles that call him everything from a brother-in-law to a cousin—and his reported age ranges between fifty-five and seventy-five. Baker's sort of like the human equivalent of the spelling of Suwarrow: hard to pin down. And it's the mysterious Baker, with his toothless grin and ruddy cheeks, who shoos us home at ten o'clock, saying we need to rest for tomorrow's adventure. We're going to Bird Island, he says, to hunt baby frigate birds. He laughs shrilly. We'll need all the strength we can muster.

With a swift slap of the flat of his machete, Totoo brings the kill total to a dozen and says that should be enough. Graeme, the hunting vegetarian, picks up the limp white body splayed across the green bush, and the two of them, fists full of wings, head back to camp.

It's been easy hunting. Hundreds of baby frigate birds line the bushes like canned goods collecting dust on a grocery store shelf. No amount of movement, noise, or proximity seems to rouse them, not even a *WHACK!* on the skull of the bird next door. They squawk now and then for food, but otherwise they seem lifeless.

And, sure enough, now twelve of them *are* lifeless and will be today's (gulp) lunch. This morning Papa John guided three sailboats across Suwarrow's lagoon to this small motu, or islet, called Bird Island. This is our first adventure with Papa John. Afterward some sailors won't be sure they want another.

I do though. I mean, I'll admit the birds are darn cute with their downy white feathers and round eyes, but I, a carnivore confined to Graeme's veg-aquarium diet, am eager for meat. So eager, in fact, that I help Totoo and Baker with the mildly nauseating task of dressing the birds. First, Totoo lops off their heads and feet and tosses them into the lagoon. Then he and Baker cut away the feathery skin, which is also thrown into the lagoon. Then I pluck the remaining neck and tail feathers, which, of course, go into the lagoon. Finally, I'm told to rinse the birds in the lagoon, which is now amok with bloody heads, feet, skin, feathers, and small circling sharks.

Did I mention sharks?

I hastily comply and put the "clean" carcasses into the pot of water with the herbs, onions, and coconut cream Papa John is preparing. Within the hour lunch is served. As sailors peer into the cauldron of boiling baby birds, the line for Papa John's other dish—dogtoothed tuna caught fresh this morning—grows inordinately long. The birds, also fresh, have to be forced onto cruisers' sagging plates and, once there, are picked at gingerly with sour expressions and hushed whispers: "How do you eat this thing?" and "Ew . . . don't dig too deep, the entrails are still inside" and "Is this enough meat to justify killing them?"

I sit on the beach down from Baker and gnaw my baby bird with gusto. Sure, the meat is gamey and the eating is a bit tricky, but what are we supposed to do? Refuse Papa John's offering? I'm reminded of the story my pescatarian husband tells of once having to eat raw dog in China. Eating any kind of bird—boiled or raw—has to be a lesser evil than slurping down dog. So I take another bite of baby bird flesh and suck on its toy leg like a lollipop. *Tastes like chicken!* I think.

Also sitting on the beach near Baker and me are two lone baby birds, white and fluffy and cute as stuffed animals. Earlier, a couple sailors convinced Baker to spare their lives since, in their words, "They're just so precious." I'm surprised Baker consented, because frigate, he says, is his favorite meal; he picks over the cruisers' half-eaten carcasses until every edible morsel is gone. But Baker is a clever man who knows his audience well. When I ask him why he spared the two birds' lives, he turns and explains loudly so everyone can hear, "You sailors are right. These birds *are* precious. I'll take them back to Anchorage Island and raise them as pets."

He gives a brisk nod of punctuation to the group and turns his attention back to his plate. He licks his greasy fingers. He smiles smugly. Then he shoots me, his fellow bird glutton, a surreptitious wink.

And it's clear to me that Baker is really going to enjoy his new "pets."

After our foray into baby bird bashing it's also clear how skilled our care-takers are at living off the land. It's a good thing, because the Cooks government doesn't supply them with much in the way of canned or dried foods. In fact, Papa John says the pay's so measly, he's practically a volunteer here. When I ask him why he returns season after season, he shrugs his wiry shoulders, holds up his brown tendony hands, and says simply, "What would the yachties do without me?"

Blank stare.

He's right. Better some cultural edification from Papa John than the typical cruiser's loll of snorkeling and lounging and doing boat repairs in exotic places till happy hour rolls round again. Every morning now follows a new routine: We cruisers dinghy ashore, say hello to Baker's fuzzy new pets, chat with Totoo about what's playing on his Walkman, and get briefed by Papa John on our next adventure. We're now enrolled, we realize, in the Desert Isle Survival School for Sailors.

It's a cross between summer camp and boot camp. It has all the chipper cookouts, craft lessons, and camaraderie of the former, and the endurance-testing, testosterone-pumping, jungle-grunting grit of the latter. Though Papa John is distinctly mild mannered, his briefings are not unlike those of a movie drill sergeant whose utterances are wholly incomprehensible except for a few choice words. "WE *gargle gargle mumble* HANG *mumble babble* CRABS *gurgle babble gaggle* TREES *mumble*, YES?" We sailors, rapt at attention, make the telltale signs of full comprehension, stroking our chins and nodding sagely. But after Papa John's detailed explanations we mumble out of the sides of our mouths:

"Hmph . . . didn't understand a friggin' thing."

"Me neither."

"Thought he said we're gonna hang crabs in trees."

"Me, too."

"Ridiculous."

"Better ask again."

With all the cross-examinations that ensue, brevity is not a hallmark of these preadventure sessions with Papa John, but the term "briefing" is nonetheless apt, since the actual information gleaned is as scanty as a Frenchman's Speedo. And so, despite Papa John's noble attempts at preparing us for our trials and tribulations, each day at the Desert Isle Survival School is full of surprises.

Like the time we learn to catch lobster with our bare hands. It's midmorning, and about sixteen of us walk the red reef at low tide with these simple instructions: Look for lobster antennae sticking out of holes.

Now, if you haven't walked a South Pacific reef lately, I should tell you there are hundreds upon hundreds of craggy holes—big ones, little ones, deep ones, shallow ones—so it feels like looking for chopsticks on the face of the moon. And we soon learn that scanning the ground is not enough. Totoo, our guide, drops to his knees, sticks his butt in the air, and plunges his mask-and-snorkel-clad face into a pool, examining every nook and cranny for hidden crustaceans. He comes up with lobster after lobster, sometimes with a machete, sometimes with his bare hands.

Soon, sailors' butts pop up like buoys for a half-mile stretch. The onlookers shout warnings when a particularly big wave threatens to crash, but regardless, sailors end up splayed across the reef, scratched and spluttering as the surge subsides. Every now and then, though, a jubilant cry rises—"Found one!"—and then half a dozen snorkel-lipped sailors rush across the pitted, slippery surface, wielding machetes to help.

Papa John sagely leaves this circus to his grandson to direct. Like a guru leading his disciples, the old man strolls along, hands behind his back, two or three quiet sailors at his side. Now and again he serenely peeks over the edge of a pool and, stabbing in his machete with precision, raises a flopping, bulge-eyed reef fish. Papa John is a skilled, if silent, leader.

Two hours later, when the bags of jousting lobsters and stiffening fish are near bursting, Papa John steers the group from the reef to the beach to cook the day's bounty. That morning, during our briefing, we'd somehow gotten the impression that our seafood would be served at tonight's Pa Pa Kew. But, with the sun still clawing up the sky, Papa John instructs us to gather dried palm fronds, sticks, and coconut husks for a bonfire. On top of this we pile pieces of bleached coral which, Papa John explains, will become barbecue briquettes when the flames die down. Then he shows us how to weave green palm fronds into sturdy plates for our feast.

Waiting for hot briquettes, lounging in the shade, sipping coconuts, we start to feel the laziness of the tropics set in. Papa John, however, puts an end to our repose. "Hup! Hup!" he cries, rousing the troops. It's time for our final test. It's time to hunt coconut crabs.

Tom Neale describes coconut crabs as repugnant scavengers—"ugly, brutal creatures," he writes—and I have to agree. They look like spiny lobsters with elephantitis. Mutantly large cockroaches with added pincers. Massive king crabs with *thwapping* tails. It's physically impossible to look at a coconut crab and not get the Yucks. (Go on. Google 'em. I dare you.) The coconut crab is like nature's own lethal Leatherman tool, each appendage a piece of weaponry: The crab's antennae smell food over large distances; its long, sharp limbs climb coconut trees; its powerful pincers rip open husks and crack the nut inside; and its smaller arms scrape out the coconut meat. This rich diet makes the coconut crab's meat tremendously sweet. Its nature is anything but.

It is, therefore, with no lack of trepidation that we set out on our next quest. Admittedly, this motu can't be more than a half-mile square, but stalking through its dense jungle is how I imagine I'd feel in the Amazon or 'Nam or the Heart of Darkness; every leaf that brushes my shoulder, every vine that twitches underfoot, gives me the willies. And yet Totoo drops fearlessly to his knees, his rear in the air yet again, to peer into the dark burrows beneath coconut palms and tree stumps and webs of decaying brush. He leans in so close it's like he's using his nose as bait. But soon he hollers, nose still intact, "Here's one!"

We all gather round to watch the fight. Totoo's first strategy is to poke his spear into the lair in hopes that the pugnacious crab will grab on. It does, so Totoo begins pulling forcefully but carefully, playing it like a fish. But soon it becomes clear that the crab has dug in its heels (all eight of them) and no amount of pulling is going to get it out. So Graeme goes around to the other side of the hole to prod the crab from behind. After much persuading, the mutantly large cockroach finally emerges, its appendages waving furiously. One pincer is clamped tightly onto Totoo's spear, the other claw is searching wildly for a sailor's toe. Confirming that the crab is male, Totoo skewers it with his machete and holds it up for all to see. The beast must weigh five pounds.

Soon sailors are hunting in the tangled brush, noses poking under palm roots, sticks jabbing into the jungle's dark places. The men are particularly intent. The pace of the hunt becomes so frenzied that our friend Chris finds himself face-to-face with a large crab he's coaxed out of its lair, only to realize he has no machete with which to kill it. "Help!" he calls in his manliest voice.

Once again, Papa John has wisely left Totoo in charge of this mayhem. After an hour of hunting, the air swags with sweat and machismo and spent adrenaline. Amnesiac to the fact that we've already caught enough reef food for a small army, the troops have killed enough coconut crab to feed a second. We trudge slowly back toward camp, happy and exhausted. We're silent. We're proud.

Imagine our surprise, though, when we emerge from the jungle to find our camp surrounded by an airborne unit of live coconut crabs, guarding the place from a few feet above ground. Seems Papa John has done some hunting of his own and, true to his word, has hung his POWs in the trees, like oversize Christmas ornaments. He warns us, "Don't sit too close. They clip off your ear, cut off your nose!"

We keep our distance. These crabs, still quite feisty, will be carried back to Anchorage Island, dangling live off a long pole carried over Totoo's shoulder, for tonight's Pa Pa Kew.

But first, we have a feast of our own to attend to. The coral briquettes, now hot and settled, are soon covered with whole fish, lobsters, and coconut crabs. As the meat sighs and sizzles, we sip more coconuts and recuperate from our exertions; living on boats, none of us has had this kind of exercise in ages. When it comes time to eat, we use our palm plates and devour the food with our fingers. The day's delicacy turns out to be what we dub "butt butter," the oily juices in the tail of the coconut crab. If you can get over the act of dipping your chunk of crab meat into a swirl of grease near what appears to be a scavenger's anus, the taste is pure heaven.

The week continues with adventure after adventure: Fishing lures, hand-carved according to Papa John's specifications, are tested on tuna, wahoo, and barracuda. Spear guns are shot, always with an escape dinghy nearby, since sharks come quickly to blood. One inflatable dinghy is actually chomped by a shark, punctured straight through with jagged teeth marks. We have sushi parties in cockpits, and potlucks onshore, because, we discover, survival school is all about food. The syllabus stretches our waistlines.

Too soon, though, the next port is calling. Graeme and I decide to set off alone, bending (Papa John–style) our rule of always boating alongside buddies. Our buddies will keep track of us via radio—and at least some of them will join us soon enough. After the last few months of traveling the crowded Coconut Milk Run, the main route from North America to the South Pacific, Suwarrow has rekindled our sense of independence. We wave good-bye to Papa John, Totoo, and Baker—and his mysteriously missing pets—alone.

Those ten summers I spent at camp growing up were my sanctuary from mean kids at school. Imagine my surprise, then, when returning as a counselor, I found a petty, cliquish behind-the-scenes hierarchy. It almost ruined my ten Kum Bah Yah years as a camper.

That's how it feels after we leave Suwarrow, when we hear several criticisms of our beloved caretakers. Turns out some rules weren't meant to be bent. Like those foreign salads brought ashore? An entomologist reports they could spread new pests to the island. She also worries that our crazy coconut crab hunts could endanger the local population. Coconut crabs, I learn, are not protected, but overharvesting can be a concern. And then there's this: Turns out, in addition to being an important stop for migratory birds (which I knew), Suwarrow is also a World Park Bird Sanctuary (which I didn't). And there I was, sucking on those little legs like lollipops. For shame!

And that's the thing about traveling the world. It's hard sometimes to navigate between people and governments, ecosystems and adventures, personal principles and cultural respect. Heck, it's hard to do this at home. One thing I know for sure though: Papa John is a good man. A generous man. A man lauded in the press for his stewardship of the trees. I don't believe he would have fed us any species whose population he thought to be in danger.

But Papa John is also an old man, a traditional man, a man accustomed to living off the land. And he loves teaching others how to do the same. But, realistically, when will any yachties actually need to put those survival skills to use? Knock wood, never.

And so the summer camp days on Suwarrow are over. A new caretaker will be installed on Suwarrow next year. Someone who'll keep the cruisers on the straight and narrow. Someone not so prone to bending the rules.

The Tutti Frutti Beauty Pageant

i *thought Dragonfly* and I had come to an understanding. I thought we'd made a truce. Heck, I thought we'd become *pals*—that she'd agreed to keep me comfy if I'd just listen to her better. Clearly, I was mistaken. Because here we are on passage from Suwarrow to Samoa and no amount of reefing or releasing or sail trim balancing will make this ride comfortable. Not that it's all *Dragonfly*'s fault. It's been windy, rainy, thunderandlightning-y ever since we left four days ago. And these big, blocky waves are making *Dragonfly* jump like a Jeep in four-wheel drive. I wish she had better shock absorbers.

The real shock, though, is that, for the very first time since leaving Seattle, I've moved beyond my usual low-grade nausea into an entirely new realm of reality called—what was it my girlfriend said?—my own personal version of hell. I'm holding my stomach. I'm groaning. I'm holding back burps and bile. And, finally, I'm puking up whatever I worked so hard to get down a few hours ago. I'm actually seasick. After a whole year of cruising. Seasick.

They say every sailor will, at some point, encounter a certain chemistry of storm and stomach that will cause seasickness. Graeme, though, *never* gets seasick. Or airplane sick or car sick or flu sick or love sick or *any* sick for that matter. He says it's because he's a vegetarian that he's so healthy. Which is all fine and good, except that because Graeme never gets ill, he has absolutely no sympathy. No nuanced understanding that he might bring a glass of water or offer to help with dishes or let me sleep a little longer or say some kind word. All that is beyond him. He treats my seasickness almost like I'm faking it or imagining it or being a kvetching drama queen who can't handle a little discomfort.

OK, so maybe I am.

The worst part is, an hour or two after I've blown bile over *Dragonfly*'s gunnels, Graeme simply forgets about it. Then he'll say in his innocent way, "Mmm . . . doesn't Pasta Puttanesca sound good for dinner tonight? Garlic, capers, lots of tangy little anchovies . . ." He rubs his tummy.

And I heave over the side again.

A week later, though, and we've got another surprise on our hands. It's no longer me who's nauseated, it's our friend Lisa, a Canadian on the boat *Nahanni*. She has a look on her face that could strip varnish off teak.

"Why doesn't anyone *tell* you that morning sickness can happen morning, noon, and night?" She sighs, her heavy head resting in the palm of her hand.

Lisa's pregnant. And while she's thrilled about the prospect of having a baby, she's not, you know, *thrilled*. She's constantly queasy, her mood's sour as unripe fruit, and the piña colada sitting before her is virgin (oh the irony of that term). *Our* fruity drinks on the other hand—Graeme's, her husband Marc's, and mine—are the slutty kind, flashy red flowers stuck in each one. We're sitting high on worn barstools on a deck at the beach, feeling like carefree backpackers exploring the world. Which, at least for the moment, we are.

We left our boats anchored off Apia, Samoa's capital, and decided to tour this green mountainous island by land. We've been doing the backpacker thing by the book: Playing cards on dusty front stoops of grocery stores. Tossing our bags onto roofs of airbrushed Jesus-Hearts-U school buses blaring Hits of the '80s. Cramming into seats with gossiping ladies, snoring old men, hide-and-seeking children, and a chicken who must have detected grain in my hair from the way he kept pecking at it. Though really the grain was beneath my feet, where a huge bag of rice propped my wet-with-sweat knees into my teeth. After hours on the bus—scent of B.O., green bananas, copra, vomit from the cute kid holding the chicken—we got off at a stop that looked right on the map but which, we realized while wading through a brown river between two villages, was one stop too soon. *Oops.*

In other words, we've been backpackers in paradise. And all this journeying has landed us here, at this small family-owned-and-operated beachside resort on the south side of Upolu, the main island of Samoa—though the word *resort* implies way too many amenities. Really it's a series of open-air, wood-and-thatch structures, the largest of which houses a small kitchen, bar, and deck with tables. The large table, where all meals are served family style, rests in the sand next to the deck. We'll gather there when dinner is served.

Tonight we'll be sleeping on raised, open-air platforms called *fale* (fah-lay), which is the traditional style of housing in Samoa, though they vary in grandeur. Fancy ones use cement, brick, or colorful tile and display five-piece living room sets to the world—like a dollhouse with its entire front wall pulled off. Our *fales*, on the other hand, are small, rickety wooden decks. Thatch roofs cost extra; so does mosquito netting. We splurge on both. At least bedding is included, though I can't help but wonder if bed-bugs are, too. But then, how can you complain when the surf is practically lapping at your toes?

The travel gods have been on our side. It just so happens that we pulled into Apia Harbor last week during Samoa's annual Teuila Festival, arguably the best festival in the South Pacific. So we put the work on hold for the week and threw ourselves into *tafaoga*—which oddly translates into English as "picnic" but which really means to go out and have *fun*. On our first day in port, we watched hundreds of men racing *fautasi*, long boats, across *Dragonfly*'s bow. I swear the rowers' biceps were as big as Graeme's (really quite nice) thighs. *Mmm* . . . And for the rest of the week we attended rugby matches, arts and crafts fairs, an adult talent contest (amazing), an adolescent talent contest (painful), and the overly serious Miss Samoa Beauty Pageant. To top it off there was the underly serious Miss Tutti Frutti Beauty Pageant.

For cross-dressers.

The four of us, Marc, Lisa, Graeme, and I, weren't quite sure what to expect. None of us had been to a cross-dressers' beauty pageant before. Not surprisingly, it was a cross between a regular beauty pageant you see on TV—multitiered stage, T-shaped runway, crisp judges' tables—and a gay nightclub—dusky lights, boisterous voices, techno beat. The decorations looked like they'd been slapped up by an overbudget prom committee, with everything from balloons and streamers to glitter and stars. We got there early enough to grab beers and metal folding seats before the crowd became a musky sea of standing-room-only.

The show opened to raucous applause, and the contestants strutted out one by one. A taut woman shimmering in a peekaboo butt cheeks dress. A broad-shouldered woman wrapped in a classy black sheath. A short, round woman in a stole and an emerald gown befitting an opera diva. The contestants ranged from toothpicked to pear shaped, short to tall, bright and bubbly to sexy and serious. The only commonality: You knew a man's body was lurking there somewhere.

The beauty pageant, like any beauty pageant, included evening gowns, bathing suits, a talent show, and of course a question-and-answer session where the contestants talked about their charity work and upstanding moral values. There was also a lot of loud music and dirty dancing. As a finale, each contestant performed a final act in homage to the theme: fruit. Miss Grape swooped and twirled to "Somewhere over the Rainbow," floaty in her purple balloon costume. Miss Cherry did a Betty Boop–style dance also with balloons, each predictably popped one by one. Miss Banana was the raunchiest, dancing to a Cher techno-ballad and gesturing with bananas in precisely the way you would expect her to gesture with bananas. The crowd squealed. During the whole event there was only one rude heckler, quickly silenced by the glares of fierce Samoan women.

The amazing thing, besides how much money the Tutti Frutti Beauty Pageant raised for local charities, is that on this 98 percent Christian island in the middle of the ocean, these cross-dressers, called *fa'afafine* ("fa-fa-fee-nay"), are integrated members of society. This is miraculous when you consider that missionaries throughout the Pacific completely annihilated other cultural practices that are, to the Western mind at least, far less taboo: tattoo, dance, traditional Polynesian dress. But Samoa, though colonized and missionized just like all the other Pacific Isles, somehow maintained much of its *fa'a Samoa*, or "Samoan way." Being accepting of *fa'afafine* (men following a "woman's way") is just one example of this miracle.

One rumor I heard about this phenomenon is that the seventh child in a Samoan family is brought up female whether he happens to be female or not. So, tonight at our beach resort's family-style dinner, I ask the Samoan woman sitting next to me about this while breadfruit, taro leaves in coconut sauce, and *oka* (the Samoan version of *poisson cru*) are passed around the table.

She says that's a bunch of hooey. She and her friend, who's sitting across from her, grew up on Upolu but have since moved to New Zealand. Every year they come back to visit family.

"But it *is* true," she says, rubbing a prominent moley birthmark on her cheek, "that everyone has someone—a son, a brother, a cousin, an uncle— who's a *fa'afafine*. My nephew is."

"And my brother-in-law's brother is," says her companion, a sturdy woman sporting short hair, stud earrings, and baggy knee-length jeans shorts. My gay-dar goes off slightly with these two ladies, and I wonder if they're partners, sneaking a little alone time away from their Samoan families. (Despite the *fa'afafine* phenom, it turns out homosexuality is *not* A-OK in Samoa.) Then again, they could just be friends; my gay-dar is by no means foolproof.

"So, are *fa'afafine* really totally accepted here?" I ask, curious for personal reasons as well as general.

"Well, yes and no," says the short-haired woman. "If a little boy shows signs of being effeminate, he's usually allowed to act and dress like a girl, and eventually a woman, if he wants. But she still might get teased a bit. She's still seen as different."

Almost as proof, the conversation goes hush every time our waitress approaches the table. She's a *fa'afafine*, probably sixteen years old, with short hair and a boy's smooth chest under her T-shirt, but she's definitely feminine, wearing lipstick, earrings, and a skirt. The latter's no surprise, though; both men and women wear traditional skirts called lavalavas.

When our waitress leaves again, the birthmark woman explains that *fa'afafine* almost constitutes a third gender in Samoa, appreciated because *fa'afafine* can do both men *and* women's work; she motions a hand in the direction of the kitchen, where our waitress has gone. This is quite convenient in a culture like Samoa's where Pink and Blue tasks are strictly divided. She smiles, "More help for mum that way."

Now this is fascinating to me, as the whole transgender/transsexual stuff actually hits pretty close to home. One of my former students, a thoughtful but awkward girl when I taught her, is now a guy.

When I went out for coffee with him back in Seattle, he said one of the hardest things for people to adjust to is the pronoun shift. Folks are understandably used to calling someone "him" or "her," he said. When we have to switch this habit midstream, or we can't tell upon meeting someone which pronoun to use, or we detect a conflict between someone's physical sex and their outward sex traits (obviously a man but dresses like a woman), we get *really* uncomfortable. And while he understands this discomfort—he said it sure would've been easier if he'd been born male in the first place—he also wishes people could just call people by what they want to be called.

It amazed me. When this kid was my student, she was kind and well liked and smart, but never seemed at home in her own skin; she slouched, she shuffled, she fidgeted. And to see her in a prom dress—oh, the agony. But now that he's a young man, he's totally at ease. Looks like a normal guy: Wears clean-cut button-down shirts, straps his chest (he's saving up for top surgery), and walks all-boy—said he had to learn that from guy friends. He seemed confident, comfortable, articulate; I was so proud of how he'd matured. Of course, you could chalk all that up to his having graduated from college—I mean, who isn't a wreck in high school? But still. He just seemed, I don't know, more *himself*.

And yet, it must be difficult for his parents. Sounded like they were adjusting slowly but surely. Still, what a shock to have your child come home from college, not the girl you raised, but the self-assured young man he's grown into—talk about a mind twister. No matter how open-minded you are, no matter how adaptable, no matter how much you love your kid, that's the kind of change that would take some getting used to.

In the 1920s, the famous anthropologist Margaret Mead was sent to Samoa to study adolescence. The question she tackled was, in her words, "Are the disturbances which vex [American] adolescents due to the nature of adolescence itself or to the civilization? Under different conditions does adolescence present a different picture?" If Samoan kids came of age without the angst American boys and, particularly, girls experienced, the reasoning went, then maybe puberty didn't inherently suck after all. Maybe it just sucked for the kids in America.

Mead, then twenty-three, lived in an American Samoan village for about six months. She collected data, performed interviews, and observed daily life, later publishing her findings in the surprise best seller *Coming of Age in Samoa* (1928). And she did indeed find that Samoan kids made the transition to adulthood more smoothly than their American counterparts—for lots of reasons. For one, children were given responsibility at a very early age, girls taking care of younger siblings and helping around the house, and boys fishing or wielding machetes alongside their fathers. There was no golden age of childhood shattered by sudden responsibility. Also, since families were large and fluid, Mead said, teens experiencing trouble at home could move to an auntie's or uncle's *fale* without a big fuss; family support ran deep and wide.

Mead cited other reasons for Samoa's angst-less adolescence, too, but her most sensational findings centered on sexuality. Mead described a culture whose attitude toward sex and sexuality was open and accepting— where adolescents could experiment with sexual partners, could wait longer to get married, and where gender was not set in stone. She used these discoveries to argue that American adolescents would be far less angst-ridden if society's sexual taboos were eased.

As you can imagine, this was controversial stuff in the 1920s and 1930s—and well beyond. Mead came under fire from both the general public and her fellow academics. Most famously, an Australian anthropologist named Derek Freeman refuted her findings in two books published after her death—conveniently after, critics said, she could defend herself. Freeman claimed Mead did shoddy work, perhaps even fabricated some of her findings, and was swayed by her own bisexual leanings. He even reinterviewed some of her subjects, revisiting them as old (piously Christian) women. They recanted their statements with the general message: "Oh, that *palagi* [white lady] actually believed us when we said we were sleeping around? We were just kidding! Tee hee hee hee."

This controversy has been one of the biggest in the history of anthropology. And while Mead's integrity has been defended by her peers and her findings largely upheld by other researchers, both anthropologists have been criticized for their overlaying of personal expectations on their research, for their biases, for their shortcomings in understanding the culture they came to study.

Which begs the question: How can we as mere travelers, in one country one month, the next country the next, even begin to understand the people and cultures we encounter? How can we avoid seeing just what we want or expect to see? How, when viewing the world, can we not be blind?

There was this guy I dated after college, the first and only guy who I immediately thought, *This is the One.* He wasn't Graeme, so obviously I was wrong. And not just in the fact that he and I didn't tie the knot. I was wrong about him in so many ways, ways I didn't comprehend until after we broke up and he said these fateful words on the phone: "I've gotten back into the habit of saying 'fag' now that you're not around."

HIM? Saying FAG??? I couldn't believe it. I'd never heard him say "fag"—a word I find abhorrent—all the time we were dating. And if I had, it would have made me see him as a totally different person. Namely, as himself.

The deal was this: I met him on that dude ranch in Wyoming—the dude ranch where I was a crappy-ass cook. A bunch of the cowboys-in-training had this horrible habit of saying "fag" and the *N*-word and other unsavory epithets. And so, in a fit of maturity, I decided that any time someone used such ignorant language, he would get a punch in the arm from me. I even told the worst faggot-sayer that my brother was gay (he's not) just to get the dude off that word. And it worked. I later overheard him saying to his friend, "Psst . . . hey man, don't say that. Janna's brother is gay." No one on that ranch said "faggot" anymore . . . at least not around me.

And yet, I'd never known that my boyfriend that summer was biting his tongue, too. That moment on the phone, six months after he'd dumped me, was such a shock—and a release. I realized I'd endowed my ex with all the traits, thoughts, and feelings I'd wanted him to have. I'd been in love with my image of the guy. Not the guy himself.

And I think the same thing can happen traveling the world, especially beautiful places like the South Pacific. It's easy to drop in for a few weeks, see the pretty sights, and leave with an idealized image or simplistic under-standing of a country and its people. Even Margaret Mead, "grandmother to the world," who went to Samoa with the sole purpose of understanding the culture, later admitted shortcomings to her early research in the same breath that she defended it.

Which suggests that, in response to the question: *How can we avoid seeing people through our own biased lens?* the ultimate answer is: *We can't.* Though certainly our vision can change. I mean, the Tutti Frutti Beauty Pageant was an eye popper, and not just because of the garish costumes and bright lights. But because clapping wildly for those ballsy women carved out more space in my brain for words like *beautiful* and *woman* and *normal.* My vision expanded and shifted that night.

What once seems odd or freakish, later seems normal once we've been exposed to it enough. Samoans shrug their shoulders, ho-hum, over the *fa'afafine* thing, just like sailing, to me, seems a totally normal way of life. We become used to what we know. And in the end, our reaction to the world says much more about ourselves and our experiences than it does about the world itself.

The same is true in relationships. While certainly I know Graeme much better than I ever did that dude-ranch dude, how I see Graeme at any given moment still has a lot to do with my own mood, my own perspective. He irritates me more when (surprise, surprise) I'm irritable. And I enjoy him more when I'm in a good space myself.

Like right now. I crawl between the bed-bug-bitten sheets of our *fale*, the scent of the sea tingling my nose, and nuzzle Graeme's neck. I say sleepily, "I love you."

Though this comment, in reality, has less to do with him right now than it does with me. Really it's my way of saying, "We're here. Together. And I'm happy."

18

High Tide

When you're skipping from country to country to country like a flat stone across water, there's a whole lot of red tape that follows in your wake. Usually it involves various offices: Customs, Immigration, Quarantine. Often it involves large sweating men in dark uniforms coming aboard to inspect your boat, drink your warm Coke, and eat your stale cookies. Always it involves pedal pedal pedaling back and forth across town from office to bank to notary to bank to office in search of paperwork, money orders, stamps, receipts, and forms. And sometimes, though rarely, it involves drug-sniffing dogs who jump on your V-berth and piss, like in Mexico, or officials who kick you out before you even get in, like in Fatu Hiva. Never, though, never has our check-in procedure been anything like it is here in Wallis Island: easy.

Wallis is an atoll in the western Pacific administered by the French government. It's disconnected geographically from the rest of French Polynesia and doesn't have even a fraction of the tourism that famous Bora Bora does—even though Wallis has that same ideal combo of white sand islets circling turquoise lagoon circling jungly center island. Maybe Wallis's isolation accounts for the simple, streamlined, laid-back procedure we followed this morning to check in. It took all of thirty minutes and occurred in two air-conditioned buildings, not far from each other, staffed by underworked, overpaid employees with senses of humor. It's like the land of opposites.

But, now that the procedure hasn't eaten an entire day like it usually does, we're thinking about sneaking around to a more peaceful anchorage on the other side of the island. Except we can't. Because the other check-in we have to perform is with the other system of governance here, the traditional system; we have to meet with the *kalea*, or chief, of the village where *Dragonfly* is anchored. This sounds easy enough, except that, despite his charming wife's assurances that he'll be back *tout de suite* (all the locals speak both French and Wallisian), he's been gone all day. So we confer with Lisa and Marc on *Nahanni* and decide to switch anchorages anyway. We knocked on the *kalea*'s door three times, and it's the effort that counts, right?

Later we'll find out: wrong.

The irony, of course, is that at 5 A.M. the next morning in the "more peaceful" anchorage, the massive sound of a tanker's horn wakes us. I had no idea a ship so huge could navigate Wallis's shallow lagoon. The mooring buoy the size of a garden shed a hundred feet away from us should have been a clue. The tanker wants to tie to it. So we haul *Dragonfly*'s anchor, move another hundred feet, then fall back into bed for more peaceful zzzs.

A few hours later, Marc and Lisa hail us on the VHF, suggesting an adventure. Marc says he wants to go spearfishing; Lisa says she wants to ride bikes. The plan, therefore, is: ride bikes. Graeme and I are game, happy that for once we won't be the only ones laughed at, since *Nahanni*'s folding bikes have wheels the size of dinner plates, too. Plus, Wallis's jungly center island of Uvéa is relatively flat; we can circumnavigate it easily in half a day.

Our first stop is Lake Lalolalo, a spectacular crater lake bound by sheer red cliffs. Uvéa has a handful of these perfectly round, deep volcanic lakes, almost as if a huge giant (as opposed to the tiny kind) pogo-sticked across the island. Our guidebook says flying foxes and blind eels live here at Lake Lalolalo, but squinting from our high perch on the edge of a cliff, feeling quite blind ourselves, all we can make out are flying dots. Still, it's a perfect spot for picnicking on soft baguettes, stinky cheese, and pâté—the benefits of French rule in the islands can be debated; the perks of French cuisine cannot.

As we continue on our bike tour we pass banana and papaya plots, flower-strewn cemeteries with elaborate stone crypts, and *artisanant* shops, where women make and sell jewelry, mats, and *tapas*. That's the painted bark cloth we originally saw in Fatu Hiva but didn't have a big enough brassiere to trade for. This time we're able to buy a set of postcard-size *tapas* without dangling our tatas; these artists prefer cold hard cash.

In addition to *tapas*, we also see a lot of churches on Uvéa. They're everywhere, all built out of dark, hand-hewn blocks with stark white mortar, all somewhat fanciful in design. It's like there's a rule on Wallis that no church can be the same. The effect is Legoland meets God. On one of the few long hill climbs, I declare I've found my favorite church. We pull over (conveniently) midhill to check it out. Eyeing it from the heaving props of my handlebars, I christen it the wedding-cake church for its circular, multitiered design. I especially like its simple panes of stained glass, each a single different color, which must cast a kaleidoscope glow inside.

The only thing we see more of than churches on our bike ride is pigs. Wallis is one of the few countries where pigs (11,000) outnumber humans (9,000). And riding the tiny veins of unmapped roads along Uvéa's shoreline, we have to dodge dozens of them. This is actually a relief, as pigs don't chase us like dogs do. Though they do laugh at us. And they do run—we've seen it. At sunset, locals whistle for their pigs like Americans whistle for the family hound. The pigs, who spend their days snouting around on the beach for edible flotsam and jetsam, gallop home, pork barrels on candlestick legs.

When we return to our peaceful anchorage, we discuss our next move with *Nahanni*. Graeme and I want to spend as much time with them as possible, since they'll be heading south soon, and we'll be heading north. Tomorrow, Marc wants to explore Uvéa's ancient ruins; Lisa thinks it's time to hit the motus. So we'll be hitting the motus for a day of sand and surf before we have to say good-bye.

Ambling around tiny Ile Fenua Fou, there's that ambiguous scent of low tide wafting on shore, half salt-pricked air, half dead starfish. Lisa stops every few feet to examine a shell; she's the consummate beachcomber, knows all the names. I'm just along for the girl time. Meanwhile, the boys are spearfishing, or at least practice spearfishing, in the pass.

"So how're you feeling?" I ask. "How's the whole preggo thing going?"

"OK," she says, brushing a straw of bobbed blond hair behind her ear. "Fine, I guess." She looks at me. "Actually, it kind of sucks."

"Why? What's up?" I lean down, pick up a flat stone, and skip it into the turquoise crepe paper lagoon; it only gives one fat *plop!*

"I've just been so irritable lately," Lisa says. "No patience. No sense of humor. Sick to my stomach all the time . . . and everything Marc does gets on my nerves."

"I've heard that happens."

"When you're pregnant," she quips, "or when you're living on a boat with someone 24/7?"

I laugh. "Both I guess." I push my sunglasses up my sweaty nose. "And see? You've still got your sense of humor."

We walk, sandals swinging from hooked fingers, bare toes digging into grainy sand, while Lisa vents. It's all the usual stuff, really. The stuff that almost sounds silly now, when she's saying it out loud, but that felt crucial and monumental and indicative of major issues at the time. It's nice to know I'm not the only one who snowballs things when interpreting my husband's behavior. I confess to her an extrapolation I made early on in our trip: He didn't brush his teeth before coming to bed, ergo, he must not find me attractive.

"Oh, God. I've done things like that, too." Lisa laughs sympathetically. "It's weird how we take *their* behavior and turn it on ourselves. Like we're responsible for it."

"Yeah," I say. "When Graeme's in a bad mood, I'll often ask if he's mad at me about something. He's actually said before, 'You know, Janna, not everything's about *you*.'" I shrug. "Harsh. But true."

A few steps on Lisa bends to pick up a Ping-Pong-ball-size shell that's symmetrically conical, like a spinning top. "A top shell, *Trochus* something-or-other," she says, handing it to me. "They make smooth buttons from these, stamp them out from the side walls." She points.

The shell's delicate pattern of pink and white contrasts prettily with its hefty weight. I rub my fingers on its rough outside and the lip of its opally inside. I go to hand it back, but Lisa's already leaning down to show me another.

Walking the beach with Lisa, examining shells alongside our lives, reminds me of that book *Gift from the Sea* by Anne Morrow Lindbergh. I read it my senior year in college and was amazed that Lindbergh, a middle-aged woman writing in the 1950s, could speak so directly to me, a young woman forty years later. Lindbergh described relationships as following an in-and-out rhythm like ocean tides. One quote in particular stuck with me:

> When you love someone you do not love them all the time, in the same way, from moment to moment. It is an impossibility. It is even a lie to pretend to. And yet this is exactly what most of us demand. We have so little faith in the ebb and flow of life, of love, of relationships. We leap at the flow of the tide and resist in terror its ebb.

This explained so much to me back then. About why that initial, giddy feeling of love always wore off. And why I shouldn't get all needy and naggy every time the tide in a relationship went out—which is exactly what I had done as a sophomore dating Graeme.

In fact, even from this distance, it's hard for me to say whether Graeme's and my connection really did just naturally wane in college (perhaps fallout from the summer camp Flurby affair), or whether it was my constant terror that our connection was ebbing that actually caused it to ebb.

I recall conversation after conversation between our younger selves—on the twin bed in my dorm room, on the ratty couch in his apartment, atop a hay bale in the wheat fields—where I, in tears, repeated this refrain: "Why don't you ever want to talk anymore? Why are you so distant?"

At first, Graeme would say, "I do, I do," and, "I'm not, I'm not," and the tide would rise for a while. But as soon as it ebbed in the slightest— one awkward conversation or one dull moment—I would sob again . . . in Graeme's rusty red pickup, on the shag carpet of his bathroom, drunk at a party. Until, over the course of six months, I slowly wore him down. And his "I do want to talk" turned into "I don't know why I don't want to talk" turned into a long, silent stare.

Our last-ditch effort to rally our relationship was a spontaneous overnight road trip in that red, rusty pickup of his down to Smith Rock in Oregon—naked. But even the starlit driving, the blaring radio, the feet-on-the-dashboard freedom, and the speel of vinyl against bare buttocks couldn't snap us out of our low tide. And soon after, on the green lawn of my gray dorm, Graeme walked out of my life forever. (Or so he thought.)

When I read Lindbergh's book just a couple years later, I embraced this tide imagery like a baby does its binkie, comforting myself with the idea that the tide in a relationship would always come back in—if I could just control my urge to "resist in terror its ebb." But, of course, I eventually figured out that that's not exactly what Lindbergh was saying. For one, some relationships weren't meant to last. Like that achingly cute guy who said I laughed too loud? He was meant to ebb and go. Though surely, I thought, in marriage—the relationship that's supposed to last a lifetime—that connection will always come back . . . as long as you work at it hard enough.

But now, married more than a year and watching Lisa on the cusp of motherhood, I realize that even this is slightly twisting what Lindbergh said. "Security in a relationship," she wrote, "lies neither in looking back to what it was in nostalgia, nor forward to what it might be in dread or anticipation, but living in the present relationship and accepting it as it is now."

That's a hard concept for me to embrace. Because I *like* how Graeme and I are right now. I've liked the rhythm of our relationship since we set out on our big crossing: Intense conversations. Exciting adventures. Even our sex life has gone gourmet since we instituted sex on a schedule. (OK, so we're no longer at it daily . . . but still.) Things are good. And I like the particular ways in which they're good. I dread the thought of change.

But change is coming. Unlike most cruisers who follow the Coconut Milk Run south to New Zealand to dodge the impending hurricane season, we're heading north to islands known for poverty, overcrowding, and environmental degradation. Partly we chose this route because sailing off the beaten tack sounded unusual and interesting. And also because we just don't have time to wait out hurricane season in New Zealand; we need to keep moving north if we want to circumnavigate the Pacific anytime soon.

Yet going north also means we won't have a steady pack of other cruisers to rely on. No more buddy boats to tell jokes to or share weather reports with on passage. No group of Usual Suspects for happy hours in port. No girlfriends, like Lisa, with whom to walk the beach, and pick up shells, and analyze life and love.

On the ocean side of the islet Lisa and I put our sandals back on. We explore the rough exposed rock of the reef, which is elaborately imprinted with swirls and arcs and cones, evidence of creatures long since vanished. These stamps of coral and shells, clear as plaster of Paris molds, would mean something to an archaeologist, I think, looking down. To me they mean legacy—how even the simplest creature can leave something beautiful in life's wake.

"Hey, Lisa, do you feel ready to be a mom?" I ask, picking my way over the reef. "I mean"—I shake my head—"I just can't imagine . . . I'm still getting used to being married." Only a handful of friends back home have kids. Graeme and I have only talked of family as a someday sort of thing.

"Well, yeah, I kinda feel ready," Lisa says. "I mean, not *totally* ready. But we still have some time to get used to it. And we've always known we wanted kids." She shrugs her tan shoulders. She's more fit and trim pregnant than I am not-pregnant, one of the few women I know who wears a bikini as unself-consciously as a T-shirt. "Plus, I'm not sure you can ever *really* be ready," she says. "Now seems as good a time as any."

I can't think of a single person I know who'd say getting pregnant while living on a small sailboat in the middle of the Pacific Ocean is as good a time as any. But then Lisa and Marc are not just anybody, even among cruisers. Just look at the gear they have aboard *Nahanni*. Gear—unlike our surfboards, which remain permanently strapped to the rail—that they actually *use*: Windsurfer, surfboard, kiteboard, scuba tanks, masks and snorkels, fishing rods, speargun, running shoes, hiking boots, bikes. They're ready for anything. They figure they'll just sail to New Zealand, have the baby there, and a year or so after that continue sailing on their merry way. I admire their nonchalance, and their gumption.

When we return to the pass side of the island where the water is flowing swiftly from the lagoon into the ocean, we find Graeme and Marc lounging on the sand. They've got a mesh bag with about five dinky reef fish and one big grouper.

"Hey, nice catch," I say, pointing to the big one. "Who nabbed that guy?"

Graeme and Marc eye each other sheepishly. Then, "That guy," Graeme says, pointing at a small human head bobbing in the middle of the pass, a speargun sticking out of the water next to it.

"The guy was amazing," Marc says. "He's local. Very experienced. Goes down and just stays there, still as a rock, for ten minutes. The fish literally come to him."

Lisa rolls her eyes. "Marc, even the very best divers can stay down for only four minutes. I read it in our guidebook the other day."

Uh-oh, I see what Lisa means about the dreaded snowball effect. I imagine her brain spinning something like: How will we teach our child honesty when my husband exaggerates even the simplest facts?

I also see what she means about being irritable when pregnant.

That night, as I snuggle up to Graeme and his pile of laundry, I whisper, "Hey, you don't think Marc and Lisa are the Bickersons, do you?"

The Bickersons is (predictably) the name we use for couples who bicker. Old friends of ours coined the term after spending a tedious evening with a couple who chastised each other incessantly—and divorced a few months later. Our friends decided they would *never* be the Bickersons, as much for the health of their relationship as for the sanity of those around them. So they came up with a secret phrase as a sort of *Psst . . . let's discuss this in private* signal when things were getting too heated. But it was such an odd saying that the moment they used it one night, I was like, "What the hell does 'Is the mongoose in need of water' mean?" I squinted my eyes back and forth between the two of them. "Are you guys speaking in code?" And that's when they explained their rule about the Bickersons. And, of course, immediately changed their secret code.

While Graeme and I have never attained true Bickerson status, I do think there have been times we've aired our dirty laundry a bit too much. I remember getting huffy in restaurants or bursting into tears at parties, usually over some snowball issue, often after one too many beers. That hasn't happened in ages. Maybe that's a positive effect of getting married.

On the other hand, I don't think sorting dirty laundry in private with girlfriends is quite the same as airing it at a party. And yet, in the year or so before setting sail, as my friends got married one by one, I noticed these conversations decreasing slightly, like no one wanted to admit her fledgling marriage wasn't perfect. So it's a relief to hear Lisa open up about her frustrations. And I suspect, when I get home, my girlfriends will, too. A year into my own marriage, I see that frustration doesn't mean failure, and venting isn't betrayal.

I nudge Graeme, wondering if he's already asleep or if he's still thinking about my Bickersons question. "Naw," he says. "Lisa and Marc aren't the Bickersons. Lisa's just pregnant. Her body's going through some crazy changes right now. They're *both* going through changes. But they're doing all right."

I snuggle in closer. His answer, for some reason, makes me feel all right, too. Like maybe his grace is transferable . . . if and when I ever get pregnant.

A few days later we say good-bye to *Nahanni*. I almost tear up watching them sail their bright yellow sailboat, loaded with Windsurfers and dive gear and Lisa's imperceptible belly, toward the pass.

"Good luck with the spearfishing!" Marc yells.

"Good luck sailing to Tonga!" Graeme yells.

"Good luck with the baby!" I yell.

"Good luck with the tides!" Lisa yells.

Graeme gives me a quizzical look over that last one, and then *Nahanni* is in the pass, and out the pass, and out to sea.

Which means it's time for us to think about heading north. So we return to the central island of Uvéa to stock up on fuel and water and, once
again, ask permission from the *kalea* to anchor off his village. Turns out a
whole group of sailors are waiting to check in with him, so we make an appointment en masse for tonight. It's time for Graeme and me to learn the
error of our ways.

At six o'clock, a group of cruisers gathers on the *kalea*'s front patio
where his wife serves us saccharine juice in small paper cups. It quickly
becomes apparent that I'm the most fluent in French among us, though I
try to warn of my poor track record as translator. No dice. I'm appointed
to make polite conversation with our hostess *en français* while we wait for
le chef to come outside. I'm complimenting her on Wallis's beautiful nooks
and crannies when the *kalea* emerges looking stern and disapproving. He's
a tall man with strong features and proud posture. He takes his seat and
scowls at the circle of gathered sailors. In rapid-fire French he explains to
me how important it is to make contact with him *before* having all the wonderful adventures he just overheard me describing.

It's quite humbling, translating my own scolding to my peers. But the
kalea makes many good points: They've had problems accommodating
cruisers' garbage, concerns about outsiders interacting with village youth,
and various cultural misunderstandings where cruisers simply didn't know
local custom. He explains that we're the village's guests, which in Wallis
invokes a precise protocol—guests ask, hosts grant. I nod and translate and
apologize over and over with burning cheeks. Thankfully, by the time everyone's offered their token gifts of baseball caps and T-shirts and tobacco,
the *kalea* is mollified. The thing that sticks with me as we cruisers retreat
into the dark, star-spangled night is the phrase the *kalea* kept saying over
and over again: "The most important thing is contact; you've got to make
contact."

Later that night, lying in bed with the hatch above our bunk funneling cool
air onto my skin, I find myself thinking about the *kalea*'s message. And
though I know the literal words he used are slightly different, in my mind
I translate his advice to that famous E. M. Forster quote: "Only connect."
It's long been my favorite saying because if there's one thing I value—in
my intellectual life, in cultural interactions, in friendship, and especially in
my marriage—it's that feeling of connection, that intensity of understanding, that quicksilver thrill when someone "gets" me. And so, instead of

recalling Lindbergh's advice to go with the flow and accept my marriage as it is now . . .

    and now . . .
    and now . . .

I send a silent wish to the universe, on the eve of heading north with my husband alone, to "only connect." As if this were as easy as it sounds.

The Good Fight

*i*f *you* were to ask one of my friends or acquaintances to describe me, I doubt words like *sweet* and *nice* would leap to mind. Hell, those words probably wouldn't even make the list. Not that I'm *mean*, but I suspect someone might offer *outspoken* or *intense* or (being sweet and nice herself) *passionate* instead. When I was young and foolish, I almost took this as a point of pride, figuring there was something valuable in standing up for one's beliefs, or fighting the good fight. But there's also something to being *tactful* and *respectful* and really listening to others. Graeme may have mentioned this once or twice.

It's something I've worked on over the years, smoothing my sharp edges so they don't jab so hard in people's sides. And, as my opinions about the world have softened from black-and-white to really-dark-charcoal-gray-and-just-slightly-off-white, this has gotten a tad easier. I've become a tad more palatable. I swear. But still, if there's one thing I can't stomach, it's unfairness. In grocery store lines, in highway traffic, on soccer fields; I'm the one who hollers to the ball hog, "Pass the ball! Pass the ball! Pass the ball, dammit!" And even though my parents said again and again, *No one ever said life was going to be fair*, I think I'm allergic to injustice—especially the social, cultural, or environmental kind. Because injustice, whether it makes me holler or cry or swallow acerbic words of protest in gobstopping gulps, never ceases to get a rise out of me.

And so, sitting on the tattered Igloo cooler beneath bouldery skies, I swallow hard and look up from my guidebook to say, "Jeez, Graeme, have you read this stuff yet? We're on our way to some pretty badass places." I dog-ear the page. "I thought the colonizers and missionaries messed with the *South* Pacific, but—"

Graeme holds up a finger. "Shhh . . . I think this is it. . . ."

And, for once, I hold my tongue and listen.

We're on a rolly sail northeast—we just passed the international date line into the Eastern Hemisphere—and we're desperately trying to tune in to radio coverage of the 2004 U.S. presidential election. When I hear "This is the Voice of America" peter through the SSB's crackling connection, I slap the guidebook shut, clamber down to the rickety cockpit table we've set up specially for this occasion, and lean toward the sound of the radio. I squint so I can hear the words better.

Now, in an effort at tact and diplomacy, and since I know intelligent, moral people come from both sides of the aisle (my dad usually votes Republican; my mom Democrat), let's just set Graeme's and my personal politics aside. If we were simply to vote the opinions of the people we've met in various countries along the way, we'd be rooting *against* George W. Bush's second term, and rooting for whatsisname. Because here's the amazing thing: People, from Mexico to Central America to all these little islands in the South Pacific—not to mention the international band of cruisers we've sailed with—have told us, usually without our asking, that the United States is in dire need of a new president. Someone, our voluntary pollees have said, who'll show respect and tact toward the rest of the world. Someone who'll end the war in Iraq. Someone who never would have started it.

The one anomaly was in American Samoa, where we did come across Bush supporters. Or, at least, war supporters, since practically every family in American Samoa has somebody enlisted in the U.S. military. The whole place was garlanded with yellow ribbons and GOD BLESS OUR TROOPS banners and THESE COLORS DON'T RUN signs. Ironically and quite sadly, American Samoa boasts the *highest per capita military death rate* of any U.S. state or territory from the wars in Afghanistan and Iraq. Yet these non-U.S. citizens still routinely exceed their military recruiting quotas. It's the only ticket off the island. One-way ticket, for some.

Well, we all know how that afternoon of election coverage, hopping from Voice of America to the BBC to stations in New Zealand and Australia (the channels kept going static), ended up. And you can guess how disappointed

Graeme and I were, on behalf of our unofficial pollees of course, at George W. Bush's win.

But here's what the nice, sweet Italian documentary filmmakers, with their high cheekbones, pouting lips, and dark hair sloshing in their eyes, told us one night on *Dragonfly* over red vino. "Don't worry," they said. "Every country has right-wing loonies. Look at the racist Jean-Marie Le Pen in France and our very own Silvio Berlusconi in Italia. Intolerant bigots exist everywhere. And sometimes they get elected to office."

Well now. That's an outspoken, passionate, less-than-tactful declaration of opinion. But I took comfort in the idea that people everywhere have conflicted relationships with their politicians. And that people all over the world understand that, like those TV disclaimers, the views expressed by a country's government are not necessarily those of its citizens.

It's true even here in Tuvalu (too-VAH-loo), a paint splattering of islands blopped halfway between Hawaii and Australia. Some years back, the government invested in a scheme of routing 1-900-PHONE-SEX calls through the country's underutilized phone lines—until an outcry from the largely Christian populace pulled the plug. In the government's defense, there's not a lot of industry here in Tuvalu since the neighboring islands' phosphate mines closed. The government has had to get creative in its search for revenue. For instance, they finally raised the funds to join the United Nations by selling the country's Internet domain (.tv) for $50 million, and this U.N. status has given them even more money in the way of charity from Taiwan. The way it works is this: Tuvalu supports Taiwan's bid for the U.N. (something China vociferously opposes), and Taiwan does sweet, nice things for Tuvalu. When Graeme and I went to check in today, the brand-new government building had a large plaque outside stating: A GENEROUS GIFT FROM THE PEOPLE OF TAIWAN. Now that's what I call diplomacy. Though I suppose when you're one of the smallest kids on the block (only ten square miles of combined surface area in the whole country), it pays to cultivate rich friends.

Tuvalu, at about ten thousand people, also has a small population. Though the guys I've got my eyes on right now aren't small at all. They're big. Maybe not as bulky as Samoans, but they're muscular and fit, zinging soak 'em–size balls back and forth at each other on the *Te Ano* pitch. ("Your Ass," Graeme translates wryly from Spanish into English for me—who knows what it actually means in Tuvaluan.) The game is indeed like soak 'em as far as we can tell, with as many players (i.e., targets) as possible on each side. Even the demure Polynesian ladies in their flowered dresses join the teams and wickedly wing balls back and forth at each other's *anos*.

Graeme and I are sitting in crabgrass under the shade of a tree, with the wind in the treetops reminding me of highway sounds back home. The breeze makes the heat bearable. We're watching the action on the field, which is not actually a field but a long strip of blacktop that tootles down the island as far as the eye can see. This pitch seems far too long for even twenty games of *Te Ano*—a curious waste of resources on this very small island, except that the span multifunctions conveniently as a kids' bike riding arena, a soccer field, a dance floor, and a place for locals to sleep on really hot nights—this expanse gets more breeze than many people's homes. Oh, and it's an airstrip, too—with the serendipitous and fitting international airport code of FUN, named after the capital town of Funafuti.

The fact that this stream of blacktop is actually a runway is made evident, not by barricades and security guards and flashing lights, but by the gift-bearing, airplane-greeting crowd that is slowly gathering behind us. A plane must be due. The *Te Ano* players take their cue and clear the strip, but they stick around, because everyone on the island comes out for the landing. Even the pigs. As the plane descends to a blaring siren over loudspeakers, a pig skitters off the runway just in time to avoid becoming pork chopped.

Now, if you've ever heard of Tuvalu, it's for one reason and one reason only. Tuvalu is the sickly poster child for global warming. Usually the headline reads something like ISLAND NATION SINKING, but, of course, that's not exactly true. With global temperatures rising and hence ocean levels rising (5.5 millimeters a year according to some scientists), the atolls, only sixteen feet above sea level at their highest point, aren't sinking; they're drowning. According to the U.N.-sponsored Intergovernmental Panel on Climate Change, the world's oceans could rise as much as three feet in the next fifty to one hundred years, and that's assuming the ice sheets of Greenland and Antarctica don't melt. (Latest I've heard, they're melting.) So the government of Tuvalu, a nation whose islands are only three feet above sea level in many places, is seriously worried.

Though Eti, a salt-and-pepper-haired local we meet in his wife's living room restaurant, is not. "I've heard the ocean has actually *fallen* in the past few years." He frowns, pulling out a straight-backed seat at the empty table next to us. He sits and looks down at his three-year-old grandson playing with a red plastic car on the floor. The dark room has about eight tables and is decorated with out-of-date calendars and dusty silk flowers. We're the only patrons tonight, though we've heard this is the best place in town. The fish served by Eti's curly-haired wife is indeed delicious, moist with ginger and soy sauce, caught fresh by Eti this morning. Sensing an opportunity to garner local fishing knowledge, Graeme convinces Eti to join us the next day, with his grandson, aboard *Dragonfly*. It will be their first time ever aboard a yachtie's sailboat.

Though the next day, on *Dragonfly*, we learn Eti is no stranger to the sea. There's a maritime academy here on Funafuti that trains young men to be seamen aboard huge oil tankers and container ships. From the age of nineteen, Eti traveled all over the world as a ship worker, often on cruise ships; that's where he learned to speak English so well. His lips scrunch into a modest smile-pucker as he describes the places he's been: Asia, South America, Europe, the United States.

"I loved seeing all these places," he says, placing his paw of a hand on his grandson's chest, who's looking over the edge of the cockpit. "But I never liked any place as well as home."

Turns out working the world over by ship saved Eti from the other work common in his day: the phosphate mines on Nauru and Banaba, both operations since closed.

"Oh yeah, I read about that," I say, picking up our guidebook from the navigation table. I fan my face with the book; it's hot out here without our unsightly bedsheet system hung for shade. To compensate, we have a clip-on fan blowing (hot) air on our guests. "It sounds like the phosphate mines were a total disaster," I say.

"For the people living on those islands, yes. The mining obliterated everything, land and trees, and so, also, many people's lives. But," Eti says, squinting at me, "the mines gave many jobs to people there, here, and in Kiribati." Kiribati is the island nation just north of us, our next destination.

I nod sadly. The dance between industry and people's lives is always more complex than my stark mind likes to admit. And yet there's no doubt that the British Phosphate Company profited far more than the workers themselves. In fact, the British made the islands a colony instead of a protectorate so they could overrule the locals' protests to new land acquisitions for mining. The Brits have since paid $10 million Australian in reparations for its admitted exploitation.

"My family is from Kiribati," Eti says, "and a relative of mine was stranded on Banaba during the Japanese invasion of World War II. He was the only one to survive the Banaba massacre." Eti wipes a trickle of sweat from his hairline with the single pad of a finger. "Have you heard of this event?" he asks.

"Oh my gosh!" My hand freezes midfan. "You're related to the guy in this book!" I stick the book in his face like a mirror until I realize this might not be the most polite expression of my awe. "Wow, here, let me show you." I flip to the index, find the spot, and open to page 254 of the *Moon Handbook for Micronesia*. "Kabunare. Was that his name?"

"Yes, yes." Eti nods calmly, handing his grandson a cracker from the cockpit table and repositioning him in a sliver of shade. Perhaps when you're related to an island hero, the glamour eventually loses its shine. Or perhaps some stories, though well known, aren't necessarily causes for glee. Eti tells us the story in his slow, careful English. Graeme and I sweat and listen.

The tale (both *Moon*'s and Eti's—they match remarkably) goes like this: It was toward the end of the war and the Japanese were defeated. Before handing Banaba over to the British, however, the troops directed the one-hundred-or-so remaining islanders to line up on a sheer cliff. Kabunare (Eti's sister's brother-in-law's uncle or some such) praised God before the guns went off. Then he fell back over the cliff, unshot. Miraculously, Kabunare landed in the water alive. He lived two months on the island before coming out of hiding, and that's when the truth came out: The Japanese had told British soldiers, who landed soon after the massacre, that all the islanders had been taken to other islands. Except for the one hundred on the cliff, this was basically true. But, when Kabunare described the Banaba massacre, perpetrated, he claimed, to cover up other atrocities committed on the island, two Japanese officers were charged and found guilty of war crimes. One was hanged; one was sent to prison.

Interestingly, the only detail of Eti's that doesn't match our guidebook's or Kabunare's direct testimony (which I'll read later) is that Eti says Kabunare's cliff dive was intentional, an act of bravery and religious faith. Whether Eti really believes this may not even matter. If Kabunare were my relative and the story had been handed down to me to pass on to my grandson, I'd probably tell it that way, too.

Though I'm not willing, like Eti, to believe that the ocean levels here are actually falling. I've heard that this belief among islanders is a reaction to foreign reports that sensationalize the situation, implying that the atoll is in imminent danger of sinking. But it's not like that. The problems are complex and insidious, creeping slowly, compounding one another, a mixture of natural and human-induced threats.

We understand this better after having a few beers with Trish, a New Zealand aid worker who travels among the islands to evaluate and fund various social "programmes." Trish reminds me of teachers who enter the classroom, young and idealistic, hoping to change the system . . . only to realize twenty years later that things have only gotten worse. She's passionate and articulate and wicked smart, but worn like the nub of a pencil eraser. Her dark cotton blouse is wrinkled. A fuzzy braid perches on her shoulder like a ferret.

Trish taps out a cigarette from an almost-empty pack. "Mind?" she says.

Graeme and I shake our heads. We're sitting on an outdoor patio at a local bar where a breeze is sweeping the musky scent of windfall coconuts past us. In between sips of beer and smoking her cigarette, Trish paints a grim picture in her chummy Kiwi accent. "Tuvalu is one of the poorest nations on earth," she says. "Average annual income is"—she pauses, doing the math in her head—"let's see, about $1,000 U.S. Mostly subsistence living. But with environmental degradation, living off the land and sea becomes hard yakka, eh."

This must be a Kiwiism. I glance at Graeme. There's a slight lift to the edge of his lips.

Trish squares her matches with her cigs and continues. "Even though the soil was never very fertile, with increasingly brackish groundwater from the rising water table, it's becoming even harder to grow anything. The only potable water on the island comes from rain catchment systems." She takes a long drag off her cigarette. "The thing people don't get is, even though the land's not visually disappearing—at least not yet—the incremental change in climate is making things dodgy *now*. The ecosystems in the reefs and lagoons are warming and becoming polluted, making seafood harder to come by. There are freakishly high tides that flood homes and erode the main thoroughfare. The landfills, during these floods, send rubbish and toxins into nearby homes and yards. And if a storm happened to hit during one of these high tides? Then you'd have real devastation." Trish sighs a cloud of white smoke. "The place is buggered."

Trish waves a hand in front of her face, then leans forward intently. "The irony about Tuvalu," she adds, "is it's probably done less to contribute to global warming than any country on the planet." She taps her cigarette into an empty beer bottle. Her fingernails are unpainted and ragged.

"And did you know Tuvalu's the only nation in the world with no human rights violations?" she asks. "The *only* nation. I read that once. Now *that's* a claim to fame." Her eyes braise Funafuti's lagoon; she looks more pissed off than proud. Then Trish stubs out her cigarette and rises from her seat. "Peaceful place. Lovely this." She gestures to the flat, darkening water. "Too bad it won't be habitable in another fifty years."

And with that, she heads to the loo.

The next day Graeme and I ride the flat paved road from one tip of this unlucky horseshoe of an island to the other. Actually, the islet we're on is shaped more like a boomerang. Eight miles long. Fifty to a hundred and fifty yards wide on average. Where the town resides you can't see the ocean on the other side, but on the southern tip of the island, through sparse palm trees, we catch glimpses of pounding surf. It feels fragile.

On our ride we carry sticks to fend off island dogs, and use them twice. And we pass three bars, a cemetery, and two landfills reeking of trash. Plastic bags float on the breeze before wrapping themselves around coconut palms, giving a whole new meaning to the term "tree huggers." There are places where the road is so close to the beach that asphalt drips like candle wax into the lagoon.

Heading back through town, where a smattering of low buildings, the new government offices, and the FUN airport reside, we sweat. This place is hot, even with the breeze billowing my skirt. Unlike the more-touristed islands we've visited, Funafuti, and all the other islands from here till Asia, require long skirts and modest tops for me—no more tank tops and shorts. This takes some getting used to on a bike; I feel a bit Mary Poppins–ish with my skirt flapping in time with my pedals.

Heading north out of town, we ride through a crowded neighborhood of neat homes and *fales*, the yards swept in lines like meditative mazes. There are small dusky stores with whole shelves bare; the supply ship hasn't come in, the clerks explain. And the bakery, we see from a sign posted on the Swiss chalet–style shutters, has already sold out of this morning's bread. We'll have to come earlier tomorrow. At the Taiwanese embassy, signaled by a bright red and blue flag waving out front, we rest our bikes against shading trees, knock on the door, and Graeme chats idly with the diplomats in Mandarin. They keep covering their mouths and tipping back their heads at the shock of speaking Chinese to this blond, bike-riding white guy out here in this foreign land.

Traveling north on the island, past the Maritime Academy, we see the remains of World War II: an old tank rusting in the lagoon, a metal pillbox of an artillery station, scrap metal, and heaps of broken cement, which children climb on like playground equipment. The island tapers again, and we glide past white sand beaches with outrigger canoes pulled up onshore. Graeme snaps a photo of colorful fishing skiffs anchored off bright orange balls in the turquoise lagoon. *God this place is beautiful*, I think.

And then, just up the road, we pass another landfill and I suck in my breath with shock. A family's home is built so close, up and above this overflowing pit, that it reminds me of Dr. Seuss's Lorax meets Sarah Sylvia Cynthia Stout who Would Not Take the Garbage Out. A woman in a pink wraparound skirt emerges on the back "porch" and empties a small trash can, straight down, into the pit. She turns to us and smiles. A man on the front stoop, on the other hand, scowls. In the front yard, children play chase, high-stepping barefoot through the rubbish strewn across the land. If they notice the stench rising off the baking garbage, they show no sign.

At the end of the road we find a weather research center whose observations confirm all that Trish told us last night. Sheltered from the midday heat, we appreciate the air-conditioning almost as much as the tide tables and charts and maps the clerk shows us. He's generous with his time, only losing his smile when pointing to particularly grim statistics. Yes, the ocean levels are rising. Yes, lagoon temperatures are warming. And, yes, the island is pretty much buggered. But have we had a nice stay here, he asks? And isn't it a lovely place?

We assure him it is. But after looking at his stats, the chilled sweat on my skin contrasts with the heat rising in my chest and my cheeks and the ocean just beyond the window.

Our last night in Funafuti a big new sailboat is in, and we accept their invitation to dinner. They're a retired couple, an older German man and his young Venezuelan wife. Magda turns out to be quiet and gracious, and an excellent cook, whereas her husband is loud and brash, full of rumbling laughter, colorful stories, and hearty pats on the back. Climbing on deck I decide he looks like a real-life Bilbo Baggins because of his short stature, barrel chest, and bulbous nose. Craggy toes stick out from his sandals accompanied by ten little tufts of toe hair. White dandelion fuzz grows from his ears.

We're having a fine time, lounging in the cockpit, trading tales of sailing.

Coming all the way from Germany, Bilbo has many. Only, as we move from drinks to appetizers to dinner, Graeme and I start to realize that, while Magda's definitely sweet and nice, maybe Bilbo, on the other hand, is not. We've gotten onto the topic of his home country. Vest Germany, he says, a vonderful place before the vall came down and it vas flooded by lazy Eastern Europeans who live off the government and don't raise a finger to vork.

I cast a look at Graeme. He dips his bread in his rice and brown simmer sauce, and cocks his head to the side, as though deep in thought. Me, I take the bait, and Bilbo and I begin debating the merits of socialized health care and welfare, and the ins and outs of immigration policy.

Bilbo complains that he pays 50 percent of his income to taxes. "It's too much," he says, "vhen all these immigrants are not even villing to make a living? Vhy should I bother vorking vhen I have to give half of it away? How can I pay ze bills?"

I look around at his fancy fifty-foot yacht with its high-tech gadgets and polished equipment. "But if you have enough money for all this . . . ?" I say, gesturing to the boat and the water beyond.

Graeme turns to Magda (whom Bilbo said he "picked up" while sailing through "Wenezuela") and tells her how delicious the bread is. Did she bake it herself?

She nods silently.

Bilbo barrels ahead: He's read many books on the subject, and these things—intelligence, skills, vork ethic—they are no mystery. Research has been done. Brain vaves have been measured. And some peoples are just more adwanced than others.

I'm in the middle of thinking, *Shitfuck, this guy is a whack job*—when Mr. Hobbit adds this: "It's clear, for example, vhy Africa is a tird vorld country and spent centuries enslaved."

I hold knife and fork midair and stare across the table at this hobbit-turned-troll of a man. His gaff about Africa being a country aside, is it possible that he's just said what he's just said? That I'm breaking bread with a man who's doing his best to conform to the anachronistic caricature of the racist, bellicose Nazi who believes in the supremacy of the Aryan race? All the while eating his brown wife's brown rice smothered in savory brown simmer sauce? This can't be real.

And that's when I take off my gloves. I am outraged, and what was once a cool, level debate has now risen to a heated shouting match. Graeme tries to change the topic. He grips my knee under the table as a secret code, a

SILENT HAND SIGNAL. He tries to diffuse the situation with appeals to reason. But neither Bilbo nor I will be reasoned with. While Bilbo appears to be enjoying the argument, egging me on after Graeme derails the conversation again and again, I am not. This is not the good fight, the healthy debate I enjoy. It feels way too personal, way too horrifying, way too important for me. And, by the end, after this man has trotted out every stereotype, every bell curve, every faulty statistic he can, I grip my head in my hands and ask, "How can you say these things? How can you see your fellow humans this way? How can you. . . ." But I don't finish. Because that's when I begin to cry.

At that, Graeme thanks Magda for the meal, nods his head toward Bilbo, and excuses us. He stands up from the table, grabs my hand, and we make our way off their boat in silence. It's warm. The stars are out. And the only sound in the black skin of night is the *putt-putt* of our dinghy's engine, which starts on the very first pull.

Graeme and I used to debate a lot. Back in college especially, it was something we really enjoyed. Philosophizing. Sparring. Arguing a particular policy or ethical dilemma over beer and vegetarian food (he converted me for a year). Only, a decade later, when we moved in together in Seattle, our sparring style had to change. First because I tended to take issues way too personally and way too seriously. I mean, I could literally hear myself thinking, "How can I love someone who's against Proposition 458?"—Prop 458 having to do with parking meters or sewer taxes or the location of the new skateboard park. (As if!) And second because I'd practically turned defensiveness into an extreme sport.

I recall a camping trip where I was sitting by an echoing lake with one of my oldest girlfriends, rehashing the day's ups and downs. She was teasing me gently for my not-always-so-tactful communication style. It was seriously getting my knickers in a twist! (As Kiwi Trish would say.) And that's when I watched as a virtual wall of television screens, like you see at an electronics store, appeared before me, each with a mental message flashing on it: "That's not true!" and "You don't understand!" and "But I have good reason!" Each TV screen screamed a knee-jerk reaction, a snarky comeback, a logical defense. Each TV screen threatened to obscure what I really needed to hear.

OK, admittedly, I was mildly stoned at the time. But still, this realization was huge for me. Because once I saw my defensiveness for what it was—static that prevented me from really listening—I was able to control it better. Later, when Graeme and I would discuss something touchy, those TV screen defenses would flash before me. But I got better at watching them, analyzing them, and then, like with a remote control, switching them off.

Now that's all nice and good, and we can all pat me on the back for this tiny, tardy, drug-induced step toward maturity, but, still, there was one other thing about Graeme's and my debate style that had to change. Namely, we had to stop trying to win. See, as philosophy majors, Graeme and I were used to spouting forth vociferously, stubbornly, and convincingly (or so we hoped) on just about anything. The goal was not to discover some Socratic capital-*T* Truth, but to outwit, outshine, outmaneuver, and outshout one's opponent. (Opponent?) For our household's harmony, this had to change. The goal, we soon realized, could no longer be to win, one person over the other, one argument over the other, no matter the carnage, no matter the cost. Because the cost, we could see, was our relationship.

Now I'm not saying we're total cop-outs, like getting married means we've turned off our brains and act like we're all Zen and shit. What I am saying is that, in the end at least, Graeme and I are—have to be—on the same side. Not his side. Not my side. But *our* side.

The next day, watching low-lying Funafuti sink into the blue of the sea behind *Dragonfly*, I ask Graeme, "Was last night really as bad as I remember?"

"What? The things he said?" Graeme asks. "Or the way you pointed your finger at him and essentially told him he was a racist jerk?"

I cringe. "All of it."

Graeme flips open the cap on the sunblock tube and starts rubbing it on his stubbly cheek and chin. "Yeah. It was bad," he says. "He was definitely out of line. And"—Graeme looks at me and cocks his eyebrows—"you definitely took his bait."

I remember how last night Graeme, much more calmly and reasonably than I, had argued against the Hobbit's outlandish statements at the beginning of the debate until he saw that it was a lost cause. That our Bilbo, like Tolkien's hobbit, was looking for fireworks, looking for spectacle, and perhaps had an insidious evil ring in his pocket to boot. That's when Graeme, besides offering occasional refereeing, had simply bowed out. For some reason, I could not.

"Well, sorry for screwing up the evening. Sorry for being so pugnacious," I say. "It's just . . . in my nature."

Graeme nods, rubs a splurt of sunblock on his nose, and says, "I know how you are with your justice thing."

In a flash, my TV wall of defenses stacks before my eyes, urging me to defend my "justice thing." I resist.

Graeme says, "You were right, Janna. You were fighting the good fight. I agreed with everything you said." He hands me the orange tube of SPF 50. "I just didn't agree with *how* you said it."

A TV screen flickers.

"Plus, we were dinner guests on their boat," Graeme adds. "So, you know, maybe your timing wasn't so good."

Another screen flares.

I reach out and rub a spot on his forehead. With his slapdash style, he never seems to get the sunblock fully and evenly distributed. But there are other things he attends to quite well, things he generally takes time and care with. Like me.

And the last TV screen fades to greenish black. And dies.

Part 6

Micronesia

20

The Mixed Bag

Our passage to Kiribati is plagued by bad timing. Not that there's a storm or a (total) mechanical breakdown or anything, but there's no wind, so it's slow crossing the equator, going the other direction this time. We throw a few jiggers of cheap whiskey over the side for the VIP ocean gods, trying to make up in quantity what our offering lacks in quality. And, practically puffing out our cheeks to blow wind into the sails, we try to figure out if we can make it to port in four days or five. I'm feeling queasy again, so I'm hoping for an impossible three. Turns out to be almost six.

Which you'd think would make landfall a huge relief. Except that Kiribati is another nation of atolls: low-lying, dry, sun-baked atolls. And, after a couple weeks already in Tuvalu, we don't experience that same surge of joy when Kiribati appears low and, therefore, late on the horizon.

Nor does the joy come when, on our first full day in port, Graeme and I get into, not the good fight, but the bad fight. I'm below, tapping away on my laptop, when Graeme announces he's ready to go ashore. He always does this, declaring that it's time to go without any warning, as though he's the official timekeeper on board. I look up from my screen. "OK. In a minute." I duck my head back into my writing.

Fifteen minutes later, having lost track of time in a particularly prickly paragraph, I look up and see Graeme sitting with his arms crossed in the cockpit. *Shitfuck.* I snap my laptop shut, hustle into the head to pee and brush my teeth, replace my shorts with a skirt, rush around the boat gathering sunglasses, hat, purse, book (just in case), and climb out into the cockpit. Then I begin slathering sunblock on my arms, face, and neck. Midslather, I turn around, scramble back below to hunt for my camera, grab a tube of chapstick, and pull my hair into what, with sunblocked hands, will be a very greasy ponytail. I emerge again. And smile.

Graeme does not.

"What?" I say. "I'm ready."

"I was ready a half hour ago," he says.

I look down at my watch, realize I've forgotten it, and go back below to get it. "Well," I say, stepping back into the cockpit, "maybe next time you could tell me the specific time you want to leave. And give me more of a heads-up beforehand."

"Maybe next time you could stop writing when I've said I want to go ashore," he counters. "There's only one way off this boat, so it's not like I have a choice; I can't go anywhere until you get around to being ready."

"Well," I say, "*I* feel constantly rushed. Like I never have enough time for anything. And I'm always worried that, at any moment, you're going to call time-out." I check my purse for eye solution in case my contacts get dried out ashore, then realize I forgot to put my contacts in. *Shitfuck.* "Plus, while I was finishing up writing and getting ready," I say, "you could have read a book or done a small project or"—I sniff the air and crinkle my nose—"brushed your teeth."

OK, so even with all we've learned, Graeme and I still don't always fight fair. And this fight in particular is nothing new. Timing is one of our oldest and stubbornest issues, one that keeps, like the cat in the song, coming back . . . if not the very next day, at least eventually. Lots of my girlfriends back home struggle with timing in their relationships, too, but unlike many issues married couples face, this one doesn't seem to divide along gender lines. Which is another way of saying that my slowness drives some of my friends crazy, too.

One of my girlfriends, for example, is on Graeme's side of the clock; she's nicknamed her husband and me the Pokey People. And, through many heart-to-hearts, she's helped me see how frustrating and annoying and disrespectful my pokiness must seem to Graeme. I *get* it—and yet there's no quick fix. I, on the other hand, have helped my friend understand that (1) managing time probably doesn't come easily to her husband; and (2) no, he isn't purposely trying to piss her off; and (3) like me, he probably just likes to have his ducks in a row (camera, chapstick, eye solution, sunblock) before going anywhere or doing anything. Things take longer for people like us. He and I have a motto when we're together: *Pokey People unite . . .*

eventually!

So, after Graeme and I torture each other in the heat of the cockpit with a long, nasty fight, we eventually cool down to solving our current timing issue. We reiterate all the old promises—clear communication, upfront expectations, respect for each other's differences, yadda yadda yadda—and then Graeme suggests an ingenious solution, one I wish we'd thought of a long time ago.

Two hours after Graeme's initial request to leave, we finally make it to shore and head to the biggest store in town. There we buy one of those dinky blow-up kayaks, the yellow kind with the breathy foot-pump and toylike paddle. From here on out we're a two-skiff family; he's got a kayak, and I a dinghy. Graeme will no longer be stuck waiting for hours, twiddling his thumbs on the boat. He'll no longer be anchored to his hokey, pokey wife.

While my husband may be punctual in his day-to-day life, I'd like to point out that he hasn't always had the best timing when it comes to love. Take, for example, how Graeme dumped me back in college and then gallivanted off to Taiwan to transform into International Business Guy. It took the man *five years* to come crawling back to what I like to call Relationship Round Two. This is the e-mail that popped up in my in-box out of the blue:

From: Graeme Esarey
Sent: Tuesday, October 27, 1996 5:59 PM
To: Janna Cawrse
Subject: Long time no talk

I just got off the phone with your mother. I called her because yesterday my father handed me one of those annual Christmas letters you write, given to him by a fishing buddy who, it turns out, is one of *your* dad's fishing buddies. Small world. At any rate, I owe my first letter to you that you stand any chance of getting (I never sent any of the others) to a bunch of fishermen. Fitting.

At this point Graeme babbles for a couple paragraphs about one of our mutual college buddies, Mike, whom Graeme says I might remember "for his sense of humor and distinct lack of hair." (I do.) Then Graeme recounts his time in Taiwan, working insane hours, sleeping on the couch in his office, learning the ropes of international business. He concludes, "Moving to Taiwan was a big step for me. I found parts of myself over there that I might never have learned about."

This sounds insightful and mature and very promising. Except then Graeme describes all the mountain climbing and kayaking and partying he's been doing since returning to Seattle. I roll my eyes. This guy's an adrenaline junkie with a death wish. Jobless and drifting.

Oh, but then there's this:

Janna, I have to say writing to you is uncomfortable for me, even now. I still get a knot in my stomach when I hear your name. But this is a letter I should have sent you long ago. Regardless of where you are now and who you want to be when you grow up, I still would like to know what you're up to. Put me on that funky Christmas mailing list you send out every year detailing your life, your most recent love, and your goals for the next year. (Rob [another mutual friend] used to read them to me over the phone when I was in Taiwan—somehow *he* managed to stay on your mailing list.)

As for me, my life is in transition. One of these days I'll find my stride again. Wonder where you'll be then, Janna Cawrse?

—Graeme

Oh yeah, my Dad says hello, and that *he'd* take you sailing anytime.

Can you imagine the shock? I mean, really. Half a decade later: "I still get a knot in my stomach when I hear your name." This was swoon-worthy stuff. It harpooned me.

Yet I was indignant, too. Here the guy tosses my heart overboard back when I'm a loveable nag, and now he cruises back into my (somewhat sorted) life to complicate things again. I'm in grad school in Washington, D.C., studying English with a minor in Saving the World. And Graeme, back in Seattle, is a directionless, unemployed businessman, climbing mountains and playing beer pong with his buddies. All play and no work makes Graeme (in my mind) still a boy.

Nevertheless, a steamy six-month e-romance ensues. We volley witticisms and flirtations back and forth—all painstakingly e-crafted of course—and eventually he flies out for a visit. We take a romantic road trip across that vacationer's paradise called . . . Delaware. It's fun. It's intense. And he finally lets me brush his teeth, something I'd drunkenly wanted to do back in college. (At the time he'd refused, and then later I'd come across photos of *another* woman drunkenly brushing his teeth—*no joke*—and we'd fought about it. Oh, the randomness of lovers' quarrels.)

But that's the thing. There's so much history between Graeme and me, both good and bad, that everything with him is loaded. Like a tray in a buffet line. Or a gun. And so—even though in tents across Delaware, Graeme and I click like Dorothy's No-Place-Like-Home slippers—I end up dumping Graeme soon after the trip's over. And I swear it wasn't just out of revenge. That's what people always assume. At the time my reasoning went something like this: Graeme's too immature, too much the same directionless, frenetic partier he was in college. I, on the other hand, have vision. Purpose. I'm moving to New Orleans to join Teach For America and save the world.

Of course I was wrong on both counts; Graeme was not a frenetic partier (just an enthusiastic one), and my New Orleans students, though they needed my teaching, did not need my saving. What I realize now, looking back, is that my inability to love Graeme at that point in my life was really an inability to make peace with myself—the naggy, needy, insecure girl I imagined myself to have been in college. The girl who, my new self cringed, relied on a man for her happiness. Being with Graeme brought up too much shared history, too much *personal* history. So I rejected that immature, insecure girl.

And by association, him.

I mention all this now because Graeme, as in his post-Taiwan year, seems to be in transition again. We're anchored off a pretty little islet in Kiribati, and he's got that parachute book out, the colorful one that's supposed to tell him what his Calling is—or at least how he's supposed to make a living for the next twenty years. Graeme is leaning over the book's slightly mildewed pages, scribbling notes in the margins, making long lists in an old, blank ship's log that, I suppose, might osmose some of its navigational juju to his task. He's hoping, like so many travelers gone before, that this bit of globe trotting will help him find his capital-*P* Purpose. Just like it's helped me find mine.

We're down below on *Dragonfly*, a fan aimed toward each of our spots at the table, and I am, of course, typing away madly. I don't use that word lightly. I am obsessed. I write as often as I can—on watch, every morning, all day if Graeme'll let me. He never does. I even set a daily alarm clock to get up to write at sparrow fart—that's Trish's splendid Kiwiism for crack of dawn. I bound out of bed at 5:30 A.M. like a flea to a dog's haunch, or a fingernail to a scab, or a cannonball prankster into a sunbather-lined pool. I'm hungry. I'm manic. I'm giddy. And lately, in addition to writing articles about sailing (some of which have been accepted, many of which have not), I've got a novel hollering in my ear. I feel downright inspired.

But Graeme doesn't. The novelty of boat work has worn off. The camaraderie of cruising, now that our community has shrunk to about two leapfrogging boats, has dwindled. And he's even getting tired of snorkeling and fishing and the new speargun I got him for his birthday when we were on Wallis Island. This is not like Graeme, to get tired of his toys. It's got me seriously worried.

The other thing that's got me worried is this crazy string of islands we're in. It's a place that, at first blush, looks pretty paradisiacal, but for us at least is anything but. The country's called Kiribati, pronounced "KIDdy-bas" because of a slightly rolled *r* and the fact that American missionaries didn't bother adding a letter *s* to the thirteen-letter alphabet they'd already developed for Hawai'i (apparently Hawai'ian has no *s* sound). The missionaries, in their divine wisdom, figured *ti* could do the *s* job just fine. You be the judge: Can you figure out how to pronounce Kiribati's easternmost island, Kiritimati[1]?

Everything I knew about Kiribati before coming here I learned from J. Maarten Troost's *The Sex Lives of Cannibals.* And even though Troost barely mentions sex *or* cannibals (the two reasons I picked up the book in the first place), it is one funny read. Plus, the man is right; Tarawa, the capital atoll of Kiribati, really is as wacky, dirty, screwed up, and beautiful as he says it is. Which is why Graeme and I checked in with the officials, bought the relationship-salvaging kayak, and scooted north into the outer islands as fast as we could.

Here's a basic primer on the atolls we've seen of late:

---

1. Answer: "Ka-DIS-mas," aka Christmas Island. Tilly mitionarieti (silly missionaries).

1. White sand beaches
2. Turquoise lagoons
3. Green palm trees

I know, I know, that's sort of the refrain out here in the Pacific, and you're probably wondering if I'll ever start singing a different tune. (I won't.) But I swear each island we visit looks like the backdrop to a MasterCard commercial: *Cost to get here? 475 days cooped up on a small boat with your spouse. View? Priceless.*

Graeme, needing to get un-cooped up, convinces me to go for a midday bike ride down the single dirt road of Abaiang atoll. It's not that Graeme's thrilled about becoming a sweaty pig in this heat, it's that he's a frustrated, hyperactive boy who needs something—*anything*—to do. I only say yes because I've already sent him off paddle paddle paddling in his ducky new kayak—twice. Its novelty already threatens to wane. So, despite the heat seeping off the crushed coral road, we head out for an all-island tour.

We haul our bikes ashore and unfold them to the delight of shrieking children. And then we start moving at a leisurely pace—pe-dal pe-dal pe-dal. Slowly we pass sunken wet pits growing green with taro, the only obvious agriculture besides palm trees. Near people's homes, hammocks hang limp. Outrigger canoes sprawl on the beach. A child drags a browning palm frond across her yard. Many of the houses here are open-air, raised structures like the Samoan *fales*—the kind where the inhabitants walk about, as if on stage—only most here are small, modest, and stick-built. No place we've visited has been more traditional than this. Or less touristed.

Micronesia, a broad swath of islands in the western half of the North Pacific, isn't nearly as well known by travelers as Polynesia. These islands are ethnically distinct from their southeastern neighbors, with an earlier timetable of settlement likely starting in 3000 B.C.E. So, even more so than Polynesians, Micronesians are famous for being expert navigators—the best in the world—translating winds and swells and clouds and stars into stick charts they laid out on the sand. Sailors memorized these maps before long voyages. One little sailing canoe we encountered a few days ago ran circles around us—even though its sail was a patchwork of old plastic grain bags.

Besides expert navigation, Micronesians are also known for their hospitality. One man, aloft in a coconut tree collecting sap for a liquor called "toddy," sees us coming. We hear him serenading the sky in a high-pitched trill like a boiling teapot. When we reach his tree, he scrambles down, whacks off the top of a coconut with his machete, and hands it to us to drink. He smiles broadly while we slurp the sweet, fizzy juice and wipe our brows. We think again: Priceless.

But Kiribati is no paradise. For one, there's the heat. It reminds me of that Robin Williams line from *Good Morning, Vietnam*: "It's hot. Hot and wet. Nice when you're with a lady, but not when you're in the jungle"—or on a breeze-deficient coral atoll straddling the equator, I might add. Even I, a woman who's enjoyed priggishly reserved sweat glands all my life, have a sticky, wet streak cascading down my back. Pe-dal pe-dal pe-daling down this dusty track, I look and smell like Pepé Le Pew.

And then there's *this* stinky fact: Beaches in Kiribati multifunction as bathrooms. We discover this firsthand when we prop our bikes against trees and walk the beach at low tide. At first we think the frequent piles of poop are an anomaly, that we've just stumbled upon the local dogs' favorite do-it-up spot. But then we encounter a couple disposable diapers, which prompt Graeme, disgusted by the litter, to say he'll never use disposables on our kids. (*Kids?* I raise my eyebrows.) A few steps on and, with the image of small humans still lingering in his brain, Graeme encounters yet another pyramid of crap. He leans forward and examines it. Almost immediately he straightens up. In a nasally I'm-breathing-through-my-mouth voice he says, "This ain't dog crap. This is human crap."

I squint at the poop. I squint at my husband. And I ask in my I'm-calling-bullshit voice, "Graeme, how on earth do you know the difference?"

And that's when Graeme reveals the unlikely but true story of the Three-Coil Steamer. Back when he was in his first transition mode, fresh home from Taiwan and partying like a rapidly aging rock star, Graeme went to Mike the funny bald guy's cabin for the weekend. There were a dozen or more people there, drinking hard, playing hard, and by sparrow fart everyone had crashed on random beds and couches and pretty much any flat surface they could find. The next morning (afternoon), when everyone was cleaning up the beer bottles and wreckage, one guy stumbled upon a perfectly formed, three-coiled pyramid of shit in the corner of the loft. "Hey!" he yelled out. "Who left the Three-Coil Steamer?" Even though by then it was no longer steaming, the name, like shit on a shoe, stuck.

Despite lethargy and hangovers, everyone at the cabin stampeded upstairs to examine the human pile of poop. (That, Graeme says, is how he gained his human poop identification skills.) But not one of the six guys who'd slept in the loft would claim it. In fact, theories were floated that someone sleeping downstairs had actually snuck up in the middle of the night (sparrow fart) and left it there as a cruel stool joke. Alibis were proffered. Fingers were pointed. No one came forward. He himself, Graeme says, almost lifting his chin in pride, remains a key suspect to this day.

OK, so maybe I was right to dump (if you will) Graeme for his immaturity in Relationship Round Two.

A week and an atoll later, we stumble upon yet another disturbing fact about Kiribati. We're lounging in the comfort of our cockpit when we're told that just last month a mob of angry islanders stoned a man to death. They dumped his body in the lagoon, there—*right there*—just two hundred yards from *Dragonfly*. I follow the pointing finger of Andy, our current guest, toward the shore of Butaritari, our current anchorage. Andy is a Peace Corps volunteer we met this morning. Since there are no other cruising boats around, we thought we'd throw a happy hour for him and his two Peace Corps buddies instead. Now they're regaling us with what it's like to live on a tiny atoll in the middle of the Pacific without electricity or running water or indoor plumbing. An atoll that's just experienced the worst mob violence it's seen in decades.

Now here's the oversimplified *Reader's Digest* version of last month's murder as told by three semidrunk, happily cheese-fed (apparently they crave cheese) Peace Corps volunteers. Off-the-record, of course.

Kiribati basically has two forms of governance. One is the official, modern British-style of government, complete with elected officials and white-wigged barristers. The other is the traditional *unimwane*, or old man, system. Essentially, old men in each village discuss issues until they reach consensus and thereby run the outer islands. Except that recently some folks in Andy's village—Andy points ashore again—had a dispute with one of their old men about, of all things, soccer. They sued the old guy. In retaliation, the order came down from the big-wiggest, badassest, oldest old man on the island that houses must burn.

So one night one month ago, Andy and Timber (another Peace Corps dude currently drinking one of our lukewarm beers) are coming back from another boat's happy hour when they hear yelling. It's late, pitch-black, still deliriously hot out, and the noise carries across the water clear and rumbly. As Andy and Timber climb from the dinghy onto shore, flashlight beams sweep the trees like searchlights. And there right in front of them, crowding the dirt road, is a mob of a hundred guys, armed with sticks, stones, and clubs.

Safe from village politics because they're *I-Matang* (foreigners), Andy and Timber follow the men to see what's going on. Within minutes, a thatch and stick-built house, just down from Andy's own thatch and stick-built house, is ablaze. Another follows. And then Tooni, "drunken Tony," as Andy calls him, walks by and makes some smart-ass comment. The mob pelts Drunken Tooni with stones. Drunken Tooni runs behind a house. Twenty or thirty guys follow and, a few minutes later, emerge, saying Drunken Tooni is dead. The mob throws his body into the lagoon—there, *right there*, Andy points again. The mob continues burning houses into the night.

"No shit?" says Graeme.

"No shit," says Andy.

"Holy shitfuck," says I, feeling a trickle of sweat run down my neck.

Timber, a shaggy dude who's stayed past his two-year Peace Corps commitment and is immune to rufflement, says, "Hey, got any more of that cheese?"

A girlfriend of mine once dated a guy whom her therapist, of all people, set her up with. He'd been the therapist's client, too, which might've been seen as a major warning sign. Instead, my friend and I decided it was lucky—because how many cute, normal, single guys do you find out there *post*-therapy? But as their relationship progressed I started to worry. When my friend would talk about him, the theme she kept coming back to was, in her words, "the mixed bagginess of it all." As in: You gotta take the bad with the good.

Now, I didn't know the guy well. And who was I to judge. But I started feeling protective of my friend, like maybe she was using this line to talk herself into loving a guy she didn't. That's sort of how I feel about Kiribati. I mean, I *want* to enjoy this place, I *want* to give it a chance, I *want* to fall in love with it. But its minuses keep subtracting from its pricelessness.

Though, regardless of the merits or misguidedness of my friend's post-therapy relationship, I now see that her mixed bag theory was dead on. At the time, I didn't really get it, probably because Graeme and I were giddy and sprung and falling in love for Relationship Round Three. It didn't feel so much like a mixed bag to me as a magical one. I blithely thought you could control the mix of traits you allowed in your bag. You know, bar things like bad tempers and jealous natures and thrusty-tongue-kissing, and welcome things like honesty and passion and humor. You could make room for morning breath and cheapness and near-neurotic punctuality, but not the "fag" word or rudeness to waiters or anyone who says you laugh too loud.

But now I'm seeing that the mix you've got in your bag isn't always apparent at the outset. Or, to mix-bag my metaphors, how someone appears in a two-inch paint square from Home Depot doesn't necessarily match how they look over time and space and in different light. People and circumstances, even love, can change.

And so I have to admit I see the mixed bagginess of my husband more clearly these days. He's casting about for a capital-*P* Purpose. He's restless and impatient and bored. And his usual fun-and-games have lost their fun. We're hot. We're atoll-overloaded. We're sailing without the safety net of cruising friends. And, to make matters worse, our SSB radio is on the fritz, so I can't easily e-mail my girlfriends back home for support. While I still love my husband (of course) and I still love cruising (for the most part), I understand a bit more about that thing called bad timing. And especially the mixed bagginess of it all.

Tick Tock

i used to be the kind of person who walked into a public bathroom and immediately, unconsciously, started analyzing which stall was the least trafficked. I figured people who *really* had to go would rush into the first. But then most people, not wanting to enter the most-used stall, would pass the first for the second. And then lots of people, seeking privacy, would go to the last stall. But if that was a disabled access stall, then they might go to the one just before that. Which would mean a middle stall would be least trafficked. But which middle stall? And if there were only three stalls to begin with . . .

In other words, my mind never sat still. I mulled over *everything*: Which brand/size/type of tampons to buy. My myriad excuses for being pokey. Why some orgasms felt better than others (not that I was complaining about any of them). I analyzed it all. And, like choosing the One to marry, I was certain that there was some Right Answer, some Best Explanation, some Most Effective Plan, and if I didn't figure it out or if I made the wrong choice, I would woefully regret it for the rest of my life. Which I often did (make the wrong choice). And did (woefully regret it)—at least for a good long while.

Harumph.

We're riding bikes along the curving, jungle-lined roads of Kosrae, and looking up, I realize Graeme's way ahead of me, not a speck on the horizon exactly, but a midsize mote floating away. There's a slight headwind, and I wish he would slow down; doesn't he realize that, wearing this flowy skirt and carrying my dog-attack stick, I can't ride as fast as he can? I hitch up my skirt to a somewhat immodest level and start pedaling harder.

Harumph.

Anyway, this overanalyzing of *everything* became somewhat of a problem, to the point that my therapist gave me a mantra to control it. OK, *mantra* is way too mystical a word for what she actually gave me. It was more like a radio jingle. Every time I found my thoughts swirling out of control, I was supposed to sing "Zippedy doo dah, zippedy . . . ." Seriously. Because the beginning was meant to remind me to turn off my thoughts like zipping my lips. *Zzzziiiip.* Plus the rest of the song was upbeat . . . about as chipper as my old roommate's "Good MOORning!" after three cups of coffee and her regular B.M. (*Very* chipper).

The crazy thing is that the zipping song worked. Well, mostly. At least I was able to identify the mental slosh I'd rather not waste my brain space on. Instead of worrying that my co-worker thought I was neurotic at the copy machine that morning, I could think about things that really mattered. Like, for example, my latest quandary, the one all childless thirty-something women are doomed to grapple with: the ticking clock of fertility.

Though that's *not* what I'm thinking about right now. Because nothing, I realize as I pedal pedal pedal past an ancient stone wall, has been as effective at harnessing my mind spew as this new obsession of mine: writing. Even though my mind still runs as fast as ever, instead of wasting brain waves on imagined explanations to cops for speeding infractions or arguments for why Graeme should put the toilet seat down, I am building characters, twisting plots, and writing constantly in my head. Which is good, since Graeme's still not willing to let me spend entire days sweating at my computer, ignoring this tropical playground. Without many cruisers around, he wants a constant playmate. And I, despite the lack of fuzzy ears and hot pink hot pants, am the mate with whom (for better or for worse) he has to play.

Harumph.

Thankfully Kosrae (ko-shry), an island in the Federated States of Micronesia, is a place that's good for play. It is finally and gloriously *not* an atoll, but rather a tall, lush, *land*-like island with mountains to hike and mangroves to explore and ancient ruins to time travel through. It's just too bad that Graeme and I have been ruffling each other's feathers lately.

Kosrae, called the Island of the Sleeping Lady, has a distinctive ridgeline that looks like an old man holding a beer stein doing a jig. Just kidding. You can't miss the reclining lady; her flattish face and flowing hair is silhouetted quite clearly. As we wend our way around Lelu Island, which is connected to the main island by a causeway, I can see the Lady every now and then through breaks in the trees. The most obvious feature she boasts are her breasts. Tits really, because they're mountains so conelike it's as though Madonna of the Blonde Ambition Tour posed three million years ago for the island's tectonic-plate-shifting Maker. Though the Sleeping Lady's fertility-goddess boobs are not what I'm thinking about right now, of course. No, no. I'm trying to figure out how Lily, the protagonist of my novel (a young woman like me and yet not), is going to fall back in love with her fiancé in any believable manner by the end of the—

BOW! WOW! WOOF! WOOF! WOOF!

"Bad dog! Bad dog!" I yell shrilly, waving my stick like a geriatric pontificate directing traffic from a front stoop. A black-and-white blur lunges at my bare ankles. I send out a spastic kick with my right foot, wobble precariously, then swerve around Graeme, who's leapt from his bike to throw stones from the side of the road. I weave on, pulse clattering, and eventually look back to see Graeme remounting his bike. He beelines two more stones at the barking dog, who is finally retreating, and waves his long stick as one last warning.

"Oh my God," I say as Graeme pulls even to where I am stopped, lungs seizing, under the shade of a plumeria tree. We look back toward the dog; it's definitely gone. "That was the closest one's ever come to actually biting me," I say. My shoulders heave. Nerves prickle my hairline.

"Yeah," Graeme says, balancing his stick on his handlebars. "He got pretty close. I was surprised you stayed on that side of the road. Didn't you see him?"

An old TV screen of defensiveness flickers on. "No, I guess I didn't. I was sort of spacing out," I say.

The wind off the beach sifts our words like flour.

"Were you, by any chance, thinking about . . . mmm, let's guess . . . your novel?" Graeme prods, leaning down to pick up a few fresh stones for ammo.

"Yeah, but what's wrong with that?" A whole wall of TV screens flashes before me.

"Well, we're not on vacation at some gated resort here, Janna. You might want to pay attention."

I say nothing. I mount my bike and start pedal pedal pedaling into the wind, my skirt flapping in time. Soon Graeme is pedaling by my side.

"I'm just saying you might want to focus on being *here* sometimes," he says. "We are in a pretty amazing place." We pass a yard with a small orchard of Kosrae's unusual green tangerines; their scent is sharp and heady. "Why don't you write about all this?" Graeme's stick motions to *Dragonfly* and one other lone sailboat at anchor in the bay.

"I'm getting bored writing for men, Graeme. It's mostly men who read those sailing magazines." I try to keep the whine out of my voice. "I want to write about something I care about."

Graeme casts another glance at *Dragonfly*, his pride and joy, then stares ahead at the road. "Is that your way of saying you don't care about this? You're bored with our trip?" he asks stonily. I imagine there's a wall of TV screen defensiveness in his mind now, too.

I hear a car downshifting behind us, and I duck back into single file. It's an old white pickup, the steering wheel on the wrong side of the cab, likely a castoff from Japan. Kids of all ages are piled in the flatbed of the truck.

I'm not sure how to respond to Graeme's question. It's not that I'm sick of sailing—though I have been getting seasick more often, and that definitely sucks. Still, I'm not bored with our trip . . . not really. I mean, look at those kids smiling and shouting at us, the crazy joy of their wide mouths and flailing arms and black hair flying in their eyes. How could I be sick of that? I pedal pedal pedal even faster to slow their progress past me.

But I suppose I am getting ready for something new. Something different. Which is maybe why I've been throwing myself so fully into my writing. Or why I've been thinking more and more about kids.

One of the girls turns her wave into more of a silly, shaking movement, her latté-colored palms flat and fluttering like tambourines. The other kids see her gesture and catch on. Now all their hands are flashing and shaking, mad butterflies, threatening to lift the truck right off the road.

I steady myself, raise my stick, and wave it gamely back.

Before coming to Kosrae, we visited one last atoll: Majuro, the capital of the Marshall Islands. While there we volunteered for a few days at a local vet clinic. Actually, it wasn't local at all; there's not a single veterinarian in the whole country, so a vet from Guam flew in and set up a temporary clinic in the high school science classroom. People brought their pets in for checkups and de-wormings and the expressing of anal glands (Scout's personal fave of vet techniques). Really, though, the goal was to put a cap on the rampant dog population, since children being bitten, even mauled, by dogs is not uncommon. It was the antithesis of a fertility clinic: The vet neutered and spayed as many dogs as she could in five days.

Figuring we'd seen enough white sand beaches, turquoise lagoons, and waving palm trees for a while (even Graeme admitted he was getting a bit bored by that particular refrain of our sailing life), Graeme and I volunteered to help. I shuffled paperwork. But Graeme, the only male volunteer, was recruited to assist the vet in catching, anesthetizing, and tying the tubes or lopping the balls off some of the most badass, mangy, flea-ridden mongrels I've ever seen.

Graeme got pretty good at using muzzles, and his once needle-phobic arms found themselves up to their elbows in dog bellies—clamping, pressing, holding back whatever intestines, bladders, and pink pulsing organs the vet pointed at. For a guy who once tried to murder a chocolate Lab by not letting her pee onshore, this seemed fitting comeuppance. At the end of the week, the vet even said Graeme had a knack for vet work. I nudged Graeme and suggested he add *that* to the margins of his parachute book.

Joking aside, Graeme really did just save, if not my ass, then at least my bare ankles on this bike ride around Kosrae. And he did it with such finesse, such verve—a new development since we volunteered at that vet clinic on Majuro. Graeme now approaches mad, barking, chasing dogs with the confidence of someone who's played God over—snip snip—a dog's nether parts.

Which I find doubly ironic. One, because, lately, the nether parts of the humans aboard *Dragonfly* have sort of been nipped in the bud, too. We're back to our old habits of trying to squeeze sex in at night, after long days working on the boat or tying dogs' tubes or, here in Kosrae, exploring the island by bike. And though this is nothing like the rat race back home, we are pretty tuckered out by the end of the day. So, well, you know. Sex happens sometimes. And then sometimes it doesn't. Which worries me, because I've always thought of sex as a barometer for the health of a relationship. Oh, but maybe that's just my whirring mind creating needless worry. *(Zzzziiiip.)*

The other part of the irony, though, is that, like I said, my mind has been mulling over something that really does matter these days. The prospect of having kids. Or, to be honest, not really *having* kids at all, but that other part: simply trying to get pregnant. Which, closing in on thirty-five, is not only whir-worthy, but actually quite worrisome.

"Why don't they teach you this stuff in school?" I ask Mom, referring to, of all things, egg-white-looking cervical fluid, which, I've recently learned, one might stretch between thumb and forefinger to gauge one's fertility on a given day. But Mom's just as baffled as I am as she watches me imitate a bird's beak with my two fingers. I'm telling her about what I read last night in the book that she brought me, across thousands of miles of ocean, from one of my girlfriends back home. It's the so-called fertility bible, and my veteran mom seems the perfect person to discuss it with.

Graeme and I have been honeymooning for a year and a few months now, and Mom and Dad are visiting for our second Christmas abroad. [Insert happy jig here.] They've come bearing four huge suitcases, two of which are filled with gifts, boat parts, and various American things we can't get out here—like Graeme's sailing magazines, Kernel Season's popcorn seasoning, a gallon jug of holding tank cleaner, and, uh, fertility books.

Mom's always liked travel, whether it's in some far-flung place like Kosrae or bumping down backroads in her own backyard. Dad, on the other hand, pretty much only goes places where there's fishing. He's in luck. He and Graeme hired a local guide and headed out this morning at sparrow fart; we don't expect them back till afternoon. Which is fine by me, as Graeme and I could use some space apart, and I've missed long talks with Mom something fierce. Plus, I've got some questions right now that maybe a mom can answer. Like: How does one go about deciding whether or not to have kids? And how do you know when you're ready for them? And, more important, how do you know when your relationship's ready? I mean, Graeme's still a boy boasting about Three-Coil Steamers; is it OK to have kids when one of you is still a kid himself?

"Oh, honey," Mom says. "Things have changed so much since I was making babies."

She twirls a huge red-and-white umbrella on her shoulder to shade her from the sun. She plucked it from a bucket of umbrellas propped for visitors at the trailhead to the Lelu ruins, a royal city dating back to the 1400s. Mom and I walk along a stone roadbed with a twelve-foot wall of huge, loglike stones towering to our right. If the wall hadn't been standing for the past six hundred years, you'd think it might topple any minute.

"Even though your dad and I waited five years before having kids,"

Mom says, "which was quite unusual back then, we were still in our midtwenties when we finally did. And you, at least, weren't exactly planned."

"Best mistake you ever made," I say.

"That's right." She smiles. "But we knew so little back then. I was breast-feeding your brother and thought I couldn't get pregnant. This stuff you're reading about fertility and family planning is light-years beyond where I was."

Little placards along our walk indicate the functions of various stone piles and rooms in this royal labyrinth. The smooth rug of gray stones beneath our feet, one says, was the kitchen; I imagine the half wall in front of me as a cupboard.

"Kids were sort of just something you did," Mom continues. "A foregone conclusion, a next step." We stare down at worn bowls in great slabs of stone where servants ground kava, an intoxicating drink popular throughout the Pacific. "I don't really remember discussing the ifs and whens of kids." Mom shrugs her shoulders. The ridiculously large umbrella lifts and falls with them. "I just put one foot in front of the other, did what was done."

It makes me sad when Mom talks like this, like she's been the passenger, not the driver, in her own life. When I've asked about her childhood and early adulthood, she usually only has faint memories; it all seems a blur, she's said more than once. Perhaps this is an effect of being brought up when children were seen, not heard. Or being a young woman when men, as she would say, "called the shots."

Though this retiring type of woman is decidedly not who I knew growing up. Strong and independent, my mom was never president of the PTA, but she taught my Camp Fire group how to provision external frame backpacks, attend to blisters on the trail, bury poop, and hang food in trees to keep it safe from bears. She was attentive and aware and expert at lots of things—never shied away, in her parenting life, from tackling the hard stuff. My mom was always and totally present for me. Still is.

So her seeming amnesia when it comes to her own life baffles me. Makes me wonder if Graeme's right, that instead of lofting my head into imaginary worlds, I should be paying closer attention to my own world right here, right now, while I still have the chance. Because maybe that's what happens when you have kids—your life becomes subsumed by all the logistics and minutiae of your family's, your children's, life. Maybe you get lost in the shuffle.

"Does it make you sad that you can't remember those details?" I ask Mom.

"Not when it comes to childbirth," Mom grins.

I snort a laugh.

"But I don't know, honey. Sometimes it's frustrating, sure. Though I suppose it's just part of growing old." We're under a cool canopy of trees now, and she runs her fingertips along the twenty-foot-high pyramid crypt, the oldest in the ruins. Mom closes her eyes and breathes in its dark, shady scent. "It's a gift, honey," she says. "Growing old is a gift."

Though getting older doesn't seem like a gift when you're thirty-four and childless. When *Time* magazine says you should have your first baby by thirty-five. When half a dozen of your girlfriends back home are struggling with Clomid and turkey basters and IVF while you sail glibly across the ocean—not even a high-powered career (like in all those magazine articles) to defend your maternal tardiness. I can hear the tick, and I can hear the tock, but it's not coming from my belly. I have no internal maternal urge shouting: *Want to be pregnant now!* The clock is outside me, ding-donging like Cinderella's good-times curfew, ticktocking like a biological croc stalking our boat.

Oh the irony. How we spend our most fertile years trying desperately *not* to get pregnant, and then . . . well, you know the drill. I recall one girlfriend saying, after almost two years of trying to conceive, that sometimes she'd see women in their early twenties and want to rush up to them, shake their shoulders, and holler, "GET PREGNANT NOW WHILE YOU STILL CAN!" It occurs to me now that maybe her message was meant for me. Though her urge seemed ridiculous to me at the time. I mean, it's not like you can click your heels and procure the partner, the finances, the emotional stability, and the overall sense that you're—*ta-daah*—ready to be a mom. Those things take time. In Graeme's and my case, thirteen on-and-off years. And counting.

The weird thing, I'm realizing, about deciding when to get pregnant is that, really, you can only decide when to stop trying *not* to get pregnant. You can pull the goalie. But after that, it's pretty much beyond your control. Even with ovulation kits and sex on a schedule and standing on your head, you might never conceive or it might take years—with or without fertility treatments. Then again, you always have to be prepared for the fact that you might get preggo lickety-split. Like Lisa and Marc on *Nahanni*, out in the middle of the Pacific. And while they were chill about integrating pregnancy and childbirth into their sailing itinerary, I'm not sure Graeme and I are there yet.

In fact, I'm not quite sure *where* Graeme and I are.

Except literally of course. Here we sit, Christmas Day, swaying to some of the most beautiful music I've heard in a church or otherwise. Only it's nothing like Christmas services back home, no matter what kind of funky, jazz-guitarist, holy-moley ministry you attend. This is Kosrae's utterly unique tradition, a practice you won't find anywhere else in the world except where Kosraens have immigrated. It's called Christmas marching.

Imagine a hundred men, women, and children—men sporting black pants and white button-downs, women wearing cotton floral dresses all cut from the same cloth—marching in precise choreography. Lines and rows. Swirling patterns. Stars and arches and box steps. Like a high school marching band, only without a football field or instruments. Instead, each competing troupe sway-marches down the aisle of the church and performs moves at the front, where it looks like a third of the pews have been removed. They march to the rhythm of their own singing, a complex soaring and dipping three-part harmony in the Kosraen tongue, with a soprano that sounds almost like wailing at the top. Some of the women hold poles topped with garlanded and glittered cardboard stars; they swing them in unison or raise them into arches for others to snake through. The men also carry decorative props, cardboard circles the size of hubcaps, some with letters spelling M-E-R-Y-R X-M-A-S (one of the little boys got out of order). These they punch forward at times, or hold up over their heads, or simply swing back and forth like a top hat in the hands of a slow-motion Fred Astaire.

Being foreigners, we are seated in the front pews as guests of honor. The ushers insisted. Children sit cross-legged and fidgety on the floor in front of us. As a new troupe enters the church, the middle-aged women of the group reach into plastic bags and toss out goodies, like in a Mardi Gras parade—only you don't have to flash anything but a smile for a prize. The most common items flung are lollipops, hard candies, sticks of gum. But there's also the occasional flying Tupperware bowl, kitchen towel, or cooking spatula. And one woman marching by in a fuchsia dress leans over my father and gives my mother a hand-carved manta ray, made from a single piece of warm, polished wood—it would retail for fifty dollars in the gift shop down the road. Mom tries to protest the extravagance of the gift, but her Mrs. Claus has already marched on.

There's no preaching, no praying, no offering plate. There are no lowing cows, no fake-bearded shepherds, no talk of Mary's conception—immaculate or otherwise. Just troupe after troupe, marching in, singing and swirling, and marching out. I enjoy watching the children the most. The girls look radiant, the adolescent boys sullen, and the littlest ones sway frequently out of step.

Maybe it's time I get in step, I think. Start working on a family. Realize my life doesn't have to be All About Me.

Maybe.

A dimpled girl marching in the front row eyes a stray candy on the floor and can't resist stepping out of line to bend and pick it up. I laugh almost out loud watching her. Then I take Graeme's hand in my left, peck him on the cheek, and squeeze. I take Mom's hand, to my right, and squeeze again. All these voices, all these families, all these children . . . this is more beautiful than any church service I've ever seen. And I feel fully here, wholly present at this joyous celebration of a little baby's birth.

The Space Between

*M*om and Dad have returned home to our old dog, Scout, and their new bird, Dave. They didn't have a bird when Graeme and I set sail a year and a half ago. And so I'm learning there are things you miss while traveling the world—the birth of a niece, the death of a dear friend's dog, weddings, the Passion Party™ where my girlfriends ate crustless cucumber sandwiches, passed dildos around the living room, and made sex jokes that (apparently) the Passion Consultant™ did *not* appreciate. Important things happen while you're gone; things change. All you get are secondhand tales.

Though Mom and Dad's bird story is pretty good even months later. Dad was over at his friend Dave's house when he saw a parakeet in a tree in the yard. Dad, who, in his twenties, had a parakeet before Mom accidentally drowned it, walked up to the tree and held out his finger. Dave (the bird, not the human) hopped on. After a halfhearted search for the bird's owner, Dad took him home and taught him to say things like "C'mere Scout!" and "I tought I taw a puddy-tat" and (in honor of Dad's friend) "My name is Dave!" Now every time the name Dave comes up in (human) conversation, it must be clarified whether the referent is Dave-the-Bird or Dave-the-Human, e.g., "Dave-the-human and I went fishing the other day," Dad'll say.

Which shows how some things actually never do change. Dad's sense of humor. My love for his stories. And the fact that a good name is hard to find.

•   •   •

"Then what name would our *kid* have?" Graeme asks a month after Mom and Dad's departure, on the island of Pohnpei, in a debate about what our married name should be. (You'd think we'd have figured that out by now.) "Gertrude Wilhelmina Esarey-Cawrse? *That's* a mouthful. And what happens when she gets married to some other victim of forward-thinking hyphenating parents? Gertrude Wilhelmina Esarey-Cawrse-Schmidt-Taylor?"

Kid? my mind jolts. But I say, "Who cares what our kid does. She can drop both names, or just one, or keep both, or make up a new one; that's her decision. But this, Graeme, is *our* decision. And if giving up your name or having a different name from your kid is so easy, then why don't *you* do it?"

This is not the first time Graeme and I have discussed (a euphemism for what's really going on) the Great Name Change Dilemma. It's one of our "issues." So big and bitter that, when Graeme and I finally got over the Royal Our (his) wedding issue, I almost thought the Royal Our (my) name issue might be a deal breaker. It felt *that* huge. Our solution was to put the decision off. We kept our own names when we got married, vowing to come up with a real solution somewhere down the road.

Which is exactly where we are right now. Bumping down a dusty dirt road in a rented blue truck with our dinghy and outboard engine stuffed in the flatbed as cargo. We're on the round-island road of Pohnpei, a lush, mountainous island with a lagoon and fringing reef—and a couple great surf breaks the local surfers are trying to keep hush-hush. Instead Pohnpei is famous, in the relative sense of the word, for the ruins of the ancient floating city of Nan Madol, sometimes called the Venice of the Pacific. Today we're road tripping south to go explore it. Only instead of having that heady, feet-on-the-dashboard, life-as-a-soundtrack feeling, we're doing that other common road trip thing: arguing.

The truck we rented for fifty-eight bucks from Senny's Car Rental doesn't have AC, or at least AC that works, so we've got the windows down and I'm holding my hair back in an effort to keep it from delivering fifty lashes to my face. We pass modest homes and sleepy roadside stores and small thatch shelters with wooden stools bellied up to the bar—all silent for this, the hottest part of the day. Though the bars won't be quiet tonight; they're *sakau* bars, where Pohnpeians get drunk (or whatever kind of high it is) on the traditional beverage made from kava roots. Peterson, the attendant at the gas dock where we come ashore each day, says it's a bit like drinking mud puddle—"But good!" he assures us, running a pink tongue over discolored teeth and smacking his lips. I've read *sakau* numbs your mouth, glassies your eyes, and makes you think the world is a pretty chill place. Peterson, a *sakau* aficionado who wears dark sunglasses and leans back precariously in a white plastic chair on the dock all day, is a pretty chill dude.

Though I personally am not chill right now. At all. I'm hot. And sticky. And pissed off.

I don't know why the name issue infuriates me so much. I mean, I've got plenty of strong, independent, feminist girlfriends who've taken their husbands' names, and their decision doesn't bother me at all. But then again, their names are not my name. And their husbands are not my husband who, seven years ago, in another rental car driving across that vacationer's paradise called . . . Delaware, assured me *he'd* be willing to hyphenate, "or whatever," for his wife. "Hell," he'd said, and I quote, "I'd even change my name to hers."

The amnesia must have set in right after I dumped him.

But the thing is, I don't *want* Graeme to change his last name to mine in a simple role reversal of the patriarchal tradition I'm trying to buck. I want something fair, something mutually inclusive, something of which we can both be proud. Hyphenation seems an obvious, if cumbersome, solution. Though I'm open to any solution, as long as it meets these two criteria:

1. I'd like to share a last name with my partner and my kids. (Kids!)
2. As a gesture toward fairness, I'd like both Graeme and me to make some sort of change, even if it's not a totally equal change. (I'm not naïve; I realize somebody's name has to come first.)

Graeme says he agrees with both these principles on principle. And yet, when the bald rubber tires of our rental truck hit the road, he just can't bring himself to agree to change *his* name at all.

"Car," Graeme says.

Which reminds me of *Wayne's World* when they play hockey in the middle of the street and have to haul away the goal every time a car comes. Though the scene in the movie isn't nearly as funny as how my girlfriend used to yell, out-of-the-blue and non sequitur–like, "Car!"—short and clear, just like that—and we would momentarily set aside whatever we were doing. And burst out laughing. And then resume our respective activities.

No laughter today though, not a tremor. And even if I could laugh right now, Graeme wouldn't get it. So I roll roll roll up my window with pursed lips and pinched fingers; the rotating knob at the end of the handle is missing. I get the window up just in time. Dust billows around us as the other car, a speeding black sedan with yellow polyester fringe hanging in the back window, buzzes by. And then, a hundred yards behind him, comes a line of cars and trucks and things that go, one after another, in a South Seas simulation of, of all things, traffic, making the biggest, baddest dust cloud you could imagine on an otherwise deserted dirt road.

But I'm not distracted. I forge ahead. "Well, what do *you* propose we do about our names?" I ask in a puckered voice, trying to keep the hot rage I feel from spilling over my eyes and onto my cheeks and into my fist and up Graeme's nose. My whole body is clenched like one big massive sphincter. I don't know how Graeme can agree with me on a rational level and yet not *act* ("I just can't do it" is his common refrain). This feels hypocritical to me. Like someone who believes being a vegetarian is the right thing to do, and yet eats meat anyway.

Oh wait. That's me.

OK. Scratch that. *Here's* what it's like. You know those issues, those BIG issues, the ones that really get to you, even if they seem small or inconsequential to other people? The ones that billow out like huge, carbon-emitting exhaust clouds and dirty everything—your partner's character, his upbringing, his judgment, your own judgment for having married him? The issues that make you look at your partner and feel like he must not know you. Or understand you. Or care about you. Or really love you?

That's what the stupid name issue does for me.

I have a girlfriend back home who dated a guy for like ten years before actually marrying him. After their wedding, I asked her if anything had really changed—because I myself, in my postnuptial months, wasn't so sure anything really had. But she said, yes, *everything* had changed. Because now, instead of having a fight and reevaluating their entire relationship, worrying if this would be where their two paths diverged . . . now, she said, a fight was just a speed bump, a diamond planter, a construction zone to get past on their mutual road of life.

And while that's certainly a perky, upbeat metaphor, I'm always caught off guard by how truly miserable the really big construction zones in a relationship are. The noise, the grit, the piles of dirt and rubble, the holes that gape open menacingly and threaten never to close. Mutual ground is hard to find. That "our side" that Graeme and I usually seek out in fights disappears amid the jaw-clattering of jackhammers and the yellow caution color of earth movers.

The dust from the passing cars clears, and Graeme rolls his window back down. He drives on silently, concentrating on the rutted road. I wrestle my window down, too. And then, after a mile or two, we come to a long line of stopped cars with a man waving a red sign far ahead. We've heard the government is paving the entire round-island road of Pohnpei. Here are the cement rollers and dump trucks to prove it. It looks like it's going to be a long wait, so Graeme turns off the engine. We bake in the deafening heat.

Finally, I can't stand it any longer. I hate it when I've asked Graeme a question and he doesn't respond. "Well?" I say.

Graeme casts me a vacant-lot look.

"Well, what do you think we should do about the name thing?" I cross my arms.

Graeme taps his fingers on the steering wheel and sighs. "I don't know what we should do about the name thing, Janna." His voice sounds drained. He wipes a trickle of sweat from his temple. "Maybe figure it out down the road?" he says. "When we really have to?"

There's a white engineer guy, sweating in shirt and tie, laying out plans across a big boulder on the side of the road. Two Pohnpeians in hard hats gather round. They nod when he points to the paper and to the road and to the paper again.

"And when will that be?" I ask Graeme, annoyed.

He looks at me. "When we have kids."

After a thirty minute wait, each of us broiling in our own thoughts, the dirt road becomes a paved road becomes a swift turn down a side road that dead-ends at a small rocky beach. Before us sheets a shape-shifty lagoon whose color, depending on water depth, goes from dark blue to turquoise to cerulean. The famous floating city, our guidebook says, is just around the corner, south of us. I crane my neck but don't see any cities, floating or otherwise, so I help Graeme haul out the dinghy, pump up its inflatable tubes, and launch it into the warm salty water. We don't talk much. Within fifteen minutes, Graeme's got the engine full throttle and I'm in my traditional spot on the bow, leaning out over the front of the dinghy, flying over the smooth water of the lagoon.

This is one of my favorite things, riding like this, a human bowsprit. It reminds me of when I was a kid and would go fishing with my dad; I'd sing camp songs at the top of my lungs, half-dreading, half-hoping that the wind carried my words in coherent phrases back to his ears. I still don't know if it did. But older now, with Graeme as my ferryman, I still sing camp songs sometimes. Or in the evenings I lean out over the water with a beer bouncing in my hand and laugh as the liquid foams and erupts down my arm.

But today I'm not singing, or toasting the lagoon racing beneath our boat. I'm sweaty. I'm hungry. And I feel unsettled by Graeme's and my unsettled argument on the drive down. My usual delight at this sort of adventure is muted, like a twelve-piece band playing some ten thousand leagues under the sea. Soon though, with the outboard engine slowed to an idle, we're entering a narrow canal into a labyrinth of man-made islands. Nan Madol.

It's a curious thing, why people would construct almost a hundred tiny islands in this lagoon when there's a perfectly good island just a stone throw's away—the jungly green shore of Pohnpei lies to our right. Carbon dating puts human habitation on Nan Madol at 200 B.C.E. Its heyday, though, came much later, during the brutal Saudeleur dynasty between 1200 and 1600 C.E. Archaeologists imagine it as a magnificent royal city of islets and canals. No one really knows why it was abandoned.

Graeme cuts the engine and we drift to the towering island of Nan Douwas, where an attendant, sitting under a spindly tree with thin green leaves, takes our three-dollar entrance fee. Nan Douwas is the fortress island, surrounded by walls twenty-five feet high built of stacked hexagonal basalt logs. No mortar. Even though these walls are hundreds of years old, and buffeted by wind and waves, many still stand without anything besides themselves holding them together. Would that Graeme and I could do the same.

We tie up the dinghy and enter the interior space of the fortress. There are many steps, many levels here, and I feel like Q*bert, hopping from cube to cube. There's a burial vault and various prayer platforms, and we climb down into a dank space that feels like a dungeon—perhaps it was. Apart from the lounging attendant, Graeme and I are alone. It's silent.

Climbing up on one of the ramparts and looking out over the rest of the floating city, it strikes me as a child's creation, Lincoln logs laid out on turquoise carpet. There once were bridges connecting the islands, and docking stations for canoes, even holding pens for fresh seafood. It's largely in ruins now, broken walls and piles of stone, perforated by water. But still, imagining it built up, roof-topped, and bustling with royalty, servants, priests, and boats, the place, like the pyramids in Egypt, seems both romantic and ridiculous. A fairy tale that, innocent enough in a child's mind, must have garnered the sweat—and lives—of so many in its elaborate creation. And I wonder if that's how it always is when building something magnificent: that it takes great sacrifice. But how do you know what is worth the sacrifice and what, in particular, is worth sacrificing? One's effort . . . one's time . . . one's ideals . . . one's identity . . . ?

We climb back into our dinghy and meander through the islands, sometimes motoring, sometimes, when it's shallow or we prefer silence, simply rowing. The place is laid out over 150 acres with an administrative district, a religious center, a communications (drumming) center, and a boulder where pregnant women used to rub their tummies to ensure easy labor. (I place my hand on the boulder and rub my tummy, too, for "down the road.") The entire compound is surrounded by a sturdy seawall.

We get out at the island of Peikapw, where the ruling Saudeleurs claimed they could gaze into the pool here like a crystal ball and observe their subjects on Pohnpei. This magic, or at least the legend of it, was one way they controlled the masses. I look into the grayish murky water, wondering if this is what Peterson's *sakau* looks like before he slurps it. It's hard to imagine finding any insight in there. Still, I wish that if I stood long enough and gazed deeply enough and tried hard enough, I could see what was going on inside my husband's head.

Two days later, back in the small capital town of Kolonia, my bike has been stolen. I was in the Internet café writing e-mails to girlfriends (Graeme and I thought it best to take a day apart) when I came out and found it gone. Of course, I hadn't bothered to lock it up with the lock I keep coiled around the handlebars for easy access. Nimbat. So I walk across the street to the police station, not two hundred yards from where my bike was snatched, and report it missing. The uniformed officer nods sympathetically and takes down my report, but he informs me it's unlikely my bike will be recovered. "Kids pull this sort of prank all the time, and then just abandon the bike in the bushes. You really should use a lock." He wags his slender brown finger at me.

I explain that it's not your run-of-the-mill bicycle, what with its elongated handlebars, folding frame, and dinner-plate wheels; it's easy to distinguish from a regular bike. I offer to bring in a photo and post signs around town. Signs will be easy because English is the common language in the Federated States of Micronesia; each of the four states and many of the outlying atolls have their own language, so even islanders use English to communicate. The officer shrugs and says he'll put in a call to his patrol cars with the bike's description.

Back on the boat, Graeme is in the same sour mood I left him in a few hours ago. After walking thirty sweating minutes back from town without my bike, I'm not in the highest spirits myself. But then I have good reason. Graeme's mood, on the other hand, is enigmatic. And ubiquitous. It reminds me a little of the space I was in the first couple months of our trip. But if I was "a bit blue" back then, then Graeme's mood nowadays is decidedly black. And even when he's not grumpy, he's just not his usual grab-life-by-the-heels-and-swiiiing self. I miss that guy.

Which brings to mind a woman I knew, a bit older than I, who was in the process of getting a divorce. Looking back she said that she and her partner had never discussed this key question: Are we married for as long as we live? Or for as long as we're happy together? It's a subtle distinction, with not-so-subtle implications. (I wanted to know if I was allowed to answer: "Both.")

My point is, while I'm not saying I want to divorce Graeme just because he's a bit of a grump right now, the concept does make me wonder: When we fall in love with someone, is it with their best self? Or their *whole* self? Sure, yeah, I know, we're *supposed* to say the latter. But if that's really true, then why is it so hard to be patient and loving and sympathetic when Graeme's whole self is acting like a sulky, grumpy, bullheaded crab?

Right now my loveable crab is up on the bow doing a project involving anchor chain, plastic twist ties, and spray paint. It's hot out (as usual), and he's sweating and scowling. It used to be that Graeme threw his best self into these boat projects with energy and optimism, excited for each new challenge, poring over six different books and consulting six other cruisers before ingeniously inventing his own solution. But now his whole self has fixed just about everything on this boat two or twenty times, and the fact that stuff continues to break, I think, is wearing him down. Boat work has finally become what it actually is: work.

Which is a serious problem, because it means a lot of Graeme's time is consumed with something he no longer finds fulfilling. Plus, unlike me, he doesn't have a capital-*P* Purpose to pursue as soon as he's gotten his Blue tasks out of the way. Despite all the time he's spent reading and high-lighting and dog-earing that dang parachute book, he still hasn't found his calling. If I were him, I'd be crabby, too.

Still, I find it hard to be patient with the worst, in my mind, major side effect of these black moods of his: Graeme's comments in conversation have become short, like splintery chips of bark. And just as gruff. Me, I prefer conversation to move and arc and segue like leaves on twigs on branches on limbs on a tree. Or at least a shrub. It's Graeme's grunt-and-nod phenomenon that worries me most.

Case in point: Graeme's response to my stolen bike news when he finally looks up from the anchor chain is bark chippish at best. He agrees with the authorities that I probably won't recover my bike. Why didn't I lock it up? Then he goes back to spraying.

I retreat below, get on the computer, and type out a STOLEN BIKE sign. I post a photo, offer $25 U.S. reward for its recovery, and print out thirty copies on our printer. The phone number I use is Peterson's at the gas dock; he offered it when I showed up sweaty and bike-less.

I ferry Graeme's bike to shore, then ride around town, taping and thumbtacking signs in every market, restaurant, and store that'll let me. Riding along I'm hunched and sheepish, worried that a cop will pull me over because Graeme's dark blue bike matches to a *T* the description of my light blue one. Though really, if I'm honest with myself, what I feel right now is not fear, but shame and embarrassment and discomfort and humili-ation. I self-consciously imagine that news of my bike's thievery has spread through town. And that everyone is now pointing and laughing, not at my *Properly Postured Circus Clown Rides Trike!* shtick, but at me, the rich white foreigner who was stupid enough to leave her bike unlocked. Me, the rich white foreigner who can afford to be careless with her possessions and pay a reward to get them back. Me, the rich white foreigner who doesn't really need that silly bike in the first place.

I pedal pedal pedal back to the boat to wait.

I'm down below writing (of course) when I hear Peterson hollering my name. I scramble up to the cockpit and peer toward the labyrinth of wooden gazebos and rickety docks ashore. Peterson's leaping and shouting and waving. This is more animated than I've ever seen our chill dude. I grab my purse and sunhat and book (just in case), and climb down into the dinghy. Then I climb back out to get one last thing: my bike lock.

Someone, Peterson says as I tie up at the dock, has located my bike! I look at my watch. It's only been an hour. Turns out it's a waitress from one of the restaurants where I posted a sign. I call her, and she says she'll take me to my bicycle. It's at her house. When I arrive at the restaurant in a taxi, the slender, shy woman gets in. She explains that she went home after her shift today, only to find my bike in her yard. Her husband said a neighbor kid dropped it off, so as to avoid raising eyebrows with his parents.

We drive on a few minutes in silence, then turn into a dusty driveway. The couple lives in a small cement block home surrounded by a dirt yard with crabgrass growing in haphazard patches. A toddler peeks out from behind her father's legs when he opens the front door. While the young dad goes round back to get my bike, I pull out my purse to pay the $25 reward. The woman protests. I insist. When her husband returns, he offers to escort me to the nearby house of the thief. I politely refuse. They politely close the door.

I go to get on my bike to ride it away, but it is unrideable. The front tire is bent, the tires are flat, the brakes squawk, and the small rack on the back hangs like a bird's broken wing. I fight back frustrated tears. Then I begin pushing my warbling bike down the sidewalk.

Of course, it's at precisely this moment when the local high school lets out. The place swarms with teenagers in blue plaid uniforms, their laughter and shouts rising up to the canopy of breadfruit trees overhead. The kids flirt and joke and litter and tease just like teenagers everywhere; I used to be so comfortable with this scene. But my embarrassment right now is intense, not just because I'm a rich white foreigner pushing a dorky broken-winged bike, but because someone among these kids is quite possibly my thief.

I train my eyes on the sidewalk. My cheeks burn with that particular brand of insecurity I used to feel in high school, walking by the smoking section, past all the kids who wore black. I always felt so prudish, so goody-two-shoes compared to those kids. I felt like shouting, through their cool stares and smooth exhales, "You don't even know me!" And I suppose that's how I feel right now. Unknown and unknowing. Like there's a chasm opening between me and this place. Like I don't have any business being here at all.

In the middle of my walk of shame, I stop. The rear end of a car is sticking out into the street, blocking the sidewalk, and I'm going to have to push my limping bike out into the stream of teenagers to get around it. My face burns hotter and the scent of too-ripe breadfruit, fallen from the tree above and smashed on the strip of crabgrass to my right, fills my nostrils. Sweat trickles down the back of my thigh under my skirt. I'm about to swerve around the fallen fruit and out into the crowd when, looking up, I realize the car is here because this house is an auto mechanic's shop. Well, I think, it's worth a try. So I knock on the wooden gate and call out to see if anyone's there. A voice booms, "Back here! Come on back!"

I follow the voice to a dark, stocky man in soccer sandals, his head thrust under the hood of a car. I explain my predicament and he looks over my bike. "No problem," he says and retreats into his garage to pull out some small wrenches and a crowbar. The man fixes each and every problem right there on the spot. He even lubes the chain and swipes off the seat with a clean rag. I try to pay him. He refuses. He shoos me out the gate, saying something about my being a guest on the island; he trusts I would do the same for him.

When I used to teach British Lit to high school sophomores, there was one thing I loved teaching so much that I'd practically jump up and down clapping in anticipation. It was John Donne's "Meditation 17," which may sound obscure but whose concept you're sure to have heard—in insurance commercials, Hemingway novels, and Simon & Garfunkel songs. Donne's message was this: "No man is an island, entire of itself; every man is a piece of the continent, a part of the main."

I loved teaching Med-17 because it was complex and beautiful, short and relevant—and I could play Simon & Garfunkel while my students found their seats. Plus it had a lovely message about the connectedness of humanity. Only now I'm starting to question Donne's rejection of island imagery. Not just because I'm out here visiting so many of them, but also because I'm starting to think, when it comes down to it, we humans might be closer to islands than a uniformly connected mainland anyhow. I'm not saying we're totally disconnected. No. But I'm realizing our connection, like the sea herself, is changeable: sometimes peaceful, sometimes swift and easy, sometimes herky-jerky, sometimes dire.

Nan Madol, that ancient floating city Graeme and I visited, literally translates to the "space between." And while anthropologists don't really know what led to the canalled city's abandonment, some speculate that the rulers, set apart from their subjects, lost touch and, therefore, control. (Apparently that murky looking glass pool on Peikapw was a bust.) And yet, in an intimate relationship like marriage, sometimes space is exactly what you need; I definitely feel like Graeme and I could benefit from some distance between us these days. Though, at a time when he's so grumbly and gray, space also feels scary. Like he might drift even further away.

When we know we're going to be interacting with strangers, where there's already distance between people, I think we expect a bit of difficulty and prepare for a bit of work. We brace ourselves for boring cocktail conversation, awkward silences, the insecurities of inserting ourselves into a new group. And when we travel, we gear ourselves up for the effort—and thrill—of bridging cultural and personal divides.

But sometimes the space between people feels totally innavigable. Which, when it's between you and the guy who stole your bike, is understandable. But right now I'm having a hard time just navigating the islands of me and Graeme—the person I love, the person I thought I knew best in the world. And even though the distance between us may only be as far as those ancient floating islands, it looks slippery over there. Gray and wet. And I'm afraid, if I attempt that leap, there won't be room for me on his side. And I'll fall endlessly into the space between.

Part 7

Asia

Typhoon Warning

a month later the good news is that Graeme and I aren't fighting anymore. The bad news? We're not talking much either. Though it's not like we're giving each other the silent treatment or anything. It's more that we just don't have much to say.

Which totally freaks me out, because I've always said I would never be one of those couples you see in restaurants, faces bland as hard-boiled eggs, eating dinner *silently*—the horror. I'm the kind of person who'll speculate on the childhood trauma of the rude waiter, launch into a diatribe against the dyed carnations, or even pick a nasty ole fight with my husband, rather than dine (gasp) silently. That said, right now is a perfect example of at least one reason why Graeme and I don't talk much anymore. Let me explain. . . .

We're walking down the village road on Suluan, a small island in the eastern Philippines, that has no electricity, no cars, no hotels, no restaurants. The modest but meticulous homes here show like a haphazard Street of Dreams air-dropped from different places around the world; there's the colorful Moroccan tiled house, the carved Swiss chalet, the shingled Cape Cod cottage, the filigreed balconied Victorian, the front porched bayou cabin, the Spanish stucco, and the Polynesian thatch. OK, so admittedly we're not seeing full-bodied replicas here, but there's the suggestion of all of the above intermixed with lots of cinder block and corrugated iron boxes, too. The mishmash shouts, "Good-bye, Pacific! Hello, Asia!"

The other fascinating thing you notice walking down the single paved road of Suluan is the second tier of smaller homes gracing the front yards of the human ones, what Graeme calls the Cock Condos. These structures are one-, two-, even three-story affairs made of bent metal, wood, thatch, or bamboo—their magnificence sometimes in keeping, sometimes in contrast to, the home behind it. (In other words, if you have a crappy house, you might yet have a luxurious condo for your cock.) Roosters are king on Suluan because the big sport here is, you guessed it, cockfighting—an event we'll be witnessing perhaps sooner than we'd like.

Now, all this stuff, the architectural hodgepodge, the cock-a-doodle-doos, the barefoot children playing soccer with an old milk carton in the shade of an acacia tree, is something I would normally relish telling Graeme about with exacting detail, colorful embellishment, and flamboyant hand gestures. But, see, Graeme's right here. Beside me. Seeing it all for himself firsthand.

Which puts me in the exact *opposite* predicament of my brother, John, who in his twenties, took a cross-country motorcycle trip in a skintight, turquoise-and-white, Evel Knievel leather suit. (Really; I have photos to prove it.) The thing is, John said he had an amazing adventure, only he wished he'd had someone to share it with. Me? I'm on an amazing adventure (skintight leathers aside), and *I'm* lucky enough to have someone with whom to share it all. Emphasis on *all*.

Which is fantastic! I mean, really, there's no one else I'd rather compare cocks, place bets, become blood splattered, and observe disembowelment with than my dear husband Graeme. Despite our recent lack in the sack, he's still my number one cock buddy for sure. And yet, when you spend a year and a half spending *all* your time with the exact same person, things are bound to lag in the conversation department; you just don't have many independent, novel, unshared experiences to report back on. Sure, you can pro-cess everything (long *o*, as my favorite fictional heroine says), but pro-cessing is just a fraction of a couple's conversation quota. You start to feel like a mama bird, regurgitating your precious worms over and over and over.

Think about it. Back in landlubber life, Graeme and I each used to go off to our respective workplaces, spend Girls'/Boys' Night Outs with our respective friends, or have private phone conversations with our respective families. This gave us some pretty good dirt to talk about. But now Graeme and I don't work; we don't have segregated social schedules; and we don't talk on the phone at all. So all the things I experience—except maybe a night watch or a trip to the Laundromat or an inspection of the egg-whitey-ness of my cervical fluid—Graeme pretty much experiences with me. And, sure, we've been in some pretty sticky spots together, but when it comes time to pro-cess and reflect on these sticky, amazing adventures, it often boils down to one simple, hackneyed refrain: *wow*.

Like yesterday. We were coming into port when a purple outrigger canoe powered by a lawn mower engine approached us. I shouted with cupped hands to the young men in the boat, "We have a message for a woman named Leah from her husband, Gordon. Do you know Leah?"

The hunkiest of them (not that I noticed) responded, "Leah? She's my sister!"

Graeme and I looked at each other in amazement. All we said was, "Wow."

Leah (pronounced "Lay-ah" like the princess) is the wife of Gordon, a Scottish sailor we met in Pohnpei. He's still stuck there making boat repairs. Has been for months. Meanwhile, his young wife and three-year-old son are stuck on Suluan, the remote, beautiful island where Leah grew up.

Every time a yacht enters Suluan's harbor, the skipper, if he's single—and sometimes even if he's not—is immediately wooed by all the marriageable ladies. Or, more accurately, their mothers. When Gordon arrived four years ago, a matronly storekeeper in a muumuu set him up with her daughter, a woman half Gordon's age. The date was actually quite fruitful, just not for the storekeeper's daughter. Gordon, instead, fell for the chaperone on the date: the quieter, prettier Leah (also half his age). They got married, got pregnant, and gave birth to their beautiful son, Iain. Not necessarily in that order.

So Graeme and I go ashore—dodging the kids' seaweed fight in the shallows, passing the colorful outriggers creeping up the beach like giant spiders, stepping around a huge hog on a leash staked halfheartedly into the sandy earth—to find Leah. We deliver a letter, and a big hug, from Gordon. She's ecstatic to see us; we are a link to her long-lost husband. And now, we realize, we've effectively secured our own personal guide for the island. Which, for two people who are running out of things to say to each other, is a nice distraction.

Leah sticks to us like a limpet to a stone. It seems a point of pride for her to walk with us, show us around. She smiles round apple cheeks to the people we pass, nodding her chin up in greeting so her black veil of hair dips down her back. Leah walks with a slow gait, feet angled slightly outward, sporting the ubiquitous soccer flip-flops everyone here calls "slippers." She takes us on a rugged hike, in said slippers, to the burnt-out lighthouse, through the palm tree plantations, over the island's high ridgeline, and down steep, rocky goat paths to the best beachcombing on the island. Her seven brothers, she says, are fishermen and divers; they've recovered huge nautilus, spider, and conch shells here. They're beautiful. Plus they fetch a hefty price at the market in Tacloban City.

Leah walks us down the beach to stone arches carved out of the rocky headland. The stone is pocked like a cantaloupe that's been melon-balled; this place smells just as fresh. Wild tropical flowers sprout from these natural concaves like flags waving in the wind. This is one of Gordon's favorite spots on Suluan, Leah says. She looks east across the water, in the direction of Micronesia and her husband. She says, "I miss him."

The next day Leah escorts us to the cockfight. We walk with her down the single paved road blown white with a fine layer of sand, the snail-trails of bicycles and slips of slippers marking it like an Etch A Sketch. Between the road and the beach, under a large tree with benchlike roots, is the cockfighting ring. The wooden barrier to the ring is crowded three bodies deep, mostly men. A match is just ending. I stand on tiptoes and am able to glimpse the final throes of the fight: When one bird is on its last legs, the referee picks up both birds, faces them off, and sets them back down to let the winner finish off the loser. I cringe at two such face-offs before the loser's neck and body go limp in the dust.

The crowd disperses. The men quickly move from standing around the cockfighting ring, to standing in a ring around . . . well . . . us. Graeme and I are the new main attraction. Certainly, we've been stared at in our travels, but it's an odd sensation when, at a sporting event, you become the de facto half-time show. After thirty minutes, I'm blushing.

"Get used to it," Graeme says, a veteran of this part of the world. "We're in Asia now. Bug-eyed staring is A-OK."

The next round is slow in starting because the cocks have to be carefully matched on the spot; there's not a prepared list of opponents, a roster of roosters, so to speak. To this end, birds are placed in mini face-offs to see what kind of chemistry (preferably bad) results. And there's a lot of posturing and politicking, hemming and hawing among the cock keepers; no one wants to sacrifice his rooster to a bird likely to kick its ass. Plus, it's not like the loser can at least take his bird home and eat it—that privilege goes to the winner. Though I imagine these birds are as tough in the pot as they are in the ring.

Finally a match is found. Each owner is given a blade to attach to one of his rooster's legs. Apparently, roosters have these sort of dewclaws that they fight with naturally anyhow. The owners attach blades, sharp and shiny, to make the killing bloody and dramatic. When the birds are ready and all bets are on, the crowd moves to the ring. Men rest their arms on top of the fence, kids peer through its vertical slats like prison bars, teenagers perch on the roofs of nearby houses, toddlers toddle on dads' shoulders. The fight begins with a blur of feathers like Road Runner—black, white, red, brown. The roosters peck and flap and lash with their heel-blades in a deadly dance.

It soon becomes clear that Mr. Black-and-White is the stronger fighter, flapping up three feet in the air and slashing his blade to great effect. Blood splatters. The crowd cheers. The brown-and-red bird stumbles. The crowd jeers. The fight takes on a rhythm—flap, jump, slash, flap, jump, slash—with a tuxedoed lead dancer. The men boo and laugh as the brown bird falls. The referee begins the final face-offs, but these don't last long because the loser is already lost. He dies, brown and red feathers breathless in brown and red dirt.

You don't have to be a vegetarian or a justice freak to feel your gut turn and your conscience gain twenty pounds watching a cockfight. This display of brawn and blood seems totally senseless to me. Disgusting, sad, cruel. Yet this is part of the culture here, the Suluan version of reality TV. And though I can't condone it, as a foreigner I'm not sure I'm entitled to condemn it either. What I can do is try to understand it.

I've always been fascinated by the relationship between the hunter and the hunted. Back when I was a cowgirl/cook on that dude ranch in Wyoming, the hunting guides expressed an almost spiritual affinity with the elk they stalked. We saw this again in Neah Bay, where, for the Makah, the act of killing a whale was also a form of worship. And here in the Philippines, these roosters are treated like royalty—up until the day they're tossed in the ring. I'm not sure honoring a creature makes it all right to kill it, but some might say it's all part of the circle of life . . . with a little sporting cruelty thrown in.

OK, so I'm not sure I buy it. But on a purely existential level, I have to admit there's something in the *passion* of cockfighting—the fluttering intensity, the fight to the death—that is utterly alive. My interactions with Graeme lately have been so dusty and gray in comparison to those whirling red talons and flashing blades. I wonder if fighting might actually be preferable to this apathy that has taken roost between us.

A true seaman would rather die in a storm than waste away in the doldrums any day.

Before we leave Suluan, we take a passel of gifts to Leah's family. They're all items we either brought on our trip expressly for this purpose: T-shirts, baseball caps, coloring pens for kids. Or items from our own goods that we can spare: a mask and snorkel for the diving brothers, fabric and thread for Leah's mom, whose foot-pedal sewing machine stands in the corner of their spare concrete house. Our simple goal is to say thank you to Leah, and by extension her family, for her hospitality. Only it backfires.

From a prominent shelf in the living room Leah's father plucks three beautiful shells—nautilus, spider, and conch—each flawless and polished. He presses them into our hands. We are horrified. These are the very shells Leah had told us about with such pride. Family treasures. And insurance, I suspect, against hard times. We try to refuse but soon realize that's more rude than our already significant blunder; we should have known Leah's family would feel the need to reciprocate our gifts. In a country where, even more so than roosters, hospitality is king, it's inconceivable that their daughter's time would seem gift enough to them. One has one's pride.

And this is too often how I feel these days. Despite my efforts to, as E. M. Forster and the *kalea* back in Wallis said, "Only connect," I keep fouling things up. Building barriers instead of building bridges. Of course it's bound to happen, making cultural missteps while traveling the world. But one so costly to Leah's family as this? It gives me a hollow, yucky-stomach feeling that won't go away.

Yucky-stomach. That's the term I've always used with my girlfriends to describe anything from the blues to relationship strife to feeling like a rich white foreigner whose best intentions turn out to be utterly misguided. Today's yucky-stomach only adds to the simmering, silent yucky-stomach I've already got going about Graeme. The one that's carved out a concave spot in my gut for weeks now.

Back on the boat, doing a final cleaning before we take off, I'm spraying our mildew-speckled cabinets with vinegar. The gunk doesn't take much elbow grease to remove, but it returns month after month. So every month (or two) I spray. My face is scrunched up all tickly and tingly when, like a sneeze I can't hold in any longer, I turn to Graeme and blurt, "Hey, are we OK?"

Graeme barely looks up from reading, shrugs, and says, "Yeah, we're fine." He goes back to his magazine.

I spray another round of mist next to the pasta bin and step back to let it settle. Again I turn. "Are you sure?" I ask.

"Yyyup," Graeme says. Then he lays down his magazine, reaches to the navigation station, and turns on the SSB radio. Loud.

The radio *phlits* and spats while Graeme searches for the weather report. He hustles a notebook and pencil from our overflowing and ever-expanding Oh-Shit Drawer and sits down to transcribe the forecast. It always comes so rapid-fire, it's hard to pro-cess all at once. But even I don't miss it when these words crackle across *Dragonfly*'s cabin: *Warning: tropical depression has formed southeast of Guam. Heading southwest to Philippines.*

I stop midspray and look at Graeme. He finally looks at me dead on. A tropical depression is the early precursor to a typhoon.

Worried about the looming weather, we race through the chutes and ladders that are the Philippines, running from what we hope won't become a serious storm. There are like seven thousand islands in this country, replete with calm waters, beautiful beaches, and several harbors identified in our guidebook as storm safe—we've set two of the latter in our sights.

This place is a cruiser's dream. And yet, like sailing through Micronesia, we're still basically on our own. Sure, you see sailboats around, but there's not the community of cruisers buoying us like during the first year of our trip. I'm realizing more and more how much I miss it.

Then again, sailing in far-flung places, you see this: an old wooden pier off our port side, empty one moment, then, as though the sighting of *Dragonfly* has been announced over a P.A. system throughout the village, the pier is teeming with shouting and waving men, women, and children, mostly children, beckoning us to drop anchor, come visit, stay. But the current in the channel between these islands is moving swiftly. We continue on.

We're off the west coast of Samar. We just need a safe place to hole up for the night, a calm spot to drop the hook. As *Dragonfly* meanders through the islets, we come even with a single, small house on the island to starboard. Below the house, planted into the hillside, there's a square cement slab the size of a driveway, except that it's not connected to anything but a footpath. A boy is there, maybe twelve years old, bouncing an orange basketball. Bounce. Bounce. Bounce. Twirl. Bounce. Under the leg. Bounce.

Bounce. Bounce. There are no court markings. There's no net. No opponent. Just this kid and his ball and the sun, an orange glow in a sky perpetually hazy with smog. He doesn't even notice us.

We turn starboard away from the first island, round the northern tip of the second, and come upon a third with another village on it. I steer and watch the depth while Graeme readies the anchor on the bow. As we circle round and round, like our dog Scout, trying to find the perfect spot, the waterfront fills with tiny bodies. I look up and see a village that appears to be comprised entirely of children. They're waiting for us.

When we go ashore at Barangay Rama (as the arcing wrought iron sign on shore proudly announces), every single child in town has gathered to greet us. Their shouting and laughter are deafening as we approach, and when we secure our dinghy and clamber up to the tiny town square, the children, about seventy of them, surround us and applaud, as though we've just performed a magic trick. We ask to see the *barangay* (neighborhood) captain; like Wallis Island's *kalea*, this is who you check in with while cruising in the Philippines. A couple of the older kids point down the single narrow path that acts as the village's main street. We begin walking, as do the rest of the children, a scene from the Pied Piper.

When we knock on the vice captain's door (the captain is not available), she informs us that it's been years since a yacht has come to visit. This explains the children's exultant reception. We complete our entry documents and walk back through town, all seventy children still in tow. I chat with girls in braids and barefoot boys, some of whose English is excellent. And then we climb in the dinghy and motor back to *Dragonfly*. The children holler and wave on shore. I've never felt like such a celebrity.

But when I suggest to Graeme that we go into town after dinner to socialize, he grunts. He's got a cold (practically the first time he's been sick in his life), and he says he can't handle walking the red carpet child gauntlet again. He's going to listen to the evening weather report, he says, then turn in early.

Me, I can't stop thinking about those kids. Their delight, their energy, the tart sound of their clapping hands. I move to the cockpit to spy on them running in the town square and throwing stones from the breakwater and dueling with sticks on the muddy shore. I'm so fascinated by these little urchins, I start to wonder if maybe I am, or at least my body is, more ready for kids than I think. Then again maybe it's just the joy of having exuberant attention aimed in my direction. It's been a while since I've felt exuberated over by anyone—other than grinning men holding squawking cocks.

And that's when it hits me. Maybe the reason Graeme and I have so little to talk about these days is that, when you're living that big, hairy, audacious goal you've dreamed of all your life, you sort of stop dreaming about the other ones—like having kids. And I suppose, in some people's book, this is a good thing. Because that way you're living in the moment, focused on the dream you've got right here, right now, not always looking to the future. At least that's the theory.

But for Graeme and me at least, this feels dangerous. Partly because of all those dreadful fertility stats I've read, telling me we should get a move on. But also because both of us grew up in families that spent as much time talking about imaginary lives as real ones: What if we added a second story to our house? What if we moved to that small town we just passed through? Or, the most common daydream in both our families: What if we bought that old boat with the classic lines, peeling paint, and rotting hull and fixed her up? It never mattered if the dream was affordable or realistic or even so much desirable; it was the act of dreaming, imagining our lives as otherwise, that mattered. I suppose it made us feel like we had options, some illusion of control. And, on the flip side, it made it seem as if sticking with the life we were actually living was a conscious and positive choice.

But Graeme and I haven't been dreaming much lately. At least not together. So maybe that's what we need: a new B-HAG. Something besides my writing. A dream we can both get on board. Especially when "cruising"—aka doing boat repairs in exotic places—isn't floating Graeme's boat quite as much as it used to. And when my mind keeps turning to thoughts of kids . . .

"Bad news," Graeme says, sticking his head out from *Dragonfly*'s cabin. He looks a bit pale, but that could just be his cold.

"What?" I ask.

"That tropical depression has been upgraded. It's now Severe Tropical Storm Roke. Heading straight for Samar. We need to leave early tomorrow morning and do an overnight run to get to a hurricane hole in time."

My eyebrows shoot up. Hurricane hole?

"OK," I say, rising from my ruminations in the cockpit. "I'll set my alarm."

Two days later I'm seriously worried. Yes, yes, of course, about the weather—the storm has been upgraded again. Now it is indeed Typhoon

Roke. But that's just part of my worry. Because, in between hunting for hurricane holes, checking weather reports, and battening down hatches, Graeme and I are still not talking. And it seems to me, if your life is about to be threatened, it might be a good time to, I don't know, *say* something.

Maybe I'm just being melodramatic. My only experience with storms of this caliber is secondhand, and my parents' typhoon doesn't instill confidence. Of course, we're not at sea like they were. But being in a harbor doesn't necessarily make you safe, something *Dragonfly* learned for us last summer when she endured a nasty storm called a Maramou in Tahiti while we were conveniently at home in Seattle for a friend's wedding. For her part, *Dragonfly* spent nine hours bashing her wooden bowsprit down and down and down against a wooden dock, so that when we returned, her bowsprit was hanging limp like a broken tree limb.

Our cruising friends, out in the lagoon on anchor, didn't fare much better. The problem with being anchored in a big storm (the Maramou had gusts up to seventy knots; a hurricane starts around sixty) is that anchors don't always hold. And even if yours does, the boat's anchor in front of you may not, in which case you might get smashed into, or caught up and dragged along, too. This happened to a dozen boats in that blow. Many sustained serious damage or at least lost their dinghies. One sailboat ended up on the beach calling Mayday.

I eyeball the sailboats in front of us. They make me nervous. We're in Puerto Galera, our hurricane hole of choice, and some of these boats are vacant—though everyone's tied to a mooring buoy instead of an anchor. I'm not sure whether this is good or bad. Just in case, we set our anchor off our bow in addition to the mooring ball, and we run two long lines ashore and secure them to sturdy trees. We also take down our ratty excuse for a bimini; it was ready to fall down anyway. And we consider taking off the weather canvas surrounding the cockpit, but decide it'll be easier to repair afterward than it will be to remove now. We take all the crap, er, gear, that normally resides on deck—surfboards, outboard engine, spare lines, gas tanks, fishing gear—and move everything below, making for a mighty crowded living space. And we read in various books about how to react to various situations during the storm—high winds, waves, a significant sea rise, dragging anchor ourselves, another boat dragging toward us. It's terrifying imagining what could happen. And it doesn't help that, when I look up from my book and ask Graeme questions, his answers are still bark chippish at best.

●　　●　　●

We go to bed early, wanting to be ready for anything. The typhoon, which is just another name for a hurricane, is set to hit sometime in the middle of the night. And yet, weaving through my worries of high winds and shredding lines and snapping shrouds and ripping canvas is this pestering thought: I wish I knew what to say to my husband to get us back to that good space, that safe place before . . . before I don't know what.

I roll over on my side to face Graeme. *Dragonfly* is rocking slightly, tugging at her mooring like a dog on a leash. The wind in the rigging is an airy wolf whistle, nothing alarming, the kind of sound we hear on any windy night. It's not at all like I've heard a typhoon is supposed to sound; I think my dad used the image of a train or a semi or some other such roaring-engine-type thing.

Graeme pushes back the single sheet we've got covering us. He must be hot. But then he climbs out over me, accidentally tugging my hair under his bare foot in the process.

Ouch. "Where are you going?" I ask. My watch tells me it's eleven o'clock.

"To the cockpit. The wind's building. I want to keep an eye on things."

I pull the sheet up under my chin. "Let me know if you want me to take an anchor watch—"

But he's already shuffling up the companionway. I can't tell if maybe he didn't hear me. Or if he didn't even bother throwing me a bark chip this time.

Any English teacher worth her sea salt will tell you that the storm is the moment in the play/book/film when everything changes. It's when King Lear realizes he's an egotistic old bastard and goes insane. When the cast-aways in *Lord of the Flies* descend into anarchy. When E.T. finally phones home. The storm signifies a crisis, a moment of truth, a turning point. And *after* the storm, knowledge is gained, order is restored, balance is reinstated. Or, in a romance, the lovers kiss and make up.

Only, real life doesn't follow a script. I wake from a fitful sleep; I've been drifting in and out for hours it seems, never really dreaming. I listen for clues about the typhoon that's supposed to be raging outside. Silence. My watch says 4 A.M.

I crawl out of bed, pad the few steps to the companionway, and stick my head into the cockpit to see if this is the silent eye of the storm I read about as a kid in *The Cay*. But, looking around, I don't think that's it. The night looks like any other night. No stars, but no gale either, just moderate wind. We're bobbing a little, water lapping at *Dragonfly*'s hull. Graeme is sleeping in his boxers on the bench seat in the cockpit. His knees curl up like a question mark.

And that's when I realize we're waiting for a storm that will never come. The typhoon that I, perhaps subconsciously, thought might snap Graeme and me out of our personal doldrums has gasped, pflitzed out, and died somewhere between the Pacific and the Philippines. There will be no magic transformation tonight. No moment of truth. Here we are, like a date stood up on prom night, all battened up with no wind to blow.

Drifting

What to do now? The sun comes up and we haul in the extra lines and anchor, return the fishing gear and surfboards and gas tanks to their regular spots, and put the bimini back up so we can have a little shade around here (emphasis on little). Back to life as normal. Except that life hasn't been normal or, my true standard, *really good* between Graeme and me for far too long.

I suppose, for a while, I was trying to be all chill about it. Trying to, for the first time in my life, *not* freak out when the tide ebbed in a relationship. But now the muddy, barnacle-covered, seaweed-strewn landscape of our marriage has been exposed too long, and the stench of things drying out and decaying is wafting across the bay. I can't hold my nose and ignore it any longer. So I pull myself up by my rubber bootstraps and go clomping about in that stinky muck. Over dinners, on dinghy rides, during happy hours, in letters I actually take the time to print out and give to Graeme, I ask questions like "What's wrong with us?" and "Are we happy?" and "Are *you* happy?" and "Why aren't we talking/laughing/screwing/playing/reveling in each other's company like we used to? Why does everything feel so different?"

At first Graeme shrugs and demurs and goes back to reading his magazine like before. But I stomp. And wade. And fling dying starfish past Graeme's nose as examples. Until, slowly, Graeme's response to my questions turns from downplaying and denial to this even more terrifying response: "I don't know, Janna. I don't know what's wrong. Things have changed, that's all."

And that's when I know that this isn't a figment of my imagination, a creation of my overdramatic, red-herring-following mind. Our relationship really is stranded in some freakishly low tide. And against the laws of love and moonbeams, it's showing no signs of coming back.

There are times when it's OK—no, not just OK, but *necessary* to let things be. To try not to control everything. To, in my mom's sage but uncharacteristically pious words, *Let go. Let God.* In the sailing world, this is when you flip on the autopilot and trust Willie or Winnie to steer for 16,899 of the 17,000 miles across the Pacific. We've done this. There are other times, however, when a (relation)ship needs hands-on attention, someone at the helm, steering, charting, navigating. Now is one of those times. Because our current course is starting to feel dreadfully akin to those six months in college when Graeme and I soul-searched on ratty couches, wept atop hay bales, and drove naked through the night chasing the loving feeling we'd lost. Back then none of it had worked.

This time it has to.

So we agree to throw ourselves into steering our relationship like a crazed Ahab hunting the cursed white whale. Our first strategy: escape. We leave *Dragonfly* for a week and embark on a romantic motorcycle (OK, dirt bike) trip through the Philippines, my arms wrapped round Graeme like on that fateful B-HAG brainstorming night two and a half years ago. We spend a full day in a paint-peeling motel room, reading *One Flew over the Cuckoo's Nest* aloud, in bed, naked—not that this can make up for months of lagging libidos, but it's worth a try. We wander small-town market stalls, buying T-shirts Graeme doesn't need and flip-flops I do, holding hands as an act of faith rather than an act of affection. One day, trying to get from one island to the next, we marvel together as a dozen men shoulder our rented dirt bike and wade with it through the surf to the so-called ferry; the boat is smaller than *Dragonfly*. We visit dusty churches and shady town squares and wild parades, and we pretend that connecting with a culture is the same as connecting with each other. The theory: Fake it until you make it.

Despite sincere efforts from both of us, however, we don't make it. A few days after our trip, our sunburnt, windswept, semirefreshed air blows out and our old relationship malaise blows in. So we try a new tack. Perhaps, Graeme says, what we're missing is community. We agree to stay in Puerto Galera for two months (far longer than our usual three-days-here-two-weeks-there schedule), and we become honorary members of the local yacht club. Immediately our social calendar is full: barbecues, birthday parties, golf games, banquets. I'm eager to bond with the local Filipina women at the club, keen to compare notes on love-and-marriage—but it turns out they're all married to retired ex-pats, white guys twice their age. Linda shows me photos of her children from a previous marriage and says, "Bill agreed to take care of my boys. I agreed to take care of him. That's our deal." Patrice's husband is so old that she treats him more like a nurse would than a wife. And Jessica—a spunky young gal I think I might hit it off with—gets in a jealous, hair-pulling catfight at the club, and despite the fact that her gray-haired hubby is one of the club's officers, she's banned from the premises forever. These marriages, I realize, operate in a different universe than mine, and I'm left with more questions about love and connection than when I started.

But maybe we're taking things way too seriously, Graeme and I say. Maybe all we need is a little fun. So we go on a binge, pretending like we're in college again, getting good and drunk. Every night. We talk loud, make jokes, dance, if not on the tables at least on the dance floor. We're the life of the party! But we all know how well booze works in bailing out a drowning relationship. . . .

OK. A month and a half into our salvation efforts, Graeme and I decide it's distance we need. We've been cooped up on this boat together too long. So Graeme throws himself into sailboat racing while I spend my days writing. Graeme flies to Hong Kong for a consulting gig. I continue writing. This independence feels good. I *relish* the time alone. And I'm not sure if this should make me feel better about our relationship . . . or worse.

So finally we pull out the big guns. Or rather, we pull the goalie. Not that we're one of those couples who naïvely thinks adding children to an unhealthy relationship is a prescription for wellness. But I want to go off the pill, which I've taken for like a decade, in order to get my body recalibrated and flush the hormones out of my system. (OK, and I'm nearing the end of my two-year stash anyhow.) The plan, in the meantime, is to use the Fertility Awareness Method—ironically abbreviated as "FAM"—which critics equate with the rhythm method you were warned about in sex ed. I'm confident, though, that with daily temperature checks, cervical poking, and those egg-whitey stretch tests, I can keep track of my cycle and keep us conception free. (If our current track record holds, abstaining during fertile phases won't be a problem anyway.) My hope is that by the time we're ready for kids—however long *that* may be—my body will be, too.

More than anything, though, I think this last attempt at relationship revival is a desperate leap of faith. A message we're trying to send to the universe, to ourselves, to each other that we know (pray?) our marriage will find its stride again. Eventually.

A few weeks later and we're on passage, sailing from the Philippines to Hong Kong, across one of the world's most dangerous stretches of water. For one, the South China Sea is notorious for piracy. All the fishing boats out here remind us of that Galápagos attack we near-missed a year ago. Plus, this area is called Typhoon Alley because it's the most active cyclone basin on the planet. Every year it sends over a dozen typhoons north to Taiwan and Japan, east to the Philippines, and west to Hong Kong and China. It is the very place that spawned the typhoon that nearly killed my parents thirty years ago. And though Graeme and I were spared Typhoon Roke in the Philippines, we know we might not get so lucky the next time a storm crosses our path.

Only it's dead calm now. No wind. No waves. And yesterday we had a countercurrent that made us feel like we were practically going backward. (The boat, at least, was not.) To make matters worse, this morning the Royal We (I) realized that the Royal We (Graeme) made a significant mathematical error in calculating how much diesel to put in the tank before we left. (Apparently I'm not the only one dismal at math.) We are therefore frightfully low on fuel. So now, on this 550-nautical-mile stretch, we have to ration engine use carefully. And flog the sails. And drift.

Which is how our relationship feels right now. Drifting. Dreary. Doldrumming. We're not Bickersoning and pissing each other off and annoying each other in that snowball way that happens. (OK, at least not constantly.) It's more like being sick with the flu but having no outward symptoms. Just an invisible migraine, and joints that ache, and that dreaded yucky-stomach feeling. Which means others wouldn't detect that we're sick, but when we laugh, it just doesn't come from as deep. When we talk, it doesn't feel as easy or meaningful or genuine. When we look at each other, we sometimes have to look away.

What a shock to feel this way after twelve years of courtship, almost two years of marriage, and the single B-HAG that we thought would bring us closer together. It's an incredible disappointment to look at this man, and feel nothing but . . . nothing.

To make matters worse, there's another reason, besides fuel rationing, that we're drifting at this moment. And that's because something's wrapped around the propeller, probably an old fishing net or a half-sunk shrimp pot or a ratty line—the South China Sea is notorious for this stuff. We lower the sails so the Royal We can go over the side and cut our prop loose. Thank goodness the Royal We, in this instance, is not me.

I'm left on deck to reimagine my old fears of Graeme floating behind us into the distance, leaving me utterly alone on this boat. (Zippedy doo-dah.) Plus there's the added horror that just a few hours ago we passed a hulking gray whale, lying like a land mine on the surface of the sea. Not that gray whales are carnivorous . . . but still . . . it's freaky. I look over the side, down into water that's clear in the same blue way huge tanks at the aquarium are. While the clarity will make it easier for Graeme to cut the flotsam loose, it will also make it easier for him to watch in horror as the man-eating whale or shark or rapacious pod of minnows attacks him. (Zippedy ay.)

We attach a line to the boat, I make Graeme tie it around his waist, twice, and he grips it in one hand. His other hand grasps a knife with a neon orange handle. Mask and snorkel strapped tight around his head, Graeme lowers himself into the water via *Dragonfly*'s ladder. He shivers, not from the cold but from nerves. When his chest enters the sea, he sucks in his breath. And dives. Our charts say it's over 10,000 feet deep here. That's 9,990 more feet than I'm comfortable with right now.

Soon Graeme's back up, gasping for breath, shaking the snorkel out of his mouth. "It's a huge nest of lines and floats," he says. "It might take me a while."

"OK," I say, "I'll tug the line if I see any. . . ." My eyes skip across the blue water surrounding him. "Well, anyway, good luck."

Graeme dives down again. And again. And again. Sometimes when he comes up, he hands me snarls of line—white, brown, Day-Glo orange to match his knife. I toss these bits in the cockpit; we don't want to leave them for some other poor soul to get caught on. Other times, on his way back up, Graeme inadvertently drifts back behind the boat a foot . . . or two . . . or three. *Dragonfly* is ghosting along at about a knot—which doesn't seem fast when you're on board, but must feel like trying to hop a speeding train when you're in Graeme's position. He is, of course, still attached (I keep checking) but has to kick like hell to catch up, holding the knife in one hand and bits of flotsam in the other. Every time he grasps *Dragonfly*'s ladder, I let out a long breath, as if I've been the one diving myself.

After about fifteen minutes of constant work, Graeme comes up empty-handed. "We're free," he says, "but a big mass of it got away when I cut the final piece." We both look back. I can't see it; it's submerged and already out of reach behind the boat. Who knows who it will grab next. Graeme climbs wearily back up the ladder. He shakes his wet head like a dog fresh from the lake.

"A sailor without his knife is a sailor without his life," Graeme says, flashing the blade and trying to sound upbeat. He dries the knife off and slips it into its sheath duct-taped to the mizzen mast.

And a sailor without his wife, I think, imagining Graeme drifting into the slow swirls behind the boat, *leaves another sailor (me!) without her life*. Not literally, of course—I now know I could get *Dragonfly* to safety without Graeme aboard—a morbid, if reassuring, thought that makes me realize how much I've grown on this trip. But losing Graeme would devastate me—take my life as I know it and replace it with a ferocious 10,000-foot-deep sea of pain and nothingness. The urge hits me to grab Graeme, squeeze him to bits, place my hands upon him to prove he's really there. Except he's salty and wet and too busy shimmying a towel across his head to notice me noticing him.

"Let's get this show on the road," he says, stepping to the GPS to check our position. His thumb flips through various screens: *Blip. Blip. Blip.*

OK. Well. Instead of him, I grab the thin, worn mainsail line, take a couple wraps around the winch, and start cranking. The sail slowly unfurls. I step to the blue genoa sheet, bend my knees, and haul back hard. I've got my head down, but my spine tells me the sail is emerging, inch by inch, foot by foot. When I'm done, I turn back, thinking now's when I'll give Graeme a hug. But he's already below, a path of puddles in the shape of feet the only evidence he was here.

I look back up at *Dragonfly*'s slack sails. No noticeable wind. No noticeable change in speed. We drift on.

It's slow and sloggy, but still there's beauty out here. Night watch I stand alone, and the darkness hides the ever-present smog and the sweat of full day and the plastic bags lapping at *Dragonfly*'s hull. The near-full moon trips across the water like an antique wedding train. Fishermen's lanterns, silent yet suspicious, hang in clusters on the horizon.

And so, under *Dragonfly*'s sway, I've thrown myself these past few nights into the one thing that's still mine, the one thing I *can* control right now. My writing. I write letters to girlfriends and entries in my journal. I work on articles for sailing magazines and a fledgling chapter in my novel. I even work on an idea for a book about our travels; maybe Graeme's right, that there is a story in the here and now. I write and write and write. And when I stand up every ten minutes to check the horizon, I watch teams of fishing lanterns advance and pass like Xs and Os across this chalkboard sea.

But now when I stand and stretch my neck beyond the cockpit, I see that one light has drifted away from the others. Toward us. I pull out the binocs and try to identify port and starboard lights, but it's only got a single white bulb. Even with that, though, I can see, gauging its movement patiently against one of our shrouds, that this is no optical illusion; this boat really is heading right for us. I turn on the radar, not that we have much extra juice, what with the smoggy skies and engine rationing. But there the boat is, a clear blip neither tanker-size nor tiny, roughly ten miles away. It's time to change course. But after turning the wheel and adjusting our sails, I realize that we're drifting so slowly, only a knot or two, that it's hard to make enough headway to get out of the oncoming ship's course. I check the radar again. Six miles away now. And gaining. So I go to start the engine—fuel rationing be damned—to motor away from the guy. But *click*. No joy. The engine will not start.

Shitfuck. For one, I'm worried about being on a collision course with another vessel. But for two, it's possible that, like the fishing boat that attacked the sailboat near the Galápagos, this one's coming straight for us on purpose. Piracy, especially in this stretch of water, no longer seems an idle threat. Time to wake Graeme.

Graeme rises fast and frenzied, swiping baggy eyes, as though physically setting aside his sleep; he knows I wouldn't wake him unless this were serious. I explain the situation—basically by pointing at the bright light off our bow—and he immediately goes to work on the engine while I get on the VHF, channel 16, and hail the boat in English. The radar says the boat is only a mile away now.

The answer that comes back from the radio is loud and clear and foreign. I have no idea how to respond, but Graeme's head cocks up from engine surfing. The guy's speaking Mandarin. This is surprising, since most of the fishermen out here have been chatting on the radio in Cantonese, the language spoken in Hong Kong. But when Graeme stops his engine ministrations and grabs the mic, he learns that this is not a fishing boat. Or a pirate (thank God). It's a Chinese research vessel whose watchman, apparently, had fallen asleep at the wheel. The ship immediately changes course to lengthen the quarter mile between us. *Phew.*

And then the man, in an official-sounding tone, asks that we—once our engine is fixed—change our course as well. He gives Graeme a list of coordinates delineating their research zone, an area he'd like us to steer clear of. Graeme then Rogers (or whatever the Chinese equivalent is) the request. He goes back to work on the engine.

A few minutes later, the guy comes back over the radio, this time in a voice that's less official. He starts asking Graeme about who we are and where we're from and how we got here. When Graeme says we're American, the guy asks if that means Chinese-born American. Graeme says no. And the man laughs shrilly into the mic, incredulous that the Chinese voice he's hearing could possibly be a white guy on a private yacht all the way from Seattle. People respond this way to Graeme's Mandarin fluency all the time, even when face-to-face with his blond hair and blue eyes. But this seaman has no visual of Graeme and so keeps asking questions, the same questions over and over, to try and convince himself that Graeme really is who he says he is.

And so at three-thirty in the morning, on a nearly full-moon night, drifting across the South China Sea, I start to wonder who my husband really is, too. Over the past six months, I seem to have forgotten. In times of crisis like tonight, Graeme seems a bit like Superman, diving into the sea, averting catastrophe, surfing large engines in a single bound. His tendency to come to the rescue has actually been one of our relationship's saving graces. Because—just when I'm ready to strangle him for his bark-chip answers or his toe-tapping impatience, at the precise moment I want to declare mutiny or make him walk the plank or file for *D-I-V-O-R-C-E*— something at sea will happen that requires Graeme's skill and gumption and courage. And my husband will swoop in like Superman to save the day, and vanquish, at least for the moment, my frustrations with our marriage.

But tonight's performance doesn't feel like a magic speeding bullet. Instead it brings to mind the unusual wedding gift Graeme's former boss gave us before we left: a fire extinguisher. Not only would it be useful aboard *Dragonfly*, Graeme's boss had explained, but it symbolized one of Graeme's best business skills: putting out fires. In business as in sailing, Graeme had been terrific at salvaging drowning deals, smoothing ruffled feathers, navigating stormy transactions. But when it comes to marriage, I'm realizing, I want more than emergency fixes and occasional heroics. I want a spark, a connection, each and every day.

Is that too much to ask?

It's been a long day, and it's not over yet. Last night, during Graeme's midnight rescue, he did indeed fix the engine. (Chalk one up for Superman.) He also discovered that our diesel problem is far worse than we thought: *Dragonfly*'s so low on fuel now that the engine can barely suck the diesel from her big, sloshing tank. Plus, the dregs from the fuel tank keep clogging *Dragonfly*'s fuel system; we're down to our last filter. We're also, for better or for worse, just off the entrance to Hong Kong's Victoria Harbor. It will soon be dark.

Entering one of the busiest ports in the world, at dusk, with a fuel-starved engine and very little wind for propulsion is not exactly the safest thing to do. However, standing offshore and drifting another night amid the threat of pirates, unlit obstacles, and asleep-at-the-wheel research vessels doesn't sound all that safe either. Plus, after thousands of miles of ocean, we're itching to step foot on the continent on the other side of the planet.

Still, my mind worries over the final leg of our voyage like one of those Choose-Your-Own-Adventure stories I used to read as a kid. It seems like every decision we're about to make could send us flipping to a page detailing our demise . . .

A. If you decide to enter Victoria Harbor's snarl of ship traffic, in the dark, with little propulsion—*flip flip flip*—you get T-boned by a drunken party boat and drown amid booze, dim sum, and Chinese techno music.

B. If you decide to turn on the engine to try to navigate this snarl of ship traffic—*flip flip flip*—you run out of diesel before you reach the marina and still get T-boned by . . . (see A).

C. If you miraculously reach the marina entrance and decide to attempt sailing (with absolutely no wind) into its narrow gauntlet—*flip flip flip*—you enter a sloshing maze of doglegs and breakwaters and, without propulsion, watch helplessly as *Dragonfly* drifts onto the rocks.

D. If you decide to turn on the engine to help navigate the jaws of this entrance—*flip flip flip*—you gasp in horror as the last fuel filter clogs . . . the fuel gets cut off . . . the engine sputters and dies . . . and you drift slowly but surely . . . (see C).

OK, so it makes sense that I'm terrified. But considering my husband's proven superhuman powers, we'll probably be all right.

Probably.

But then what? Say we make it into port. Say *Dragonfly* actually lands safely on the other side of the Pacific. Then do we start our slow drift again? Our relationship not sinking, but not really swimming either, until some near-disaster makes us leap into action once more? Is this our wallowing waltz: drift-flounder-leap . . . drift-flounder-leap . . . drift-flounder-leap . . . ?

I've heard this happens to married couples all the time. They coast through their marriage on parallel tracks that, like lines emerging from a Da Vinci sketch, grow farther and farther apart. Looking back, I wonder if this is why Graeme and I have drifted in and out of each other's lives so many times already. Because every time we grow as individuals, we also grow apart.

I'm down below, pumping the remaining fuel from *Dragonfly*'s big tank into the white plastic bucket from which we hope (pray) she will be able to draw cleanly for the final minutes of our voyage. When I left Graeme in the cockpit, he was squinting into the fading light and assuring me that our Hong Kong charts are detailed and up-to-date—not like those coffee-stained ones we used for Mazatlán. I half-expect to run aground any moment.

My forearms ache. My back aches. My frontal lobe, swimming in diesel fumes, is threatening to do a swan dive to the floor and take the rest of my noggin with it. The bucket between my legs contains what looks like the piss of a dehydrated horse.

"I think that's all I can get," I holler up to Graeme, the plastic pump in my hands farting golden drips into the sloshing bucket.

"OK. Good. Fine," Graeme yells down from behind *Dragonfly*'s wheel. "Hey, you should come up here, Janna. See what we've gotten ourselves into."

I look up, fearful. His eyes are locked on whatever's looming in front of us.

I know I should move fast, I know I should leap into action, but I step wearily toward the cockpit. I feel so drained by this crossing, as if the drifting and worrying and pumping have sucked all the liquid elements from my body and replaced me with straw. I mean, don't get me wrong, I'm excited—sure, I'm excited—to get to Hong Kong. But my shoulders and chest and the trunks of my thighs don't seem to have gotten the message.

I climb out into the cockpit, step up onto the teak bench where Graeme stands, and turn. On our starboard side steep hills rise, jungly with trees, bulging green even in the fading light. To port the hillside is stacked gray with hulking apartment complexes and elaborate, stepped cemeteries, concrete stairways for giants. And floating all around us are dozens of other vessels, moving in crisscrossing patterns like electrical wires. Rusty fishing boats. Corklike water taxis. Old Chinese sailing junks with upswept bows. Barges. Tugs. Cone-hatted fishermen in narrow canoes. Three-storied party boats with red lights and Chinese banners and techno music pulsing from their decks.

I suck in my breath. "It's beautiful, Graeme," I say. Forgetting the fact that my temples are pounding sweat and my palms are stinging with diesel.

He looks up at the wind indicator. It indicates: no wind. "Just wait," he says. "Just wait."

And he's right. Because, as *Dragonfly* coasts slowly on and night descends, the gray cutouts of skyscrapers fill with pointillistic light. The sounds of the city—horns and highway hums—waft across the bay. And as we turn the corner stretching west, a double skyline appears on either side. Kowloon, on the mainland, glows with light, window after window, silent and steady. But Hong Kong Island, on the south side, is brighter, brassier, constantly reaching out to grab hold of the night. Building-wide neon signs shout: SONY! PHILIPS! AIG! Reds, blues, and greens scratch up and down skyscrapers' spines. Searchlights rotate like whirlwinds from building tops.

"Wow," says Graeme.

"Wow," says I. "It's even more spectacular than I remember it."

And that's when it hits me how remarkable it is that we're in Hong Kong—*Hong Kong*! Remarkable not just because we sailed and stormed and drifted 17,000 miles to get here. But because this is the place where, five years ago, Graeme and I officially launched Relationship Round Three. Where we wrote "the end" to the Harry-met-Sally saga that, over the course of a decade, pushed Graeme and me together and apart, together and apart, together and . . .

I thought that story had already ended happily ever after.

I turn my head to examine the man next to me, his face framed by neon and night. I love Graeme, but after spending almost two years on a boat with him, I miss him, too. I miss that intense feeling of connection we had when we fell in love—right here in Hong Kong—for the third and, I thought, lasting time. Back then I'd thought it was fate that brought us together. That he'd come back into my life because he was finally different.

And *I* was finally different. But right now, considering how we've struggled for the past six months, it feels less like fate that put us in the same boat. And more like farce.

Looking back over this journey aboard *Dragonfly*, I see that I've accomplished so many of my personal goals. I escaped my harried, perfectionist, workaholic lifestyle. I fulfilled my high school dream of sailing to the Southern Cross. I became, if not an expert, at least an Above-Average-Joe sailor. I even started writing.

I look at Graeme. He's peering through binoculars toward the silent and steady Kowloon lights.

My life's biggest, hairiest, most audacious goal, I now realize, could be this: *Figuring out how to make love last.*

Full Half Circle

*t*o *recap:*

Relationship Round One

When I was nineteen years old, I fell in love with a fisherman.
  He dumped me.

Relationship Round Two

Five years later, he came crawling back.
  I dumped him.

And that's when fate stepped in . . .
  A couple months after Graeme's and my romantic-but-not-romantic-enough road trip across Delaware, I hung up the phone, heaved a sigh, and crossed Graeme Esarey off my list forever. *It's just not meant to be*, I told myself.
  Though later that year, in New Orleans, the tarot card reader in Jackson Square had another theory.

  TAROT LADY: Your love card looks like someone you've been with
    before.
  ME: Mm, nope. Not possible.

TAROT LADY: Why not?

ME: I've dated and redated. I've *x*ed off all my exes.

TAROT LADY [singsonged skeptically]: o-KAY-ay.

The Tarot Lady flipped the next love card. She said, "Uh. No. There it is again. This is *definitely* someone you've loved before." She looked at me with shrewd eyes. Then, in her best woo-woo voice, she added, *"The cards do not lie. . . ."*

Two years later I moved back to Seattle, to a salty old neighborhood called Ballard (rhymes with mallard). Every morning before work, I walked Scout to the park to do it up. There, Scout took a shine to Milo (a mutt). Milo belonged to Dave (a human—not to be confused with Dave-*the*-human). This Dave was tall, dark, and married. But we got to be friends anyway, partly because we were both dog-loving teachers living a mere block from each other. And partly because we had something else in common: Graeme.

It turned out, of all the places I could have chosen, I'd moved in down the street from one of Graeme's Very Best Friends. *Sheesh*. I was certain my cover was blown. Certain Dave would tell his VBF Graeme that I not only lived down the street, but also had earned the neighborhood nickname of "Headlamp Lady" for walking Scout after dark while grading papers by flashlight. (*Spaz*.) So I half-expected another e-mail from Graeme (bitter? swoon-worthy? mocking?) to pop up in my in-box any day now.

Ah, but forces were at play that I could not understand. In deference to Graeme's then-girlfriend (Dave's wife's best friend), Dave kept my presence *secret* for the better part of a year. Until, that is, Graeme announced he was quitting his job to go climb mountains in Peru. Emboldened with this news—and the knowledge that Graeme's relationship was on the rocks— Dave decided to stage an intervention. The night before Graeme's departure, Graeme's buddies gathered in a bar. They looked somber. They sat stiffly. They fidgeted nervously. Until, finally, the truth came out: "Look, man," Dave said, clutching his beer like a billy club, "I've been walking dogs with Janna Cawrse, every morning, for the past nine months. . . ."

That summer my ghost walked Graeme up and down the Andes. When Graeme returned home, his relationship fizzled and he set out on a fishing trip with his dad. Somewhere motoring down Alaska's Inside Passage, Graeme's dad said, "Why don't you give that Janna girl a call when we get home? *I'd* take her sailing any day."

Returning to Seattle, Graeme installed himself on Dave's old couch to look for a new apartment, a new job, and a new (old) girlfriend. He sent me an e-mail that was neither bitter nor swoon-worthy nor mocking. Instead, it was downright charming: "Dave says you're his neighbor," Graeme wrote. "So I figured it would be neighborly to write a 'hello neighbor' note. Except that I don't live in Ballard. I live in a 1973 Winnebago. But try as I might I can't find any place to park it. . . ."

I chuckled. Then remembered I was a harried, perfectionist, martyring workaholic who'd crossed Graeme Esarey off my list forever. So I didn't respond.

But Graeme is nothing if not persistent. Four days later he sent another e-mail reiterating: "Write me! Otherwise I'll have to sneak around Ballard worrying about getting busted at my favorite fish shack before we have achieved détente."

Relationship Round Three

And so it was that on a brisk Friday evening in October of 2000, I strolled with my double-ex to a pub called Bad Albert's. We talked and laughed and talked some more. On the walk home, Graeme wheeled me through a parking lot in a shopping cart; I couldn't remember having laughed so hard. We clicked like the heels of Dorothy's red slippers, snappy yet comfortable—*There's no place like home.*

That weekend Graeme took me sailing. And then he offered to frequent-fly me to Hong Kong, where he would be working for the next month. He was leaving the very next day. Before he could rescind his offer, I said, "Yes!" And it was agreed that, a few weeks hence, I would fly halfway around the world to the City of (Neon) Light.

The moment I got home that night, I crept down to the basement. From a low shelf I pulled out an old wooden box that had once held wine and cheese. Now it was filled with letters. I rifled through Christmas cards and air mail stationery and sheaves of legal paper and envelopes until I came to what I was looking for: a postcard dated June 6, 1997, sent from Hong Kong to Washington, D.C. Graeme had sent it to me during Relationship Round Two. His cartoonish script read:

Top 10 Things We Should Do Together in Hong Kong:
10. Take the Star Ferry to Aberdeen.
9. Buy jade "soul rings" on Jordan St.

8. *Stroll along the waterfront at night, holding hands.*
7. *Eat steamed lobster in pepper sauce, and throw the shells on the floor.*
6. *Kiss in a glass elevator 80 stories up.*
5. *Stay at the Peninsula.*
4. *Play roulette in Macao on a hydrofoil.*
3. *Drink Chinese beer at the Yeltsin Tavern.*
2. *Go whale watching in a small boat.*
1. *Watch the sun come up from the Peak.*

Well, we didn't cross *every* item off that list in Hong Kong, but we sure did try. What I remember most, though, isn't the sweeping view from the Peak, or the precipitous roll of the Star Ferry at the loading dock, or even the silky sheets at the Peninsula Hotel. What I remember and cherish most is this: One afternoon, in a vegetarian restaurant on the Kowloon side, I looked up at the man sitting across from me. He was holding his chin between forefinger and thumb, a smile teasing his lips. We were in an argument, a heated argument, about socialism and capitalism and greed. He'd just laid out an impassioned speech in between heaping mouthfuls of tofu. *Now,* his eyes dared, *what's your response to* that?

And in that moment, looking at that sly grin, staring into those glinting eyes, I thought, *This is it.*

This is what I love.

I want to continue this *conversation, with* this *man, for the rest of my life.*

Half a decade now has passed since Hong Kong was officially registered as Graeme's and my Special Place—like how some people cherish the coffee shop of their first blind date, or the seaside town they got married in, or the exact spot, next to the pond, under the willow, where they got engaged. (The latter having, unlike me, an engagement story at which they don't cringe.) But a lot changes, I'm learning, when you've been with someone for five years, two of it squeezed into a space the size of most people's bedroom.

Reading back over old e-mails from Graeme, archived on my laptop like blackmail evidence for old right-doings, I don't know whether to rejoice or despair. Passages like: "YOU MAKE ME FEEL LIKE SHOUTING FROM THE MOUNTAINTOPS—SOUL-SCREAMING, EARDRUM-PIERCING HAPPINESS!!!" Or, in one of his more steamy e-mails: "We fit together in that sweet tangle of arms and legs and blankets." *Mmm* . . . Is that how it was when we first (re-)fell in love? So ecstatic that we expressed ourselves in ALL CAPS, exclamation marks, and XXX? O! how the flighty have fallen. O! how the lovebirds have landed.

Landed, that is, in a sloshing Hong Kong marina girded by swaying skyscrapers. Yes, we made it into port safely; Graeme's superhuman powers and the diesel in the white bucket prevailed. And while Hong Kong is superromantic in general, and is our Special Place in particular, e-mails between Graeme and me these days are perfunctory: "Been a busy day." Or "Trip to China on Wednesday." Or "Where should we eat tonight?" The urgency? The intensity? The electric displays of affection beamed across cyberspace? That's over and out.

I'm reminded of a story I heard on NPR once about a woman who ran into her old high school flame at the frozen yogurt shoppe. He was the manager. She, on the other hand, was happily married to a successful business guy, had a couple kids, a nice house, yadda yadda yadda. But she became obsessed with this yogurt dude. She'd go in and flirt with him, and he with her; they'd even pass notes like in high school. She thought about the guy all the time. Until finally, unable to stand it any longer, the woman confessed everything to her husband. But he didn't freak out. He didn't act jealous. All he said was, very sincerely, "Oh honey, I'm sorry I don't give you that feeling anymore." And her obsession was gone. *Phlit. Phlat. Phlew.* Out the window. Because she was reminded that giddiness, like those rubbery carrots that sat in our bilge for eighteen days, is a perishable good. It never, ever lasts.

And I guess that's where I am right now. In Hong Kong with my husband, realizing the honeymoon is definitely over. Trying to figure out what to do next. On the logistical level, we've talked about staying here the rest of the year so we can restock the cruising kitty—we're broke. Graeme can do some consulting work and I can write. Then, I suppose, if everything goes OK, we'll sail the cold North Pacific route home. Not as honeymooners anymore, but as regular married folk: Ho and Hum.

Which gets us beyond the logistics to the stuff that really matters: love. While I'm no longer expecting yogurt-shoppe giddiness, I do need to feel connected to the person I'm supposed to spend the rest of my life with. And I *know* we need to keep trying. But it seems like, over the past six months, we've already tried everything. Escape. Talking. Distance. Not talking. Community. Sex. Crying. Talking. Drinking ourselves silly.

Superman heroics. Talking. Talking. And more talking. Here in Hong Kong over the past month, we've tried all of these things and more . . . then all of these things *again*. Yet our spark is not sparking, our boat is not floating, our love engine is not turning over.

So is this the moment, as in the Green Box Theory of Love, when "human skill and effort can do no more"? Is this when our love chips get cashed in, when the chipbooks are balanced, when the Green Box gods decide whether or not we'll weather the storm? Because, when it comes to reigniting this romance, I, for one, am running low on ideas. And, while I'm not about to file for D-I-V-O-R-C-E, I can't help but wonder just how long we can you go on drifting before we end up on the rocks.

To complicate matters, my grandmother is visiting my family in Seattle next week, and I'm flying home to see her. I'm actually looking forward to the trip—I could definitely use a change of scenery—but Graeme refuses to come. Too many business opportunities, too much boat work, too expensive, he says. He'll see me when I get back. Which, I suppose, he will. But I'm disappointed. Upset that he's not prioritizing my family, upset he's not prioritizing *me*. And leaving like this—adding even more distance to the already disquieting space between us—it's hard to imagine just how I'll feel about coming back.

"I don't know. It just feels different," I say, huffing and puffing alongside my friend while jogging Seattle's Seward Park. It's a typical drizzly day in June, the pavement a maze of puddles. My girlfriend, who hasn't seen me in a year, listens while I vent.

"I mean, we still love each other," I say, adjusting Scout's leash in my hand. A stitch builds in my side. "But we're just not connecting lately." I squint at the sheet metal of lake. "Actually," I add the hardest part, "we haven't been for a while."

We jog past a sign, overgrown and almost unreadable: POISON IVY. I give Scout, who's not sure what to make of me being home, a bit of a tug. It's scary telling my friend all this. Part of me worries she'll rush to judgment, think I've made a horrible mistake, marrying Graeme, quitting my job, sailing to the other side of the world.

My girlfriend cocks her head and says this instead: "OK. So let's put this in perspective. You've been cooped up on a boat together for two years now."

I nod.

"You've been spending twenty-four seven with the same person for a looong time." Her body bobs up and down next to mine.

"Yup," I say.

"But when's the last time you actually had a deep conversation?" She shoots me a look. "I mean a good one. With Graeme, or anyone else. Something other than fighting about your relationship."

I think. Shake my head. "Can't remember."

A few steps on, she continues. "Well, no one I know likes deeep conversation more than you, Janna." She emphasizes the word *deep*, long and low. "So have you ever considered that maybe that's what makes you feel connected to someone? *That's* what makes you feel loved?"

She lets this sink in for a moment, the syncopation of our running shoes and Scout's jingling dog tags the only sound.

Then she adds matter-of-factly, "And so, even though you know rationally that Graeme loves you"—she raises her hand to her face—"and that you love him"—she wipes rain and sweat off her brow—"without that intense conversation in your life, you just don't—you know—*feel* it?"

Dag, I think, *she's GOOD*. I lick a raindrop from my upper lip and cast a sly smile sideways. "What are you, a marriage guru or something?"

She snorts at my irony—she and her girlfriend aren't legally allowed to marry. But, of course, she knows a ton about love. And a ton about relationships. And, being one of my special people, a ton about me.

Being home again, the thing I'm remembering so palpably about my girlfriends is this: I LOVE THEM. Individually, yes. Because each is (in my very biased opinion) stellar, each friendship unique. But I also love my girlfriends in some general woo-woo way, as though they form a single collective being—a friendly phantom limb or a floaty rainbow aura or the rowdy cheering section of my soul. My girlfriends are my sounding board and my mirror, my safe place and my silly place, my favorite blue jeans, my damp snot-rag, my cuppa tea. They fill needs for me that Graeme, being a guy, just doesn't get. Or even if he *does* get, my girlfriends—all put together—fill needs that Graeme, bless his heart, couldn't possibly fill alone.

Back when Graeme and I set out on our voyage, I thought marriage was about mutual reliance. Being a team. Being whole unto ourselves. In my naïve eyes, it was (dah-da-da-daaah!) *Us v. World*. But now I can see that relying solely on Graeme and—let's not forget—*me* for the last chunk of our voyage, well, that hasn't exactly filled me up. In fact, it's done just the opposite: Our relationship well has just about run dry.

I've installed myself for a morning of writing at Seattle's best little-known coffee shop, the Ugly Mug at the south end of Lake Washington. Every morning when I walk in, Willie, the proprietor, asks, "Are you havin' the uuzsh?"—*uuzsh* being short for the *usual*. I've only been home a week or so and the guy already knows my drink. Willie, a large, bearded man who wears pink glasses and a baseball cap, considers it *his* job to provide the pick-me-up, not the coffee's.

"Yup, the uuuzsh," I say, drawing out the word. Willie rings me up and we chat a bit—about God and politics and all the stuff you're not supposed to. Then I head to the stool in the window. Meanwhile, Willie's working on a double-tall mocha, extra whip.

Today's first order of business is to check e-mail. So I pull out my laptop and scan my in-box.

Re: book club
Fwd: Women's dinner tonight?
Re: Coffee Thurs.

And that's just the first three e-mails. My girlfriends are filling every nook and cranny of my calendar for the three weeks they've "got me home" (their words). It feels good to be fawned over like this. Of course, booking my trip like I did—longer than my grandma's five-day stay—means more time away from Graeme. But when Graeme refused to come, I thought to myself, *The more time away, the better.*

But now my eyes scan down my in-box. Searching. *Anything from Graeme?*

Scroll.

Scroll.

My knee jiggles anxiously.

Scroll.

Scroll.

Nothing.

"Here ya' go," Willie says.

My hands leap off the keyboard and every joint in my body jumps.

"Whoops. Didn't mean to scare you." Willie sets my drink on the high counter in front of the window. He puts his hands on his hips and stands there, head tilted, observing me for a moment. "You doin' OK?"

I nod silently, my cup already to my lips.

After another moment, he raps his knuckles on the countertop—*rwap rwap*. "OK then. Let me know if there's anything else you need."

"Sure, Willie. Will do," I say.

Willie pushes his pink bifocals back up the bridge of his nose, nods his head as though affirming my health and well-being, and heads back to the coffee bar. I turn back to the window.

Is there anything else I need? Willie wants to know. My gut answers instinctively: *My husband back.*

I take a sip of my mocha and begin answering e-mails.

> What can I bring? Dessert?
> I've already got a ride—see you there!
> Let's make it 3:30 instead. . . .

But somewhere between REPLY and SEND, my fingers stop typing. I think about Graeme and, more than that, the things my girlfriends have said about Graeme. The things they've said about everything. . . .

"I'm so sorry you're going through this."

"I know how you feel."

"Have you instituted date night?"

"*We* went through this last year. . . ."

"Oooh, those are the cutest jeans!"

"At least *your* husband's willing to talk."

"So we went on this couples retreat. . . ."

"Well, did you *say* that to him?!"

"They must have therapists in Hong Kong."

"Have you thought about sex toys?"

"Mint chocolate chip or Chubby Hubby?"

I've been skipping over the surface for so long now, but here my girlfriends are grounding me, pulling me back to myself, and getting me to see outside myself. They ask questions. They hear hard answers. They ask tougher questions. And they share their stories, too. If there's anything I've learned over the past week, it's that Graeme and I are not alone. My friends' relationships have gone . . . are going . . . will go through these low tides, too. They're in the same boat as I am. So, no matter how distant Graeme may be, *I* am not alone.

The other thing about spending so much time with my girlfriends again—besides commiseration, affirmation, sympathy, advice, laughter, perspective—is the reminder that Graeme does a few things for me that my grrls *don't* do. Yes, *that*, of course. But other things, too. Like, none of my girlfriends, bless their hearts, has signed up to live with me for the rest of my life. None has vowed to have and hold me, to shoulder a mortgage and eat three square meals with me. To share the morning paper, fight about finances, put up with my pokiness, overlook my bad cooking, laugh at my puns, and argue about travel plans. None has promised all that. And not a single girlfriend has braved wind, water, and flour weevils with me. Quit a job, sold a car, and abandoned family for me. Sailed across the Pacific Ocean with me—all in the mad pursuit of a dream I concocted when I was fifteen years old. A naïve dream about the sea and transformation and love and the Southern Cross.

Graeme has done all these things.

For better or for worse.

I'm down to the end of my mocha. I swirl my cup to mix the last sips of coffee with the remaining blop of chocolate. Sip. Swirl-swirl. Sip. It's thick and saccharine, lukewarm now. I look out the window at the first blue-sky day since I've been home. From Willie's window I can't really see the lake, but I can see a seaplane, its pontoons wobbling slightly in the breeze, coming in for a landing. For an instant a TV screen of frustration flares. Graeme should have flown home with me. He should be here. Especially now, I think, when we're in Mayday mode. When our relationship is sinking.

But then it hits me. The real reason I want Graeme home has nothing to do with shipwreck or obligation or expectation or keeping score. The real reason I want Graeme home is simple. I miss him.

If you had asked me two weeks ago, in Hong Kong, if I thought there was even a remote chance that I'd miss Graeme while I was away, I would have shaken my head: *No way, José.* We'd tried distance, we'd tried time apart, we'd tried doing "our own thing." None of that had worked. In fact, what I was most worried about was the opposite of missing Graeme. I thought I might enjoy being away from him too much.

And, admittedly, I have enjoyed being away. But—what's that

saying?—distance makes the heart grow fonder? Or maybe, in my case, distance makes the heart go ponder . . . about my strengths and my failings, about my wants and my needs, about my expectations and my good fortune and my blessings. What I'm realizing is that, when my life is filled with friends, I don't need or expect or even want as much from Graeme; the pressure I put on our relationship goes way down. I mean, I'm less likely to fuss that he didn't notice my cute outfit. Less likely to kvetch about shaved hairs peppering the sink. Less likely to offer up for analysis *every single detail* of my day. My girlfriends are better for that stuff anyway.

When Graeme and I were out there alone, sailing off the beaten tack, all we had was ourselves and each other. And for that particular chemistry of history, it wasn't enough. I had my love of writing, but I craved community and connection. Graeme didn't mind the isolation, but he needed a capital-P Purpose. Our diverging desires and needs knocked us out of balance, and we drifted way off course. But now, surrounded by friends and family, I'm coming back into trim again. And I'm ready—no, not just ready, but *able*—to pour everything I've got into this marriage.

When I left Hong Kong a week ago, I felt like I was at the end of my rope. That I was at that crisis point where, according to the Green Box Theory, "human skill and effort can do no more." But now, I realize, I am nowhere *near* the end of my (as a proper sailor would call it) line. I have support and resources and ideas and help. I have strength and gumption and courage. I am nowhere *near* done trying. I am nowhere *near* giving up on my mate.

And finally I understand what Anne Morrow Lindbergh meant about the tides. Pure and simple: Things change. How I felt in Hong Kong last week, how I felt in Kiribati eight months ago, how I felt bumping down that dusty dirt road in Pohnpei, is not how I feel today (thank goodness). Likewise, what I feel today is not what I'll feel next week or next month or next year. This is both the most terrifying and, now I see, the most *heartening* thing about marriage. Because, even though the honeymoon ends, so, too, do the storms. We just have to stick around long enough.

And so it is at that the moment our tide shifts, the moment Graeme and I Turn the Corner back into love does not take place over a candlelit dinner or while watching the sunset. It's not some sweet thing Graeme says or a gift he buys or a Superman feat he does. There's nothing heroic or Hallmark about it. Instead, I Turn the corner for the Royal Us, alone, sitting nine time zones, 6,500 crow-fly miles, and 17,000 *Dragonfly* miles away from my husband. Because that's when I decide that there is no construction zone too big, there is no sailboat too small, and there is no ocean too wide for this marriage.

I lift my head from the palm of my hand, a tentative smile bending my lips. How ironic that it took flying halfway around the world to come full circle—back to my husband, back to my self. I feel more *me* than I have in ages. And I suspect that will allow Graeme to be more *him*, too.

I take a deep, audible breath.

When I touch my mouse pad, the screen saver on my computer, photos from our trip, instantly disappears. My in-box stares me in the face. And there, *right there*, is an e-mail from Graeme.

Subject: Coming home

Every joint in my body jolts. I double-click his message and my smile stretches to a grin.

> Been doing a lot of thinking lately. I miss you. And since you can't come home to me right now, I figure I'll come home to you. Got the ticket today. I arrive Friday. Any chance you'd like to act out one of those cheesy airport reunion scenes? If not, I'll grab a cab and wander around Seattle till I find you. At any rate, hope you don't mind me being your hot date this Friday night. See you soon. YIP! YIP! YIPPEE!!!

And it's not just the ALL CAPS and XXX and exclamation marks that get me feeling giddy again.

Graeme is coming home. He's coming home to me.

The Motion of the Ocean

i '*m sitting* in Pizza Express, waiting for Graeme to join me.

Hold on. Remember we're talking about the ultimate Pokey Person here. Lemme repeat that.

I'm sitting in Pizza Express, *waiting* for *Graeme* to join *ME*. Yes, that's right, the tide has definitely turned. We said we'd meet at six and here, at 5:59, I'm already settled at a table, I've ordered a virgin margarita, and now I'm just *waiting*. I look up from the phone in my hand every time I hear the door *whoosh* and *jingle*. Not him. But no rush. I love unexpected, unscheduled time like this where I can read my book or file my nails or program numbers into my shiny blue Hong Kong phone. *Beep-be-be-beep.* I'm chillin'.

Pizza Express is a place that, if it were in the States, would be some orange-Formica'd hole-in-a-strip mall with red flames and blurred running shoes for graphics. But this is Hong Kong, baby. Pizza Express here is sleek and metallic, airy and hip, and they've got a fried-egg-and-rocket pizza that's divine. It's also one of our favourite (as the Brits would say) people-watching spots. I'm seated against a wall of windows overlooking the stairs, ramps, and escalators that snake up Hong Kong's Mid-Levels. It's rush hour, so the sea of dark hair, business suits, and dresses flows steadily uphill, the workforce heading home to the high-rises.

Whoosh. Jingle.

There's Graeme.

I give a little wave and feel a shiver of anticipation. I'm not giddy, not in that fleeting yogurt shoppe way, I'm just honestly excited to see my husband. Things have been good, ALL CAPS good, since our relationship reunion in Seattle. Plus, we've got a lot to talk about tonight.

Graeme approaches the table, leans down, and plants a kiss on my lips. "You're on time," he says.

"Early," I correct him. "Not everyone showed up for writing group today, so we got done early." I tug at the fluttery shirt I'm wearing. "I even had time to get this."

"Where'd you get it?" He examines my new top as he pulls out his chair.

"A little mom-and-pop stall on the way down the hill. Do you like it?"

"MmHM," he says. "I do."

"Lately, people are looking at me, thinking I'm getting—"

"No-no," he says, wagging his finger, "not the *F*-word. That is unless you were going to say fffabulous."

I smile. "Actually, I was thinking fffantastic."

"Fffenomenal?"

"Infffuckingcredible."

"OK. Glad to have that settled. Now let's get down to business." And Graeme rubs his hands together, as though he's starting a fire.

Tonight's our second (not-exactly-annual) B-HAG Brainstorming Summit. Last time we did this, all options—move to Mexico, live in a Winnebago, become outdoor sex aficionados—were on the table. Tonight our options are a bit more limited—like I said, things have definitely changed. But at least we're back to dreaming again, envisioning the next leg of our journey—together.

Graeme and I work nine-to-fiveish these days, wear clothes in addition to our skivvies, and act a lot like Average-Joe Joes. Only we still live aboard instead of aland, and still consider the word *cheap* a compliment. Ironically then, *Dragonfly* is moored at the Royal Hong Kong Yacht Club, one of the fanciest yacht clubs in the world. Though it's not the British-accented staff or the dress code in the upstairs restaurant (where we have yet to dine) that lured us here. No, it's that there's just no better place to be in Hong Kong than right here, actually *in* Hong Kong. The MTR subway is a short walk west, forty-seven-acre Victoria Park a few blocks east, and all the restaurants, shopping, people-watching, and neon we could ever want are just beyond *Dragonfly*'s cockpit. The significant downside is that a sewage drain dumps directly into the yacht basin where we live. We're talking used condoms and full-fledged logs. *Gehck!* Gives a whole new meaning to the English translation of *Hong Kong*: "Fragrant Harbor."

Fortunately, everything else about our life in Hong Kong makes up for the severe grossitude of living in raw sewage. Graeme, for his part, is swimming in work like a drunk fruit fly in a wineglass. He has a steady stream of consulting jobs that challenge him and reward him and give him a clear purpose every day—none of which involves fixing diesel engines. Even though it's the same kind of work he's always done in his workaday world, now Graeme's his own boss, setting his own hours, building his own company—and his frequent business trips to China no longer result in jet lag. Plus, in his spare time, Graeme's crewing on shit-hot boats in the yacht club's regular races. His obsession with incessant sail tweaking is finally being put to good use.

And me? I, of course, write every day. On the boat, at the yacht club, in Starbucks, and, my favorite spot, at the Hong Kong Central Library, a massive landmark of a building that overlooks Victoria Park like a lighthouse over a harbor. Walking to these locales, laptop on my back, my body surges with a Janna Meets The Wide World energy. I crane my neck like a tourist, gaping at hand-tied bamboo scaffolding, laundry hung six stories up, and dancing Chinese signs. But then, just as often, I get that I Belong Here rush—when I flash my frequent rider subway pass, when I buy my daily mango at the fruit stand, when the dry cleaner greets me by name. This thrilling juxtaposition of the exotic and the quotidian is what I love most about living abroad. It makes me feel like I could be plopped down in any country, anywhere in the world, and make my way. I have yet to find a feeling as empowering.

And the best part is that this thrilling independence is balanced by community. Despite the yacht club's hoity-toity reputation, we've made fast friends with some other sailors, and I've ensconced myself in a group of girlfriends who meet regularly for dinner-n-drinks. Plus, I've joined the Hong Kong Writers' Circle. Their weekly critique groups provide the professional community I've craved, and the feedback my writing sorely needed. The biggest thing I've learned about writing so far? I've got a lot to learn.

"Fine," Graeme says. "If you want to be fair, the first kid takes your name and the second kid takes mine." He says this almost as a threat, since he knows sharing a name is important to me.

Here we sit at Pizza Express, where we're supposed to be enjoying a romantic evening getting our dreams and goals and lives aligned—and we're fighting instead. Our B-HAG brainstorming session has gotten derailed by our old Name Change Dilemma. And now I'm gripping my fork more tightly than I should.

"What? And have a halvesies family?" I say. "Siblings with different names? How confusing would *that* be?" I stab the yolk on my fried egg pizza so it yellows the green arugula around it.

"Siblings in step-families have different last names," Graeme says. "People are used to it these days."

He lifts his oversize beer stein casually. I put down my fork, cross my arms, and watch him take a sip.

"I *don't* think step-families should be our role models, Graeme. That's exactly what we're trying to avoid." I lean forward and pick up a pizza slice. It drips yolk onto the slices below. "OK, remind me again," I say in between messy bites. "What's so wrong with hyphenating? People are used to *that* these days, too." I motion innocently with my pizza slice. "What about that politics professor you liked in college? Tim Kaufman-Osborne? Everyone called him T.K.O. and his wife, Sharon, S.K.O. What's so bad about that?"

Graeme turns the edges of his mouth down. "Graeme Esarey-Cawrse. So I'd be called G.E.C., huh? Sounds like a crappily made truck to me."

He's right. And honestly, I'm not sure I want to go by my initials either.

"Or"—Graeme lifts his eyebrows brightly—"people could call me *Gec*." He spits out the word comically, like a cat hacking up a hairball.

I crack a smile.

"Hi, my name is *Gec*!" He looks like he's hocking a loogey. "And this is my wife, *Jec*!" His expression this time is pure vomit.

"Ew . . . ," I say, my shoulders jumping with a reluctant giggle. Graeme's always been good at sound effects.

"Yup, that's us, *Gec*!" (Loogey.) "And *Jec*!" (Vomit.) "*Gec*!" (Loogey.) "*Jec*!" (Vomit.)

He continues this for a while until he sees he's got me. I'm seriously laughing now, pressing on my cheeks, willing them to stop, because I'm supposed to be mad.

Then he changes tack. "And this is our daughter, Rosalind. She's a *Rec*!"

he says melodramatically. Now he's cracked himself up, coughing into his fist, eyes watering.

My laughter, on the other hand, has stopped abruptly.

"Ew. Rosalind. How'd you come up with *Rosalind*?" I cross my arms again and make a face.

"Shakespeare," Graeme says, in between coughs. "Rosalind is from Shakespeare." *Cough. Cough.* "I thought you'd like it."

I push a glass of water toward him. He drinks. Coughs again. Drinks.

"Rosalind? RAAAH-zuhlind?" I say, stretching the word out snidely. "Great. This is just great. Now we're going to have to fight about *first* names, too." I lower my head and fake-furrow my brow at him. He's still coughing. And that's when it occurs to me that maybe the reason he's laughing so hard is because he's joking.

A sliver of a laugh bursts out through my thin-lined mouth, and now we're both laughing and coughing again. Because that's the thing about arguing when our marriage is in a good space, a solid space. Fighting's still no fun. It still sucks. But it feels more like a speed bump than a bridge to nowhere. And the distance between pissed off and all right isn't so far to travel.

Still, though, I think as our laughter subsides, we need to find a solution to this Name Change Dilemma. Really. We need to find a solution . . . soon.

The night before Graeme and I left Seattle, we attended a Fourth of July party at a friend's house on Lake Washington. It was one of the few Fourth of Julys I could remember in Seattle without rain. Still, instead of being outside, my girlfriends and I were gabbing in the kitchen—the kids were outside; the wine was with us. And that's when, leaning up against the counter behind me, I announced Graeme's and my big decision, the one we'd come to during the past ten days in Seattle: "We're bagging the kid thing for now," I said. "We're reinstating the goalie."

The reaction was swift.

"Good," one friend said. "You're smart. You don't want to have kids until you're damn well ready." She glanced out the window at her two children playing *Mine! No, Mine!* on the green lawn.

But another girlfriend, also a mom, looked pensive. "I don't know," she said. "Can you ever *really* be ready? I mean, *nothing* prepares you for motherhood."

And one by one, my girlfriends—some moms, some not—put in their two cents.

"It changes everything," one said.

"I'm scared of the exhaustion," said another.

"Yeah, but it's easy to gripe about the hard stuff," said a new mom. "You can't really explain the good stuff." Moms' heads nodded in unison.

But my girlfriend who'd chosen a life sans kids said, "I like being an auntie; I enjoy the little ones, then send 'em home."

"Oh, but there's nothing like your child saying, 'I love you.'"

And while I was happy and confident with Graeme's and my decision to wait until we were *really* ready, I liked hearing my girlfriends' thoughts. The way they arced and swayed like limbs and leaves on trees.

But, of course, all plans are made in Jell-O. Once Graeme and I returned to the other side of the Pacific, back to our home on *Dragonfly*, we discovered the true upshot of the motion of the ocean. Not shipwreck. Not seasickness. But morning sickness.

Soon after re-Turning the Corner with Graeme, soon after telling my girlfriends, "We're reinstating the goalie," soon after being careless with basal body temperatures and cervical checks and fertility charts, I found myself peeing on a stick in a hotel room in Shanghai. And while I'm dismal at math, I knew exactly what that + sign meant.

So I'm pregnant!

Now don't go getting your knickers in a twist. I know that, for two people who've just traveled a rocky road, who said they're not ready for kids, who're living on a small boat amid raw sewage in a foreign country, this might not seem like the best timing. But, just as we learned off the coast of California two years ago, sometimes it takes losing your steering to get exactly where you need to go.

So here we sit, aloft in a lighted Pizza Express window, talking and fighting and laughing and talking some more. Funky jazz-fusion freckles the air, and conversation hums in multiple languages around us. I lean in toward Graeme and say, smiling, "Psst. We're having a baby."

Graeme leans in, too, his voice beaming. "Yyyup. We're having a baby."

And that's why we've got to hash out, lickety-split, not only the Great

Name Change Dilemma, but also our new B-HAGWB (big, hairy, audacious goal with baby). Because, while we're both thrilled to be expanding our tiny family, we're not sure we're ready to move back to Seattle. Hong Kong is our Special Place after all.

In the middle of my third virgin margarita (on the rocks, extra salt), I say, "What the hell, Graeme! Let's go for it!"

"Have the baby in Hong Kong?"

"Sure. Have the baby in Hong Kong. People have babies abroad all the time."

"That's right," Graeme says. "*Nahanni* did it."

"Yeah, Lisa and Marc did it." Remembering Lisa, I look down at my belly bulge, semi-masked beneath the flutters of my new blouse. "You know, it's not that I mind getting a big belly and looking *pregnant*," I muse. "It's that right now I'm in that stage where I just look plain—"

"Fffooey!" Graeme says. "You look fabulous. And fantastic. And—"

"Fffar out," I say, motioning the girth of my ass as opposed to my belly.

Graeme sighs. "You look great, Janna. Seriously. You're more beautiful now than I ever remember." He grabs a hold of my hand. "And I've got lots and lots of years to compare to."

Graeme looks so sincere that I decide I better believe him. With my free hand I touch my belly, the bulge I really don't mind at all. And I whisper, "Thank you."

I ease out of our bunk at sparrow fart. Graeme's still asleep. It's still dark out. And Hong Kong's skyline, necklaced in white light, looks silent without her neon jewelry. Someone turned off the Technicolor while we were sleeping. Standing in the cockpit, in one of those pinch-me-I'm-dreaming moods, I'm tempted to breathe in deeply like I used to, to smell coconut palm and hibiscus and other South Pacific scents. But, like everything in life, this Fragrant Harbor is a mixed bag—not the place to go getting yogic with deep breathing. Instead I stifle a yawn, press my hands against my growing belly, and do a slow pirouette. Hong Kong's lights dazzle even in black and white.

Down below again, I go through the slow, familiar motions of making coffee. My fingers grip our stove-top espresso pot (a wedding gift) and untwist its aluminum frame. Before setting sail I didn't even know how to make coffee. I only drink it with lots of milk or lots of chocolate, or, prefer-ably, both. But Graeme loves the stuff—hot, strong, black—so whenever I get up first, I brew it for him.

On passage, brewing coffee began just before 4 A.M., when the Southern Cross hung like a kept promise in the sky. If the seas were heavy, I'd hold the coffeepot on the stove so it wouldn't topple out of its clamps. (I learned this from experience.) This ritual, to me, meant it was finally time to sleep. For Graeme, though, waking to its deep, round scent signaled something else. He once told me, in a fit of sentimentality, that it made him feel loved.

Funny how the simplest things can take on meaning. When I used to scrub the hull, Graeme would always set out the sun shower for when I emerged salty and algae-strewn. Or, when Graeme threw himself into a boat project, I'd create an elaborate maze of fans to cool his boxer-clad ass. Nautical love notes, if you will. And that's the thing about living in such a confined space with your spouse; while the day-in, day-out life of cruising created a sometimes monotonous togetherness, it also provided constant illumination for the little things, the simple things, that make us each feel loved.

The coffee on the stove gurgles. I click off the flame and turn off the red propane switch. Steam fills the cabin with the rich aroma Graeme loves. I retreat back to the cockpit to sit, arms wrapped around my knees, for just a little while longer. Gazing at the imperial Hong Kong skyscrap-ers, now gray with the dawn, I roll these final moments of solitude over my tongue.

Graeme stirs in the V-berth. A sleepy voice calls out, "Good morning, Janna Marie Cawrse Esarey." I can hear the smile in his voice.

"Good morning, Graeme David Cawrse Esarey." I smile back. There's no hyphen, it's still a mouthful, but at least we're both fully there. Our baby, we've decided, will get both names, too.

"Hey, do you hear that?" Graeme asks.

I cock my head. "Hear what?"

"Wait. Listen," he says.

I wait.

"There. The sound of the kites," he says.

The birds' screeching banter emerges through the wash of city sounds. Not exactly melodic, but lively—pretty in its own way. Their dark shapes swoop above the harbor masts in fluid contrast to the urban landscape around us. This place, the passage that got us here, it's all a mixed bag. But it took every mile, every up and every down, to deliver us to this precise moment. This precious moment. Now.

"There's coffee ready for you, Graeme."

"Mmm . . . I know."

Silence.

Then he says, "But the coffee can wait."

My eyebrows rise a fraction and the corner of my lips twitch. I take one last look around. Then I pad down the companionway and crawl back into bed with my husband. Through the open hatch above us, we watch the kites and masts and skyscrapers soar overhead.

Epilogue

i *remember before* Graeme and I set sail, our friend Dave-the-dog-walker told me: "Look, Janna. If you want to change your life, you don't just run away from it. You make different choices. Because, even if your stress doesn't follow you on your trip—which it probably will—it will certainly be here waiting when you get back."

On the one hand, Dave was right. When I was a martyring, workaholic, perfectionist teacher, I now see that I was *choosing* to be. (It just took me a little distance—namely, seventeen thousand miles—to realize this.) But here's where Dave was wrong: My stress actually *didn't* follow me on our cruise. And it *wasn't* waiting when I returned. Don't get me wrong; I'm no Zen hen. But I'm no longer Chicken Little.

I count this among life's miracles, though I think there's actually a rational explanation. It has something to do with Choice. Because clearly, buying a boat, quitting one's job, and sailing across the Pacific Ocean requires a clear choice, a conscious decision, an act of will. So much so that all along the way I kept reminding myself, "Hey! This is your dream! You chose this! Enjoy it!" It was like a pinch on the arm—or a kick in the ass—and often that little reminder was enough to ratchet down the stress or sing away the fear or give me perspective or make me buck up.

But, of course, Real Life poses different challenges than those faced cruising. With bottoms to wipe, on-line checkbooks to balance, and writing deadlines to meet, my days aren't like that tampon ad—*Carefree!*—anymore. Yet, amazingly, the same mantra still works. When I feel my nerves spinning out of control even now, I *zzziiiip* my thoughts and remind myself, "Hey, pal: You *choose* the life you live every day. You *make* it the One you want."

And, somehow, this little pinch unwinds the wind-y thing in my brain, stops my nerves from fraying like *Dragonfly*'s old dock lines, and helps me breathe deeper. Because, while being a mom and a writer and a wife may not seem as sexy or exotic or ambitious as sailing across an ocean, they are my choices, my Life Dreams, too. As big and hairy and audacious as the Southern Cross.

Still, though, the motion of the ocean is full of ups and downs. Winds shift. Seas change. Tides ebb and flow. And I can't end this journey without a few final stops along the way.

The truth is we never did complete the Ring of Fire. Never did sail, as we had dreamed, from Hong Kong to Japan to Alaska to home. We realized that navigating new parenthood without family, friends, and (not to be fussy or anything) refrigeration, and then crossing the chilly, stormy, unfrequented North Pacific with a "Baby on Board" sign might not be the big ball of fun we'd imagined. So we packed up our boat-size life, ate our last fried-egg-and-rocket pizza, and returned from whence we came, though not in the way we'd come. *Dragonfly* followed via container ship.

And here we are now. Home in Seattle. Anchored by our families. Buoyed by our friends. Simultaneously drained and filled by our motion-of-the-ocean daughter. When we returned, Scout, miffed at our long absence, made a valiant effort at giving us the dog version of that middle-fingered SILENT HAND SIGNAL. But then she'd forget and wag her whole body like a paint shaker in spite of herself. We had two more good years with her, dogwalking, fetching, highchair-licking, and, of course, sailing near do-it-up-worthy beaches. And then Scout was diagnosed with a fatal bone tumor. She went to sail on angel shoulders in the sky. I respectfully mark her passage in these pages because her passage through my life indelibly marked me.

But they say a hatch never closes without a porthole opening. Not long after Scout's passing, Graeme's mom celebrated five years cancer-free. That's five years she spent messing about in boats. Five years she spent traveling. Five years nurturing everyone, from her aging parents to her first granddaughter. Needless to say, Vickie's laughter on her cancer-free celebration was the full, round laughter of Life.

Which brings us full circle to the fact that my shockingly huge belly is bumping the edge of my laptop as I write this. Soon (like, get a catcher's mitt, sister) I'll be giving birth to another daughter—which, in Graeme's and my book, adds up to just the right number of crew. His motto with his daughters hearkens back to that old refrain: "*She*'ll go." Because we're definitely going again, loading the hold with strollers and sippy cups, training wheels and coloring books, favorite giraffe-blankets and *Goodnight Moon*. Sailing, which started as a harebrained escape, is now a part of us. A shared passion we can both get on board.

In the meantime, though, people are always amazed that I, the mom pushing the buggy, sailed across the Pacific Ocean. They seem impressed by the magnitude, the supposed glory of it, but I want to tell them this: It's not so important *what* Graeme and I did—like a bullet point on a résumé or a notch on a belt—it's more important *how* we did it. Though that's not easy to explain in ten minutes at the playground. I suppose that's why I wrote this book, so my girlfriends and I could finally hash over *every single detail* of those two years they missed. And so I could understand our journey better, too.

I see now that Graeme and I made it across the Pacific in the same way all committed couples make love last: By giving to each other, by relying on each other, by seeking support when "each other" wasn't enough. And, of course, by trusting that the tide rises. Eventually.

Five years ago now, off the coast of Mexico, on a night watch silent but for *Dragonfly*'s hums, I saw the Southern Cross for the first time. And, as the lyrics promised, I understood instantly why I'd quit my job, sold my car, and abandoned my Labrador retriever. But, of course, I didn't embark on this journey just for some kickass stargazing. I endeavored to change my life at a time when my life needed changing. And while a goal that was smaller, less hirsute, more modest may have done the trick, in the end I'm glad I ended up on *Dragonfly*. Definitely glad I ended up with her skipper.

But, of course, it doesn't take sailing across an ocean to learn a bit about oneself. It doesn't take a Harry-met-Sally saga to find true love. Whoever we are, whatever we're doing, it's not *what* we do, but *how* we do it. Sitting in traffic, making love, selling widgets, raising a family. Not the what but the how.

Dragonfly knew this. Over the course of seventeen thousand miles she showed us—on night watches, in nasty blows, through the doldrums, under the Southern Cross—that little people can do big things simply by daring to try. Or, as she might say in her cheeky way, it's not the size of the ship that matters, it's the motion of the ocean.

Glossary

Above: Above (i.e., standing on) the deck. This is where Graeme goes when I'm below-decks (see "Below") and he's trying to get as far away from me as possible.

Aft: Back or rear, e.g., the aft cabin is the room at the back of the boat (opposite of "forward").

Aloft: Above (i.e., suspended in the air over) the deck. This is where Graeme goes when he's *really* trying to get as far away from me as possible.

Anemometer: A gizmo that measures wind speed (aka wind-o-meter). *Dragonfly's* very old wind-o-meter only gave loosey-goosey approximations.

Autopilot: The nifty electric gizmo that steers the boat so we don't have to. (Ours is named Willie after its maker, Wil Hamm.)

Below: Below (i.e., in the cabin beneath) the deck. This is where Graeme goes when I'm above-decks (see "Above") and he's trying to get as far away from me as possible.

Bilge: The lowest, coolest part of the boat. If you lift up our floorboards you'll find eggs and veggies stored there—along with dust bunnies, mold, and lots of oily gunk.

Boom: The long, horizontal log-like thing that holds the foot of the sail and threatens to knock your head off whenever the boat tacks.

Boom Vang: One of the many lines Graeme likes to tweak when he's pretending *Dragonfly* is an America's Cup yacht. (The vang micromanages the boom.)

Bow: The forward or, as Mom would say, "pointy" end of the boat (as opposed to the "stern").

Broach: When the boat tips so far over that water pours over the deck and into the cockpit (precursor to a knock-down).

Cabin: The living space, or spaces, below the deck of a boat. *Dragonfly* has an aft cabin (the bedroom we use underway) as well as a main cabin that houses the galley, the settee, the head, and the forward bunk.

Companionway: The stairway that connects the cabin to the cockpit.

Capsize: When the boat overturns completely, i.e., the mast sticks down into the water instead of up in the air where it belongs.

Clipped In: To be tied to the boat with a harness and line so (A) you don't fall overboard, or (B) if the boat knocks down or capsizes, she hauls you back out of the water with her.

Cockpit: The outdoor seating area on a boat where you do things like steer, adjust the sails, and eat sardine dip during happy hour.

Fall Off: (1) To change course so as to point farther away from where the wind is coming from; generally results in a slower, more comfortable ride, (2) fall off, as in, the boat.

Forward: (1) The forward part of the boat (opposite of "aft"); (2) the way Graeme acted in order to convince me to date him a third (and final) time.

Galley: The boat's version of a kitchen—and, when tilted and bashed by big waves, my very own version of hell.

Genoa: The forward sail on a boat, often called the "Genny."

Head: The boat's version of a bathroom—and, when tilted and bashed by big waves, my very own version of purge-atory.

Helm: The boat's steering device, in *Dragonfly*'s case a rust-stained steering wheel or—in a pinch—the long, phallic emergency tiller.

Helmsman: The person steering the boat or using Willie or Winnie to steer.

Hull: The body of the boat that floats in the water, aka an airtight shell great for growing mildew.

Knock-down: When the boat is blown so far over that the sail hits the sea (precursor to capsizing).

Line: Quite simply, a rope (though no self-respecting sailor would call it that).

Luffing: When wind blows parallel past the sails and, instead of filling them and propelling the boat forward, makes them holler and shriek and flap.

Mainsail: The center sail on a boat, called the "main" by Average Joe sailors, or the "mains'l" by old salts.

Mast: The long stick that holds the mainsail up in the air. Big stick = big sail = big speed. When we saw an America's Cup yacht in California, Graeme told me he had mast envy.

Mate: (1) Marriage partner; (2) Sexual partner; (3) Sailing partner.

Maximum Hull Speed: 1.34 x (length of hull at waterline)$^{1/2}$ (No, I'm not joking, this really is the magic formula. Which is a prime example of how some things in sailing can make perfectly intelligent people feel really stupid.)

Mizzen: A small, secondary mast and sail behind the cockpit, which adds forward propulsion or comes in handy as a backrest.

Port: (1) The left side of the boat (as opposed to "Starboard"); (2) A place to go ashore.

Reef: (1) To reduce the size of the sail in order to avoid broaching, knockdown, or capsize; (2) A shallow spot where you could potentially run aground; (3) A coral ridge with colorful fish that's pretty for snorkeling.

Rig or Rigging: The sails and masts, and the shrouds that hold them up. *Dragonfly*, with her two masts, is called a "ketch" rig, whereas most sailboats only have one mast and are called "sloops."

Rhumb Line: The path a boat takes following a specific compass heading to travel the shortest distance between point A and point B.

Roller Furling: When the sail rolls up on a tube like fabric at the fabric store, as opposed to being hoisted up like a flag on a flagpole. Roller furling makes for slower but easier sailing.

Rudder: The large, underwater paddle at the back of the boat used for steering.

Sail Trim: The pulling, pushing, hauling, and tweaking of sails to optimize their position and shape so the boat will move forward at maximum speed.

Settee: A table surrounded by built-in bench seats, which, on 99 percent of cruising boats, have wine-stained cushions.

Shroud: (1) A vertical wire that runs from the deck to the mast to hold the mast in place; (2) A vertical wire that Graeme leans against when he's pissing off the side of the boat.

Skipper: (1) The person who runs the ship; (2) The guy you realize is an asshole fifty miles off the coast of Oregon; (3) Your husband.

Starboard: The right side of the boat (as opposed to "port").

Stern: The rear end of the boat (as opposed to the "bow").

Tack: (1) To change direction in such a manner that the boom swings over the cockpit like a club swinging for your head; (2) The charted course or direction.

Tiller: A long stick, attached to the rudder, used to steer the boat. *Dragonfly* normally steers with a wheel but has an emergency tiller for, well, emergencies.

Watch: The three- to five-hour stretch of time when it's your job to watch the sky, the horizon, the wind, the water, the sails, and Neptune's mood— or curl up in the cockpit, read a good book, and check for ships every ten minutes.

Willie: See "Autopilot."

Wind Indicator: The thingamajig at the top of the mast that has an arrow indicating which way the wind is blowing. *Dragonfly*'s works about as well as the finger lick test.

Wind Vane: A nifty paddle gizmo on the back deck that steers the boat without electricity (ours is named Winnie in honor of the wind).

Winnie: See "Wind Vane."

Yaw: To deviate from a straight course, aka. the inexpert zigzagging method Janna uses whenever hand-steering *Dragonfly*—also an apt metaphor for how she steers her marriage and her life.

Acknowledgments

P inch me. Hard. Because arriving at the acknowledgments page of a book (*a book!*) means I must've had either (A) ridiculously good luck, or (B) a whole lot of help from a whole lot of people. Or both.

First and foremost, thank you, Mom and Dad. You instilled in me a love of adventure, song, dirty jokes, and stories—all of which made this voyage and this book possible. And thank you for Tali Tuesdays, which gave me precious time to write. I am also grateful to Jon and Vickie Esarey, who fed my daughter green eggs and ham (literally) while I pecked away at these pages. Both sets of parents gave Graeme and me a roadmap for making marriage work.

If Graeme had written this book, he would have told a very different story. (Loads more about the sea. Nada about our love life.) By necessity, I left HUGE amounts out, which means the majority of our cruising friends aren't even mentioned. And yet they are the very people who kept us safe, supported, and highly entertained all the way across the Pacific. So thank you to our dear community of cruisers. Special ahoy to Judy Lin.

I also owe my gratitude to the sailing rags that gave me my writing start: *48° North, Cruising World, Blue Water Sailing, Latitudes & Attitudes,* and *Sail*— we still armchair sail through your pages. Other folks who helped me on my path to becoming a bona fide writer I met through the Hong Kong Writers' Circle, Travelers' Tales, and the Book Passage, Whidbey Island, and PNWA writers conferences. Thanks to the *Seattle P-I* for hosting my blog "Happily Even After," and thank you to my loyal blog readers. I'd also like to thank the Jack Straw Writers Program, poet Judith Roche, and my Jack Straw comrades of the pen for listening to excerpts over the year this book was born.

I thank my lucky stars every day for my agent, Rebecca Oliver; she's been my advocate and my adviser—and I just *love* her laugh. Huge thanks to the folks at Touchstone/Fireside, and especially to my wonderful editor, Michelle Howry, whose advice was always spot on. And no one ever seems to mention this, but it was a successful nonfiction book proposal that allowed me the opportunity to write this book. So thank you to Waverly Fitzgerald for her helpful class on the topic, and thanks to early readers Madeline Crowley, Christie Walker, and Allison Cohen.

Sincere appreciation goes to my network of friends and family who attended book readings, endured longwinded e-mails, and, when they received my calls for help, freely gave it. All your good juju (especially yours, bro) buoyed me along the way. Thanks, Ashley, for your fellow writer's eye. And cheers to the Seattle coffee shops that doubled as my office space, especially to Willie and the regulars at the Ugly Mug.

To my girlfriends near and far, I am indebted to you. Your friendship and laughter—and your willingness to analyze relationships with me ad nauseam—amount to some of my greatest joys in life. Your thoughts pepper this book and give me insight and perspective every day.

This book could not have been written without the unflagging help and uncanny wisdom of my dear friend and writing partner, Sarah Callender. She read every word of every draft a dozen times, giving comments verbally, in writing, and (I swear) telepathically—often at a moment's notice. Plus, our daily phone conversations saved me a heck of a lot of money on therapy. All the best lines are Sarah's.

Finally, my sincere gratitude goes to *Dragonfly* for taking us away. To Talia for bringing us home. To Savai for providing a very real book deadline (her birth)—and for skillfully nursing while I typed my edits. Writing this book has not been easy, but Graeme has ever been the fire in my belly and the wind in my sails. Graeme, I doubt you ever cared to star in a book, particularly one about how challenging love can be. Thank you for sailing with me to the Southern Cross, and for letting me tell the tale from my biased perspective. I love you. I love you. And, what's more, I love you.

The Motion of the Ocean

For Discussion

1. The book opens with the author thinking her husband is an asshole, but after they survive a small calamity together, she says she's never felt so in love. When have you experienced this sort of flip-flop of emotions about a loved one? Throughout the story, how does Janna reveal both the positive and negative aspects of marriage? Of her husband? Of herself?

2. When looking at the mint color of the walls in her foyer, Janna says, "Those little color squares are cruel jokes; they trick you into thinking that you know what you're getting when really you never can tell." Is this an apt metaphor for choosing a life partner? Why or why not? What can prepare us to make this monumental decision? How does one choose the One?

3. Throughout the book Janna demonstrates that she finds it difficult to be on time or do tasks in a timely manner—she is a "Pokey Person." Graeme, on the other hand, is "one of those superefficient so-called humans who gets twice as much done in half as much time." What are the pluses and minuses of these approaches to time? What kind of person are you when it comes to time, and how does this affect your relationships?

4. The Pink-and-Blue division of labor challenges Janna's sense of worth aboard *Dragonfly* and raises questions about her new role as wife. How do the Pink and Blue play out in your own life? Do these divisions impact your sense of worth as they did Janna's, or do you instead identify with the attitudes of Janna's cruising girlfriends? Explain.

5. At the outset of their trip, Janna wonders if marriage is about agreeing to drink only from the relationship's cup and being satisfied with whatever sustenance it offers. By the end of the voyage, however, she argues for a couple's need for otherness in order to thrive in their togetherness. Do you agree with this? Why or why not? How does a couple build otherness while staying close and committed?

6. What does Janna mean when she says, "It's the space in between, the getting from point A to point B, that terrifies and teaches us most"? How is this sentiment borne out in both the actual and figurative crossings that Graeme and Janna experience on their journey? What do they learn about themselves and their relationship in these spaces in between? Identify some of your own crossings from one stage of life to another and how you met the challenges of the space between— whether it be between a new and old self, or between you and a loved one.

7. Back at home in Seattle, Janna says that what matters is "not the what but the how"—that one can have an extraordinary existence no matter how ordinary one's life appears. How is this philosophy true or false? What is your own big, hairy, audacious goal? What have you done or might do to pursue it?

A Conversation with Janna Cawrse Esarey

You present your depression in a very straightforward manner in this memoir. Was that deliberate? Have you always struggled with depression, and do you continue to struggle with it? What would you recommend to readers who see parallels in their experiences of depression?

I wanted to be frank about my experience with depression because when we keep things hush-hush, we endow them with more power than they already have. Dangerous. My depression has visited me since high school, dropping in now and then like an uninvited houseguest, but it doesn't define me. My strategy is to talk about it to a friend or loved one, or—if it keeps banging on the door—a professional. And, yes, I still deal with it. In fact, one of the many factors in our decision to come home was a bout of pre-baby blues in Hong Kong, which made me worry I might later have postpartum depression (thankfully, I didn't). I didn't mention this in the epilogue because it felt like a can of worms. But, since you ask, there go the worms.

You explored the question of what can and cannot be fulfilled by one's partner and determined that it's best to diversify how one's needs are met. Has your thinking about this changed the longer you've been married?

Core needs must be met within the partnership; otherwise it's not a partnership. With the chaos of kids, though, connecting with Graeme can go by the wayside. But one of the best gifts I can give my girls is to stay deeply in love with their dad. Often this is accomplished by spending more time with him. Sometimes it's friend time or alone time. Being my best mom self means taking regular time *away* from my children. Paradoxical but true.

What were the challenges you encountered as you strove to tell your story? What did you leave out that you wished you could have included in the memoir?

In terms of writing, the biggest challenge was the insane schedule—drafting a chapter a week—while piecing together child care for a toddler. There's a reason *juggle* rhymes with *struggle*. Also, I got the green light to write this book literally the same week I conceived my second daughter, so I wrote my memoir while pregnant, which is a small miracle considering how a pregnant woman's brain shrinks in inverse proportion to her belly growing (at least it feels that way). I delivered my book-baby just a few weeks before I delivered my real baby, and then I was typing edits in between—and sometimes even during—nursing sessions. In fact, my youngest is sitting on my lap, mauling a monkey rattle as I type this.

In terms of story, I found it very difficult to edit my life down to a single storyline. I mean, just think of the myriad things you do, think, feel, say, hear, and see on any given day. Your day is like a quilt square with a very busy pattern. And if you sew that together with another seven hundred some-odd crazy quilt squares, you've got the fabric from two years of life. So I had to extract a single, solitary thread, stretching diagonally from one corner of my quilt to the other, to have a story that was short and coherent enough for anyone besides my mom to read. Think of all that leftover fabric—days and months, ports and storms, best friends and entire countries—undulating out beyond that thread. It almost gives me a yucky-stomach feeling thinking of everything I had to leave out (e.g., *Sorry, Central America, you didn't make the cut*). But I feel better when I remind myself that my book is a single thread from my life. It's not my actual life.

You introduced us to a whole community of cruisers, particularly women. Do you still maintain contact with the women you met on your voyage? What can you tell us about these sailing women and their approach to living such a unique life?

We keep in touch with cruising friends mostly via e-mail. Some are still cruising. Most are not. That's the thing about big adventures; they don't have to last forever, and when you return to your old life it's with renewed vigor. My best girlfriend from cruising (who doesn't even appear in the book) is the perfect example. She was a high-powered, burning-out businesswoman. One night, while watching *Dawson's Creek* reruns, she saw that episode where Pacey and Joey sail into the sunset. My friend thought, *Hey! If they can do it, so can I*. The next day she googled *sailboat crew* and signed on for a voyage across the Pacific. She ended up having a wonderful romance with the captain of the sailboat she was on. When my girlfriend returned, she easily found another job, which totally disproves the idea that stepping off the treadmill for a year or two means you won't be able to get back on. In fact, I think she'd say that sabbaticalism makes for happier, more productive people. Makes me wonder what her next adventure will be . . .

In your role as a writer, you seem to have zeroed in on the complexities of women's lives as they strive to balance love, family, work, friends, and self. What continue to be the prevailing concerns for the women you encounter and the unique strategies they employ to stay grounded in their lives?

Now isn't this *the* question? I mean, who doesn't struggle with balance when we have so many competing priorities? And just when I think I have a semblance of balance, life goes and changes on me!

One of my girlfriends says the problem is we women think we can have it all—since that's what we've been told—when really we can't. So women try to be the perfect worker, wife, mother, daughter, sibling, neighbor, housekeeper, cook, hostess, friend, and lover—all while looking fabulous. In trying to do everything, and to perfection, we drive ourselves nuts and/or end up feeling like we're doing nothing well enough. Men, in contrast, (according to my friend) cherry-pick a few roles and don't throw their backs/psyches out trying to do them perfectly. I'd be curious to know what others think about this theory.

As for me, I'm loathe to admit I can't have it all. But I have come to realize that I can't have it all *at the same time.* So I suppose my strategy—and that of my girlfriends—is to prioritize what matters most to each of us right now, and then let a whole mess of stuff slide. For me this means: I don't shower much; our oh-shit drawer is now an oh-shit room; I don't read my mail as often as I should; and our neighbors are usually the ones to wheel in our recycling bins, for which I hereby publicly thank them.

What keeps the women in my life grounded? That's easy. Each other.

What advice would you offer those inspired by *The Motion of the Ocean* to tackle their own big, hairy, audacious goals?

Take good notes! And share your B-HAG on my website (www.byjanna.com). If you're blogging about it—which by all means you should—leave a link so others can follow you on your journey.

What is on deck for you and your family's next B-HAG?

My personal B-HAG is to finish that novel I'm so scared to write. Our family B-HAG is to cruise again—with kids this time. And Graeme's and my B-HAG is to make love last. Forever.